PHYSICAL BODY ASCENSION TO THE NEW EARTH

Instruction Manual

Robert E. Pettit, PhD

Emeritus Associate Professor

iUniverse, Inc.
New York   Bloomington

Physical Body Ascension to the New Earth
Instruction Manual

iUniverse books may be ordered through booksellers or by contacting:

iUniverse
1663 Liberty Drive
Bloomington, IN 47403
www.iuniverse.com
1-800-Authors (1-800-288-4677)

ISBN: 978-1-4502-3171-8 (pbk)
ISBN: 978-1-4502-3173-2 (cloth)
ISBN: 978-1-4502-3172-5 (ebk)

LCCN Number: 2009923350

Printed in the United States of America

iUniverse rev. date: 5/19/2010

Contents

Acknowledgments

To each Research Associate who has participated in the Subtle Energy Research program for the past twenty years, I thank you for your dedication and the contributions that have made possible the assembly of the information presented within this book. Your suggestions of references, Internet Web sites, and workshops, in addition to your spiritual talents, have opened up many new avenues of knowing. The many insights have provided a foundation for working with subtle energy and how to conduct remote spiritual healing sessions. Over these twenty years, more than 850 individuals throughout the United States have helped open up new understandings of a multitude of procedures and techniques that have helped guide the design of many research experiments.

Writing and summarizing the material for this book has been an exercise in responsibility, dedication, discipline, awareness, and a willingness to be open to receive guidance from many Spiritual Assistants. This book has been designed to help those who are on a spiritual path to the New Earth. Special thanks to the editors, Betty Pettit, Patricia Pike, Irene Jennings, Harriett Gray, and Isa Ra. Also a special thanks to the staff and assistants who respond to the many calls for help from throughout the United States: Larry Sorensen, Suzy London, MD, Linda Case, Francosis Pellissier, Betty Pettit, Sharon Berry, Don Yows, Jackie Cohen, Janet Rainey, Kim Notz, George Ward, Maurice Portilla, MD, Nayda Portilla, Steve Fox, Nira Granott Fox, Cheryl Bright, and Carol Handing.

Also, thanks to the Research Associates who have remained faithful through the years:

Annette Gore	Tom Lynch	Valerie Lynch
Bridget Sorensen	Delwin Houser	Kelly Lousey
Bradley Smith	Dorothy Combs	Leonard Ripley
Maria Smith	Leroy Wood	Betty Wood
Jennifer Hudspeth	David Hudspeth	Vicki Miles
Shellie Hudspeth	Mindy Hudspeth	Michael George
Sharie Cochran	Martha Moore	Irene Jennings
Martha James	Debbie May	Donald Miles
Cynthia Luttrell	John Luttrell	Geoffrey Luttrell
William Luttrell	Joanna Himes	Loretta Lines

Rosie Kuhn
Alicya Simmons
David Pettit
Rebecca Winks
Cher Barlevi

Kenneth Shaw
Vicki Buffington
Sharon Pettit
Christopher Pettit
Faina Engel

Stephanie Flanders
Rebecca Thomas
Lisa Christian
Sandra Letson
Jason Wagner

Patty Kumm
Kathleen St John
Christy Campassi
Kathy Middleton
Brad Eberhart

Lea Carleton
Bonnie Thompson
Christine Lurski
Michael Middleton
Rick Pinckert

Amy Wagner
Steve Thompson
Dorothy Gilkes
Barbara Baine
Paula Bordelon

Marlene Coats
Gregory Coats
Harrison Spiegel
Venetia Poirot
Shelly Hume

Randy Scherer
Jason Ellis
Lorie Spiegel
Judy Modglin
Vicki Bolton

Sandra Schaff
Shannen Twaddle
Geddy Hamblen
Pat Janus
Donna Taylor

Jody Janati
Bonnie Hansen
Chris McCombs
Barbara Blevins
Marina Pierce

Donna Reiber
Judith McClung
Elaine Checkly
Lea Carleton
Jacque Tindel

Frances Hebert
Deborah Massey
David Massey
Elynn Light
Toni Tindel

Simone Little
Marvin Kubik
Jan Pryor
Lei Hill
Cathleen Howard

Rosemary Lanza
Nina Miller
Kelly Norri
Bruce Thomas
Carolyn Jones

Patricia Kubik
Paul Gryglas
Patty Kumm
Chareen Thomas
Lawrence Hansen

Mauricio Portilla
Russell Barrett
Susan Neander
Gary Batten
Tyson Goodman

Barbara Johnson
Lisa Glover
Allese Hauroutunian
Paul Gresham
Nancy Evans

Charles Kuchulis
Frances Townsend
Jennifer Kenning
Inbal Farber
Deborah Oakes

Peter Jurouskis
Rosemary Lanza
Nancy Coats
Carla Stine
Carol James

Janice Eicher
Nancy Kriesky
Mariett Laneer
Tom Stine
Terry James

Annette Murphy
Dana Morris
Jessica Schuman
Anne Hartikka
Pamela Boyke

Katharina Spurling Kaffl	Michele Francesconi	Jesse Nochella
Robert Parma	Sharon Amber Louise	Letitia Jackson
Linda Stowe	Adele French	Lyle Christensen
Roxy Baxter	Betty Axthelm	Stephen Bredesen
Lucy Lutkowski	Juli Ann Benett	Neal Anderson
Arlie Paulson	Jack Frazier	Suzanne Frazier
Jamie Ware	Daly Smith	Kathy Slentz
Sundi Bright	Cyreal Burgett	Greg Slentz

Thanks also to the hundreds of additional individuals throughout the United States and the world who have periodically assisted the research program in many different ways.

Thanks to the faculty and staff of the Department of Plant Pathology and Microbiology at Texas A&M University, College Station, Texas, for their encouragement and support during my twenty-seven years with them. Thanks for the grant support of the Agency of International Development, Rockefeller Foundation, United States Department of Agriculture, Peanut Growers Association, Pesticide Producing Companies, and many other supporters of our research activities. These grant funds provided an opportunity to travel, conduct research, and attend conferences in forty-four states of the United States and twenty-seven different countries of the world.

Credit for book cover art "The Blue Marble West Photo" of the Earth is given to the National Aeronautic and Space Administration, Goddard Space Flight Center. The composite photograph was taken 700 km above the Earth onboard the Terra satellite in 2001. This was the most detailed true-color image of the Earth taken from space up to that date.

Finally, I would like to thank my wife, children, grandchildren, and great-grandchildren for their support throughout the eighty years of my incarnation on planet Earth. I have been grateful for the patience, support, and encouragement of my mother and father, brother, and family as I have journeyed down a road still unfamiliar to me and many others.

* * * * * *

Section I: Changing Times and Historical Perspectives

1

Very Dramatic Changes Are Happening on Earth "Now"

Introduction to the Changes Taking Place on Planet Earth

According to material I have received from many sources, many humans on Earth are still spiritually asleep, unaware of all the changes taking place around them. Not only are they unaware of what's happening on Earth, but many are unaware of the changes taking place throughout the Milky Way Galaxy and beyond. Because of an urgent need to better understand these changes, a majority of those individuals listed in the acknowledgements have requested that I research the subject of the "End Times" and "The Shift" and write this book. *You Can Avoid Physical Death* has been designed to help you and others understand what's happening. The book also addresses how these changes will affect everyone and how you can prepare for a different future.

During the latter part of 2008, Earth's inhabitants became aware that some truly dramatic changes in the economic, political, social, religious, and educational systems of the world have been quietly taking place. As these changes became more intense, humans witnessed a significant economic downturn that resulted in loss of jobs, homes, and retirement savings, resulting in considerable fear and stress about an unknown future. Costs of gasoline, home heating fuels, food, clothing, and various services increased significantly and caused economic hardship for many throughout the world. Along with these events, significant climatic extremes caused hardships for many. Humans all over the world lost their homes and peace of mind as a result of hurricanes, tsunamis, tornadoes, firestorms, rising sea levels, floods, and landslides. Many of these events will continue during the transition period between 2009 and 2012. Many people who had put their trust in religion or in a stable planet, financial systems, or their government's ability to control the economy have begun to experience a profound loss of trust in these old, outdated illusions. People are wondering what can be done to keep society from falling apart.

From a spiritual perspective, the current global financial system can be described as extremely evil. The banking, taxing, and pricing systems have all been designed to take from the masses and allow those in positions of power to control humanity on Earth. These dark, powerful financial, political, religious, and social controllers have as their goal "Service to Self" as opposed to "Service to Others." Any social system designed to take advantage of others will not survive upon the New Earth. The group that has been in control of a majority of the world's social systems for the past several thousand years has been called the "Illuminati." Recently, these powerful individuals have begun to realize that their control is coming to an end. Watch them closely, and keep in mind they will not give up without fighting to preserve their way of life.

Many humans are waiting on their governmental leaders to correct the current economic situation. Notice they have written a check for billions which cannot be cashed. Spirit indicates it is *insanity* to expect to fix a problem with the same actions that created it.

Not only are economic changes occurring, but many other changes are taking place that influence all life on planet Earth. For example, the polar ice caps are melting, migratory birds have stopped returning to their nesting grounds, and indigenous native tribes throughout the world have stopped having children. The jet stream (high-altitude, one hundred-mph wind currents) recently touched ground for the first time in recorded history. Locations in Mexico have recorded ground temperatures above two hundred degrees. Why are these events and many more occurring? It may be helpful for everyone to monitor these events to better understand how they are affecting your life.

In reality, everything humans experience on Earth is like a dream, a conscious, illusory dream created by mass consciousness. When you dream, you are not really present; you are where the dream has taken you. Dreams are as real or as false as you make them. Enlightenment and the search for new perceptions are to a great extent about awakening from the dream to seek truth. Waking up from the dream happens through forgiveness. When you forgive your experiences, you are no longer bound to the illusions because you know the illusory dream is not real truth. You realize you had been participating in the illusory dream that humanity's consciousness created.

As you look around the planet Earth, you quickly realize time and energy are changing very rapidly, at quantum speeds. They are changing faster than ever before in recorded Universal history. Time is rapidly collapsing every day. All of the major cultural and religious traditions on Earth point to this time in history as the end of the world, as we have known it. The Mayan calendar, the Bible, the pyramid calendar, the Vedic scriptures, Hopi prophesies, and other records point to the coming End Times. By End Times, we are referring to the end of one cycle and the beginning of a new, very different historical cycle. The dream of a new civilization and New Earth, which many have wished for, is "Now" taking shape. The American dream has come, peaked, and is "Now" giving way to a new dream— Heaven on Earth. To make way for the new way of life, the old ways will have to be removed, cleared from your consciousness. As part of the clearing process, humanity's way of life is rapidly being replaced, leading to a dramatic increase in confusion and chaos.

It's becoming very difficult to understand what the future will be like. Many individuals are becoming very concerned about their futures. Things and events that you previously called real experiences and held on to—the old way of life on planet Earth—will of necessity have to pass away to make room for the new. In many cases, these changes have resulted in various mental, emotional,

> ## Alert—"Wake Up!"
> **The current third-dimension Earth will cease to support human life relatively soon.**

and physical imbalances. Consequently, one important way to adapt to these changes is to request spiritual help. Request understanding and guidance on how to adjust your bodies and daily activities to regain and maintain balance.

Life on Earth is not about suffering, and it's not about getting out of here. Nor is life all about having Earthly pleasures—just keeping busy doing something all the time. Those doings are merely part of the third- and fourth-dimensional illusions. To transition and pass through the Star Gates and into the fourth- and fifth-dimensional states of consciousness (via Ascension), the first requirement is for you to gain a clear understanding of *who you truly are*. This is the one key ingredient that lays the groundwork for your transition from a planet of low frequency to a planet of higher frequency. That transformation of understanding about who you truly are will totally change your perception of the Universe and your eternal future. Whether you believe in a Creator or not, you are a spiritual creation, created by The Creators, (God/Goddess), (ALL-THAT-IS), (I-AM-THAT-I-AM).

The Creators (Elohim) have gained support from throughout the Universe to restore the planet Earth to its originally designed path of love and responsibility to the whole. The behaviors previously instilled by the Interlopers (negative entities) are destroying the Earth and its diversity. These activities will be put to an end. These restoration events were prophesied to have occurred sooner. However, they were delayed so that a larger number of humans could participate in the creation of the New Earth.

Those who plan to graduate and Ascend to the New Earth may have a tendency to want to convince others to join them on the path they have chosen. You can share your beliefs, but it is not your job to judge or try to change another's chosen path. The New Earth will be the manifestation of Heaven on Earth for those who have prepared spiritually and believe that they have an opportunity to choose that path.

A phase shift is taking place within the Milky Way Galaxy, the Solar System, and on planet Earth. "The Shift" on Earth involves the receipt of newly arriving energies from outside the Solar System that are being absorbed by the molecules that make up humanity's physical reality. These molecules are moving faster and faster, which means their rate of vibration (frequency) is increasing. As this Ascension process continues, all the physical forms that we are so familiar with will be undergoing a frequency (phase) shift. Simultaneously, the planetary frequency is shifting upward, as are all other natural objects on the planet. As this process takes place, all biological forms are shifting to the fourth-dimensional state of consciousness. It is a purification process. The only things that will remain on the other side of "The Shift" will be those creations whose higher-frequency wave forms are compatible with that of the New Earth.

Similar changes have happened on Earth ever since it came into existence. The ice on the poles has melted before. Extraterrestrials have been coming to Earth ever since it was created to assist in "The Shift." Erratic weather occurs constantly, and pole shifts have occurred before. Movement of the Earth's tectonic plates is commonplace. There is nothing new about these events, but humanity's awareness of these illusory events has increased. Humans are realizing they are not alone. There are other, parallel realities and worlds beyond worlds—right here, right "Now." Excitement is building, and many are asking what is really coming, how it will affect them and what should they do to prepare?

You have had billions of years to explore various parameters of Universal Laws by creating many parallel versions of your Oversoul. These parallel versions have been called parallel lives. Each parallel life was created and designed so that your Oversoul could explore and simultaneously experience many realities on different planets. Every time your soul incarnates on a planet it comes in with an approved contract that will be used as a guide for that life experience. That sequence of activities has come to the end of a seventy-five-thousand-year cycle. Therefore, it is time to hit the restart button to clear out all old programs, false beliefs, and dangling fragments of thought forms that lack any semblance of usefulness. That is, to clear out all the fragments from the experimental screen left over from previous experiments on various planets. All of the possibilities and choices you have included in each of your life contracts have been nearly exhausted, and it is time to bring those lives to an end. The drama is over. The old play is over. The set and props will be dismantled; the play will be closed and removed from view.

Preparations have been and are underway for creating the new play. It will have a whole new set of props and some new, exciting experiments. All of the parallel realities you have been exploring will terminate, and a whole new set of possibilities and probabilities will emerge for those choosing to graduate and Ascend to the New Earth.

This book has been designed to provide you with an explanation of current and future events, and to provide you with tools to help you prepare for "The Shift," graduation, and Ascension to the New Earth.

Human Ego May Protest the Magnitude of These Changes

Remember your ego may greatly protest the magnitude of the message you are sensing in the world around you and reading in this book. In fact, you may observe the ego attempting to clamp down on your consciousness to keep your body and soul together. Be alert, and realize that this attempt by your ego is not in your best interest. It is a falsely assumed, protective measure. When this measure manifests, a sense of fear may come into play. As this happens, your breathing will become shortened, which indicates all systems are on red alert. That is, until the perceived danger is identified and dealt with. When the red alert occurs, take a deep breath and give your consciousness, body, and ego a message that everything is safe. Your objective will be to avoid reacting from a position of fear. Avoid responding to the ego; rather, respond from your heart and God/Goddess within. React from a position of strength, stability, love for self, and calmness in order to remove all fear-related emotions.

> ## Caution!
> **The human ego may protest your reading this book because it will feel threatened. Why? Because you're established false beliefs may be challenged.**

As a help for you in this transformation process, spirit requested that I write this book. It has been written for those humans who are ready to "Wake Up" and realize they are much more than a physical body. Every human has a spirit and a soul that have chosen to ride around on Earth in a physical body. Since the real you is spirit and soul, it is about time to take care of your most important evolutionary aspects. The process of "Waking Up" is a spiritual endeavor, not a religious one. Failure to "Wake Up" is a choice to remain stuck within the third dimension of duality consciousness, where the challenges of pain and suffering predominate. If it is your choice to remain within a third-dimensional state of consciousness, then you will be required to transfer via the process of physical death to another third-dimension planet. You can continue your third-dimension lessons on another low-frequency planet. There is no God/Goddess or Creator making this judgment; you have free will to make a choice in line with your chosen contracts. If your current contract contains an option to shift your consciousness to the fifth dimension through graduation and Ascension to the New Earth, then this book can help you along that path. If your choice is to stick with the third-dimension duality patterns your contract was designed for, then you will proceed down a different path, and that is perfectly OK. As you go over your contract and contemplate your appropriate choice, remember that the old, third-dimension Earth and the new, fifth-dimension Earth exist right here in two parallel realities. The old Earth is scheduled to go through a rejuvenation phase and will cease to support human life. The new, high-frequency, fifth-dimension New Earth is also right here in another parallel reality.

Some may ask the question: Dr. Pettit if these cyclic patterns and events are truly taking place, why haven't we heard of them on the news, within the educational systems, in the churches, or from the government and politicians? All of these groups have been designed to control the masses and limit spiritual development. By limiting their spiritual development, the masses are held in bondage to those in control. All man-made institutions have a vested interest in maintaining the status quo in order to hold society together as a third-dimension reality. If the leaders of these institutions relinquished their power, it would destroy their third-dimensional beliefs, their erroneous economic security, and their conservative way of life.

However, humanity has reached a point in its evolutionary cycle where the old way of life (duality consciousness) must give way to the newly evolving, fifth-dimensional way of life called Unity/Christ consciousness.

The old, third-dimensional world is now beginning its rapid fall. Many are finding that their financial status, job status, living quarters, and lifestyles are fading away, and there is not much left to hold on to. People want to know if there is anything left that will give them security. It is scary to lose one's secure, familiar way of life and venture out into the unknown. The conservative approach has been to cling to those familiar patterns and beliefs in hopes that they will meet your needs. Those behavior patterns and beliefs were designed for the old, low-frequency, third-dimension Earth. If you plan to remain upon a third-dimension planet, these conservative patterns may meet some of your needs. I repeat: the third dimension of planet Earth is in need of rejuvenation and soon will no longer support human life. Humans have been destroying Earth for many generations and are currently accelerating these destructive patterns. Yes, the third-dimension Earth will still exist, but in a structural form you may have difficulty recognizing. Many predicted Earth changes are still a possibility. Spirit indicates that the cleansing process for third-dimension Earth will involve regions of the Earth sinking into the oceans. In order to create balance, others regions will rise from the ocean floor. The regions that rise will have had their soils replenished with life-giving minerals.

Because these events were anticipated many years ago, Earth requested permission from the Creators of the Universe to shift to the fifth-dimensional state of consciousness. That request was granted, and the New Earth is rapidly shifting and taking shape. The New Earth will have a thriving population of humans and other life forms vibrating within the higher frequency ranges. If you would prefer to transition to the new, fifth-dimension Earth, you have to prepare to shift your consciousness, and thus graduate and Ascend.

If you have a completely closed mind about the concept of individual or mass Ascension, this book may help open your mind to that possibility. The objective is to provide you with evidence that humanity is connected to cyclic patterns that extend throughout creation. One of those patterns is an opportunity for your soul to spiritually evolve. Humanity is "Now" at the end of a cycle. New spiritual opportunities, never before envisioned, are available.

Right "Now" the concept of a New Earth may be outside your understanding. You are not alone. As you observe others, you will note that a majority of the human population is unaware of the coming "End of the Age." Many have closed their minds to trying to comprehend these concepts and changes because they appear complicated.

You can observe these closed-minded individuals. They stroll around like unconscious robots, acting out their feelings without trying to discover what causes those feelings. Many have become so deeply programmed by their controllers (the Illuminati) they have become trapped in the illusory dreams playing out on third-dimension Earth. Some have labeled these dreamers zombies. They appear to be caught up in pursuing the pleasures of Earth. They cling to their material possessions and are blinded by an unrestrained drive to obtain more. Many have no desire to venture into uncharted waters; they feel safe with their familiar social and religious beliefs. Many become fearful when they try to understand difficult spiritual concepts. Some of these individuals are trapped in the duality of self-centered behavior patterns. They will not be going to the New Earth.

For those who are ready to understand, those who are open-minded and ready to "Wake Up;" the opportunities are unlimited. This means reenergizing your spiritual capabilities by clearing out those thought forms that would bind you to the low-frequency, third-dimension Earth. The spiritual path will be void of political, religious, economic, and social dogma, and of a multitude of illusory dreams and dramas. Humans have been waiting for centuries in anticipation of the coming changes that bring into being Heaven on Earth, The New Earth.

The concepts of a New Earth outlined within *You Can Avoid Physical Death* will open up a whole new world of alternative realities. To enter this new world will require setting aside time for your spiritual development. Also, those of you who desire to create Heaven on Earth should select a time line (pathway to the future) that is most appropriate for you. Once you have created your time line, you will have started to prepare to create your dreams, that is, implement your desires of what Heaven on Earth will be like.

Trust That You Can Adjust to the Many Changes Taking Place

During this time of collapse, it is very important for you to remember to increase your ability to trust in yourself. You will be able to get through these dramatic changes if you remember to trust in who you are. I'm not talking about trusting some guru or an unknown God/ Goddess for guidance. I'm discussing the need to trust your internal guidance system. Throughout this book, we will be emphasizing the need to trust your spiritual self right "Now," knowing that in each "Now" moment you have everything you need to survive and make it through these changing times. Always keep in mind you will have choices to make during every "Now" moment.

As these events continue, everyone should strive to avoid any form of fear, such as stress, anxiety, tension, and worry. Remove all past fears that could surface again. You can help yourself and those around you by mentally avoiding the fearful consequences of economic, social, and environmental events.

> **Avoid all fear and know you can accept and adjust to any future changes taking place on Earth—starting now.**

Think positively and live your life in appreciation of what is being given to you. From this position of strength, you can give love to all others on the journey with you. Make every "Now" moment a happy and joyous time. One additional objective of this book is to provide you with the techniques and tools to help you have a successful, joyous experience during these changing times. To accomplish the goals of removing fear, accepting, and adjusting will require the removal of old behavior patterns and instituting new approaches to solving everyday challenges.

The new social systems that will emerge during and following the coming changes will be designed to serve the greater good of all. The greater good of all is based on the concept of loving thy neighbor as thyself. The state of consciousness associated with this concept is called Unity/Christ Consciousness. It is a feature of fifth-dimensional consciousness, as opposed to the old Earth's third-dimensional duality consciousness. That duality consciousness, which emphasized the extremes of good and evil, was never intended to become a permanent way of life. Thus the time has arrived to make changes that will create a new way of life upon the New Earth. The predominately fifth-dimensional consciousness will be designed around Unity/Christ consciousness concepts, where love is the prevailing way of life.

What we are experiencing is a shift in consciousness where all the components of Earth and its inhabitants are changing frequency. This vibratory shift and acceleration in consciousness will continue during the coming years, up to 2012 and beyond. To become a vital part of "The Shift" realize that there is no need to wait for 2012

> **Duality consciousness was never intended to become a permanent way of life on Earth.**

and beyond, when "The Shift" will reach a turning point in many ways. It is your responsibility to use every "Now" moment up to the end of 2012 to help create the new you and the New Earth. This means you will need to dedicate considerable time and effort each day during the intervening years to create your new reality. For those who were unaware that graduation time is near, the information within this book is you're "Wake Up" call. For those of you, who are awake, continue your preparations.

Your creations will be guided by what you think and believe. It has always been true that your thoughts create your reality. All humans create their reality by what they think, imagine, and visualize into becoming a part of their everyday experiences. Every sickness and challenge you have experienced on third-dimension Earth was related to a thought or an out-of-control negative emotion you mentally created.

In the past, human existence on Earth has been a constant cycle of reincarnations involving death and rebirth. This repetitive process has been caused by the soul's lack of sufficient awareness of who it is. As a result of this lack of awareness, humans have seemingly become victims of disease, tragedy, or adverse circumstances that resulted in their physical death. Many consider this sequence normal. Just yesterday, someone stated it is natural to physically die. That is a false belief. Your body was designed to live for thousands of years—when you take care of it. On many other planets, physical death would be considered a very abnormal process. However, because of a series of historical mental, genetic, social, and emotional mishaps, most humans die and leave their physical body in less than one hundred years.

> **Your physical body was designed to live thousands of years when taken care of.**

For those who die with limited spiritual development, this process takes them into the third overtone of the fourth dimension. In the history of the Earth, souls that have moved to this third overtone would most likely reincarnate on Earth again and again. In fact, over the past seventy-five thousand years, a majority of souls currently residing on Earth have repeated this cycle for thousands of lifetimes. This pattern of repeating one life after another on the same planet needs to be upgraded to a more spiritually based pattern designed to accelerate the soul's spiritual evolution.

After death, while within the fourth dimension, as you become aware of your spiritual essence as an eternal consciousness, other opportunities become available. With that awareness between physical lives, you may be given a choice to request and a capability to recreate a new, less dense physical body. That new body will allow you to enter the tenth, eleventh, or twelfth overtones of the fourth dimension. Remember, reincarnation (returning to some third-dimensional planet) originates from the lower overtones of the fourth dimension. From the higher overtones of the fourth dimension (the tenth to twelfth), you *do not* have to reincarnate on a third-dimensional planet.

Regardless of the spiritual path you chose, everyone on Earth will experience firsthand, in one way or another, a majority of these dramatic events. All aspects of these changes are part of a cycle where an opportunity is made available to become a part of the Ascension process. If you are in denial about these potential chang-

> **If you are in denial about the changes taking place on Earth, get over it "Now," while there is time to prepare for graduation and Ascension.**

es taking place, get over it "Now." You have no way to stop the cyclic changes that have been put in place for hundreds of thousands of years by the Creators of this Universe.

Open up your ears and eyes. Take a look around. Try to find out what is going on. You won't find out everything you need to know by tuning into the communication media. For example, avoid reading and watching what the controlled and manipulated media presents on television. Instead, search the Internet, study this book, and read other books listed in the reference section.

Then use your God/Goddess-given capacity of discernment to find out what's really happening. Go within during meditation to listen to the still, small voice that originates from spiritual sources to provide you with guidance. Then work hard to regain an understanding of what it means to make a shift in your consciousness.

Everyone on Earth has been struggling with their own feelings of separation, unworthiness, and loneliness. In relation to these feelings, there is currently an ongoing separation of souls occurring on Earth. Humans are subconsciously separating themselves into major groups. Two of these major groups are those who have awakened and those who have chosen to remain asleep. Those who have awakened have been called the "light workers" because they have opened their hearts, minds, and eyes to the light of God/Goddess to observe what is happening. These individuals are preparing spiritually for the coming changes. Those who remain asleep will have chosen other options.

Many different changes will be required to complete the newly designed procedure for Ascension. These changes are under way, and there is no way to stop them. The changes were designed, approved, and are being implemented by the Creators. Many of these changes on Earth have been sensed by Extraterrestrials from other planets throughout the Universe. They are here in large numbers to observe how these changes will affect the Universe, and to help when their help does not interfere with human evolution.

As a part of our journey within the Universe, we each volunteered to come to Earth. In the process of surviving, we have created the illusion of being victims. The victim illusion was created to assist us in our spiritual evolution as a part of the duality of the third dimension. We must "Now" realize that when we take on victim consciousness, we become a victim. One concern is that if we become victims, we could also take on warrior consciousness. Warrior consciousness correlates with Service to Self (STS) one of humanity's main challenges to overcome within duality consciousness. To Ascend, we must take on Unity/Christ consciousness and Service to Others (STO).

In the STS version of reality, people keep or hold their power for self-satisfaction. They try to keep STO people from remaining on their spiritual paths. Those of the STO persuasion realize there is an endless supply of energy; STS people believe energy is limited and that they must take it for themselves. To remain within the STO persuasion, the best protection is love for all of creation, including those in the STS persuasion.

Realize you are in control, and the only one you can truly control is you. This understanding of your control capabilities allows you to receive the power to heal not only yourself, but to help heal those who request your help. As you heal yourself, realize that you are connected to everyone and everything within the Universe. Then, as you heal, everything within the Universe also receives a degree of healing. By setting the example of love and acceptance of self, you have helped create a New Earth. Also, as you apply the concepts of STO, you become an example for others—someone worthy of following. Every time someone (anywhere in the world) calls for your help, all you need to do is ask their inner spirit, their God/Goddess within, to un-create or transmute an imbalance or infection, and it's done. There is nothing complicated; believe, and it's done. But it won't work if you have doubt or believe it will not be done; the imbalance or infection will persist with a limiting belief system. Your belief helps create the reality you experience in everything you put your attention on.

The years of 2009 and 2010 will be a dramatic period for the reconfiguration of every element of society. There will be no exact roadmap to help in reconfiguring your inner and outer worlds. The way in which these Earth changes and reconfigurations take place will be a brand-new process. Never before in the history of the Earth have such rapid changes taken place within such a short period of clock time Thus you will be called upon to have patience and persistence in striving to create your new reality. You are being called upon to have faith, believe, and know that everything is in divine order as you align and think with your God/Goddess within.

As you shift from the third dimension to the fourth and fifth dimensions, you will be unable take physical objects with you. For example, you will have to leave all of your money and physical belongings behind, just like you left them behind when you experienced physical death in the past. The frequency vibration of third-dimensional objects and fifth-dimensional objects are dramatically different. They are incompatible.

Another important challenge most humans have is becoming aware of current events. People who are unaware are drifting with the flow on autopilot. They have lost control of their destinies and lack a sense of knowing what might take place in the near future. They let others or circumstances control their lives. To become conscious of current events will require constant alertness and study on your part. This means going within and listening to the heart, the still, small voice within, to know what is important and what applies to you.

When you are unaware of some beneficial energy arriving on Earth, then that energy event is very slow to manifest in or adjust to your energy system. The moment you become aware of an incoming energy event, that awareness can help you shorten the time required to manifest that beneficial energy. For example, if you are unaware of the many cosmic light dispensations (divine light) currently arriving on Earth, you will only slowly utilize that healing light to help transform your bodies. As you become aware of this divine light arriving on Earth, you can make connection with its source and request that these light energies heal your body of any imbalance. You can also request and create new body parts.

As another example of energy changes, spirit has announced that there is a need to prepare for the second wave of Ascension during December, 2008. You should prepare "Now" for this second wave of Ascension. Without knowing what to ask for, you could inadvertently become fearful and miss out on this opportunity. Without knowing, you will also be slow to integrate the new energies. You may also have more difficulty accepting other new energies that will be coming through the portals to help shift your consciousness. Remember, these new energy adjustments are not to be feared. These adjustments will provide you with a higher degree of awareness, a deeper state of understanding, and a stronger presence of self (the God/Goddess within) — to offer direction and help guide your life.

Throughout 2008 and 2009, a series of portals (Star Gates) have been and will be opening. These portals will continue to open in order to provide a new wave of awakening about the New Earth. There are many books and Web sites available to help you stay informed about coming changes. It will become very important during the next few years to spend some time reading various books and Web sites to find out the latest helpful information. Always use discernment to reject false information. Then go within to receive direct guidance.

Releasing Old Realities and Taking on the New Realities

To take advantage of the upcoming opportunities to graduate and Ascend from the old Earth plane, you will be required to release the old and accept the new. This requirement is part of a graduation process within cycles of seventy-five thousand and twenty-five thousand years that take place as the Solar System moves around the Galactic center. The most dramatic changes occur at certain points within the seventy-five-thousand-year cycles. For example, scientists have discovered that seventy-five thousand years ago, the human organism had a massive increase in brain size. This was when third-dimensional consciousness developed in the human organism. Since we are "Now" coming to the end of a similar cycle, and to the end of three twenty-five-thousand-year cycles (as of December, 2012), planet Earth and the Solar System are shifting consciousness. As a result, we can anticipate another physical body change. This specific transition will be somewhat different than any past experience. Thus, humans are having difficulty in knowing how to prepare for "The Shift." From historical records we do know dramatic changes occur within the Universe every twenty-five thousand years.

According to an advanced Spiritual Being called Ra the normal allotted time period required for a soul to graduate is at the end of three twenty-five-thousand-year cycles. Generally, at the end of each of these cycles, a smaller number of souls graduate from a planet. However, it is more likely that a larger number of souls will graduate at the end of this seventy-five-thousand-year cycle. This will occur somewhere around December 2012.

Those who are prepared to shift to a higher state of consciousness (an inside job) are the ones who will graduate and Ascend to the New Earth. Those third-dimensional humans unprepared to shift to the higher, fifth-dimensional state of consciousness will be required to make another choice.

> **Those who are prepared to shift to a higher state of consciousness Will graduate and Ascend To the New Earth**

Keep in mind that within this Solar System, different planets commonly vibrate at different dimensional states of consciousness. For example, Venus has already shifted to the higher dimensions. The Hathors currently reside on Venus within this higher dimension. The remaining third-dimension Venus is a hot, dry desert. Likewise, Mars is currently devoid of life within the third dimension; however, in the past, third-dimension life did exist on Mars.

The good news is that this is essentially the first time in twenty-five thousand years that humanity has had an opportunity to be a part of a newly designed graduation and Ascension experience. Many of you reading these words came to Earth during this incarnation to help in the Ascension process and co-create Heaven on a New Earth. Many of you reading were purposely chosen as crack team members, approved by your High Self Spiritual Council, because you would be capable of helping make these changes successfully. Thus, it is time to "Wake Up" and accept your responsibilities as the vast, multidimensional Master that you truly are.

Try to understand that unless the suggestions within this book are learned thoroughly and integrated through the heart, all these ideas will remain as mere information. Helpful information in any form, unless applied in your daily activities, will clutter the mind and be soon forgotten. It will be very important to reconcile the difference between reading about good ideas and doing something with those ideas. The value is only real when those ideas have helped improve your well-being and prepared you for graduation and Ascension.

The process of Ascension and going to the New Earth *is not* based on your old belief systems about how some speaker told you about going to Heaven. The general plan does not provide for a rapture to get you out of the mess here on Earth. The plan, under very specific circumstances, could include your being beamed up to an awaiting Extraterrestrial

> **All thoughts and information you will receive within this book will have value when applied. Otherwise, you will only have information which clutters your mind.**

craft. Such a scenario has been put in place if and when an emergency develops to save those who plan to Ascend in their new bodies. I repeat: the whole process of graduation, Ascension, and movement though the Star Gate to the new Earth *is not* about what you believe; it's all about spiritual evolution, soul growth, and an internal shift in consciousness. It's about knowing who you are and your ability to be of Service To Others (STO) as opposed to Service To Self (STS), love all of creation, and taking on Unity/Christ consciousness. It involves many other internal shifts in consciousness. Not even God/Goddess within or some advanced Spiritual being can interfere with your free choice. Your shift in consciousness is an individual decision and should only be made when you have prepared and are ready to make that shift.

Remember, many humans will have no interest in graduating and Ascending to Heaven on Earth. Everyone has a choice to make as to whether they Ascend or remain on a third-dimension planet. Go within to find out what your divine plan is. The path to the New Earth will not stop developing, regardless of what anyone thinks or believes. The Creators and God/Goddess has already approved and given permission for the Earth to Ascend to the fifth dimension. The current third-dimension Earth will remain as a part of the multidimensional Earth; however, it will be uninhabitable during its recovery period. Those who are destined to move to the New Earth will know who they are; so will those who have chosen other paths or time lines. As difficult as it may seem too many readers, all of the physical illusions of the third dimension will soon pass away as third-dimension Earth prepares for its renewal and rejuvenation.

There is nothing to be gained by engaging in debate with those who don't have an understanding of what is taking place on Earth. There is nothing to fix, including the beliefs and understandings of others. You have no need to alter another's evolutionary path. To assist your family members and brothers and sisters within the world, you must first help yourself. Before you can help heal another, you must first heal those aspects of yourself that are still in separation from who you truly are. The best way to assist our brothers and sisters is by example. We then give them a rope to hang on to or a road map to follow through their jungle of doubt and confusion. We must cease all judgment of their behavior and our own behavior, and then ask for forgiveness. You must also develop compassion for yourself and others who are suffering. Without suffering in the third-dimension reality realm, none of us would have gained understanding or learned how to convey compassion to those who call for help.

Those on the Ascension path will separate themselves from those who claim to know all the answers about what is happening and have different agendas. If you plan to Ascend, stay clear of those struggling to hold on to the conservative, warrior-type false beliefs. If you observe them closely, you will note that their true objectives are the control and manipulation of others. These deceivers and judgmental individuals are in reality working for the Interlopers, entities that have inserted themselves into the original design to create duality for this planet and maintain control of its inhabitants.

The aim of the Interlopers was to slow spiritual development, and they have done a good job. The original plan set forth by the Creators Elohim (a vast spiritual group that designed this sector of the Universe), was to have a planet based on love and responsibility toward all components of creation. It was to be a location in the Milky Way Galaxy where the entire planet and its occupants would be concerned about each other's well-being—a planet dedicated to (STO), as opposed to (STS). The Interlopers diverted the original plan and put individual interests above that of the whole, called STS. They also inserted the concept of destructive competitive behaviors and superiority by race and rank. As a result, they distorted the valuable concept of STO.

A good example of their diversion techniques is illustrated by the massive expenditures on competitive sports. The drive for competitive sports has been created as a diversion from humanity's spiritual path. The goal of sports is to gain a conscious following that distracts the followers from reality. Romans and Americans have been key manipulators in this diversionary technique. You would be wise to avoid being pulled into the trap of wasting time participating in or viewing sporting activities.

For you to Ascend to the higher states of dimensional consciousness, you will be required to clear out all those low-frequency; adverse energies trapped within your energy bodies. The flushing or clearing process will be most noticeable in social relationships. For example, the clearing process will cause economic instability, the breakup of families, increasing violence, road rage, street and school shootings, a breakdown of law and order, food shortages, and international crises. These external events are the outward manifestation of an internal cleansing. Some of these adverse energies created by humans over many lifetimes have also been stored within the Earth. Third-dimensional Mother Earth cannot continue to store these discordant energies and is in the process of releasing them. Many of those discordant energies are returning to those who created them.

The Earth and humans who plan to graduate must purge all past fear, anger, rage, and other lower forms of emotion to evolve spiritually. Simultaneously, the higher-frequency emotions of love, a desire for peace, compassion, and forgiveness will need to be installed to fill the voids left after these clearings. The whole process is moving humanity toward healing and wholeness, even though it seems like everything is coming apart. "The Shift" is underway. You are breaking away from the confines of the false, limited beliefs that held you within time bound duality consciousness. As a result, you are moving out of time-bound thinking into a new reality of no time and your no space. You're moving into a new reality realm, where unlimited possibilities exist. Also, those souls who have chosen to graduate are pooling their thoughts to help create the New Earth.

There are still pieces of the puzzle being organized and put in place within you. These new pieces will fit when the old pieces have been removed and the new pieces are placed in their proper positions. To put your puzzle together, follow the urges from your heart, take a chance, and open each new door (your next challenge) with confidence that it will be the most appropriate one. Recall that the main reason that Jesus the Christ came to Earth was to show you how to Ascend to the New Earth. You may need to review Christ's real instructions in books like, *Love Without End* by Glenda Green (1999) to come up with more accurate interpretations of the old, modified "holy" books.

Pay close attention to some spiritual Web sites shown to be relatively accurate, such as lemureanconnection.com, www.operationterra.com, www.matthewbooks.com, and www.godchannel.com.

These Web sites and others have frequent updates about current events. For example, Matthew's message, posted on March 23, 2008, indicated that worldwide consciousness will influence the withdrawal of troops from Iraq, starting after the U.S. presidential election. In another message posted on May 21, 2008, a prediction was made that the new U.S. president would be Barack Obama. Any time you receive outside information, use discernment and pendulum dowsing to determine its accuracy. There are many books on dowsing, and the American Dowsing Society, Web Site; www.dowers.org, can help provide you with information about how to use this very important technique.

The whole evolutionary process can be symbolized by the arrival of a newborn chick. When the chick emerges from the egg, there has to be some destruction of the eggshell that held the chick within the enclosed chamber where it began its growth process. In like manner, the rigid structures and patterns that have held third dimensional humanity in place must break down. Many humans fail to recognize how these rigid structures have bound them to third-dimension Earth. These structures need to be broken, just like the egg shell. As each individual works to break these old structures, associated with third-dimension illusions, some cracking sensations may be felt. It certainly won't be comfortable. Be prepared to accept these inner Earthquakes.

After the stuck emotions are released, we are open to accept the new, high-frequency energies coming to Earth. Resistance to these clearings and to the acceptance of the new energies will be overcome. The processes of change are so great there is no way to stop them. Anyone and anything that cannot ride the waves of change will not survive. All third-dimensional frequency patterns will be too low to adapt to the higher frequencies of the New Earth. Anyone who cannot clear out the old patterns and accept the new energies will go through the physical death process and enter the lower octaves of the fourth dimension. There they will appear as spirits or souls without some of their physical bodies. In contrast, those who accept the new energies and create new physical bodies will eventually Ascend to the New Earth in those bodies.

Many currently reading these words have incarnated on Earth at this time in history to Ascend to the New Earth. Once they increase their awareness, they will begin to realize that all those physical "things" around them are merely illusions, consciously created for the lessons they provided. More and more humans are "Waking Up" and beginning to understand that there must be something better than all the illusions humans have created and are experiencing.

After we begged to come to third-dimension Earth, we strutted around and bragged, saying *I got me a journey over there on Earth. Of all places, I was approved for Earth.* As part of our approved agreement to come to Earth, we had to take on physical bodies and adopt

> **When we accepted an opportunity to come to Earth, we really set ourselves up for some major challenges.**

veils of forgetfulness. As a result, we forgot our pasts and forgot who we were. We really set ourselves up for challenges when we came to Earth.

As you read, hear, or see anything, realize that your understanding comes from within. Everything that we experience is within. There is nothing out there except illusions. What appears to be out there must first be within; otherwise, there is no understanding. There is nothing outside of you to create an understanding for you. As you study the metaphysics of the Universe, you realize that when an astronomer looks through his telescope at distant stars he is in reality looking at the walls of the outermost portions of his inner conscious reality. Everything out there is a reflection of what is within the observer.

If you observe a weakness in someone else, that is a reflection of what is weak within you. What you see out there is an aspect of yourself experienced within. For example, Extraterrestrial beings are really visitors from within our consciousness. Yes, the Extraterrestrials have existences separate from us. But realize that all Extraterrestrials are within our consciousness, and we exist within their consciousness. We are all connected. Each entity, regardless of its physical features, is facilitating the evolution of all other entities throughout the Universe.

As we each request that our God/Goddess Self within help us remember who we are, we can begin to renew our capabilities and pull in more of God/Goddess light. As a result, you can energize your Love Body, activate your "Light Body" (described later in the book), and prepare to receive a new physical body for Ascension to the New Earth. Yes, you will need a new, high-frequency body to Ascend, to experience, and be compatible with the fourth– and fifth-dimensional states of consciousness. Always keep in mind that Ascension is not about going somewhere. Ascension is an inside job. It is about knowing who you are "Now" so you can arrive consciously, being in the right place at the right time. Then you will be able to arrive consciously in a new "Now," Heaven on Earth.

All those souls still asleep, those committed to the third-dimensional illusion of separation and duality, sense that the light workers are moving farther and farther away from them. As a result, those who are still asleep are struggling to hold the light workers in their matrix of duality or in their obsolete set of conservative belief systems. Has anyone judged your behavior patterns and asked, *Are you off your rocker, or you are living in a dream world?* Some people who believe you are living in a dream world are afraid you may be correct, but they don't understand why you are so different. One of their challenges is to overcome their lack of discipline and lack of open-mindedness and then create a willingness to try and understand. Many with closed minds have become trapped in a world of false beliefs and useless illusions. Yet there is hope that they can "Wake Up," at least in time to graduate before the end of the next twenty-five-thousand-year cycle—that is, twenty-five thousand years from "Now" on another third-dimension planet.

Those who are asleep are still our brothers and sisters, since they have also been created by God/Goddess. They may be our family and friends, work associates, or others everyone around us. So we must be willing to help them. One of your first tests is to be able to totally accept that everyone is your divine brother and sister. Then you must realize that you are to love them just as they are. However, we have some challenges in terms of knowing how to help them. Helping will be a difficult task, since many of us still remain within our old duality-energy fields. Those energy fields embody the consciousness of enemies, lack, and separation. We will need to *let go* of these illusions, attachments, and false beliefs in order to be able to help those who request help. It will also be helpful to clear the victim and the warrior mindset from our consciousness. We must realize we are not separate, and that we already have everything we need to help our brothers and sisters.

Many people want to leave planet Earth because they are bored, tired of separation, tired of pain and suffering, and just plain tired of the confusion and chaos. Do you fall within this group consciousness? Would you like to shift into a different state of consciousness? Most everyone senses the many changes occurring and realizes there is something better beyond this current "Now." If you believe and prepare, there will be something better. Then you can help create a New Earth. Many will refuse to change, and that's OK. They will prefer to physically die rather than change the old, conservative beliefs that have been their foundation for many lifetimes.

Graduation and Ascension Will Require a Shift in Consciousness

The main requirements for graduation from the third-dimension Earth and Ascension to the new, fifth-dimension Earth involve knowing who you are and raising your consciousness. Residents of Earth long ago lost their ability to understand consciousness. They have forgotten how to move from the lower frequencies into the higher frequencies of dimensional consciousness. Many on Earth speak of consciousness without really understanding its depth, or have given up trying to understand this highly important concept. Many think they are conscious of events around them when they use their intellects to sense and analyze physical observations, events, or various developments. What they think they know is based on accumulated knowledge from their pasts. That knowledge is made up of illusions and false beliefs, all of which have been based on the individual's intellect during many lifetimes.

Thus, many humans have subjugated the consciousness to their intellect. The intellect is far removed from reality and an understanding of consciousness. Humans who emphasize the use of their intellects are short-circuiting their understanding and the use of all their "awareness factors." The awareness factors that are most commonly ignored or seldom taken are into consideration are the sensings from telepathic information which is available from beyond traditional physical communications. By ignoring telepathic sensing from spiritual sources and other more advanced entities, many humans have ceased to evolve spiritually. The graduation and Ascension process involves the utilization of all awareness factors. Learning how to utilize all of your awareness factors will help shift your consciousness to the higher dimensions.

Just as your soul exists at various stages and levels of development, your conscious awareness factors exist at different stages. These awareness factors are a healthy form of energy which can be drawn into the body under specific physiological and psychological conditions. When an individual holds on to various constraints imposed and programmed by religions, governments, educational systems, and society in general, these awareness factors cannot be forced through these massive physiological and psychological blocks.

The concepts and understandings presented within this book have taken advantage of the intellect, as derived from scientific evidence, and also information gained from utilizing all components of the awareness factors. That is, the author has been in constant communication with the unseen Spiritual Hierarchy. Within the non-physical higher dimensional realities there are multitudes of Archangels, Ascended Masters, Extraterrestrials, and masses of information that can be telepathically received from all parts of creation. Telepathic information is not only available from the Spiritual Hierarchy but it can also be received from trees, animals, and Mother Earth herself.

By ignoring some of our awareness factors, humanity has suffered dramatically. We have used our physical awareness to move forward technologically, but we have failed to move forward spiritually. We brought this tragedy upon ourselves by losing our connection with Creative Source energy. Think of spiritual consciousness as the awareness you have through your sensitivity of mind, your intuitive sensitivity to various aspects of your God/Goddess within, and the Spiritual Hierarchy. Keeping your connection to Source Energy is highly important. Spiritual awareness encompasses an unlimited pool of knowledge and wisdom stored within all components of creation.

All of life is predicated upon levels of awareness. You have attended schools to become aware of the physical aspects of the world around you. Through the programming of the educational system, you have been taught to concentrate on using your five senses as a means of determining reality. The archaic and restrictive pattern taught in the schools has been designed to force students to verbalize or write their thoughts rather than imagine and visualize their thoughts. Once thoughts are imagined and visualized, those thoughts should and can be sent and received telepathically. As a result of the archaic educational system, humans have been dumbed down to where they have lost their natural manner of giving and receiving information telepathically. A consciously aware individual can receive valid information from all components of creation. Most humans live within a world of illusion and false beliefs. They lack understanding of what is real, because they lack an ability to communicate telepathically.

True consciousness involves the fine tuning and utilization of all of your outer and inner sensing systems. Those who lack the drive and will to utilize all of their awareness factors, including their telepathic abilities, will fail to soar to greater heights of consciousness. Many humans have allowed their intellect, with all of its false beliefs and limiting imprints, to limit their spiritual development. Those who fail to gain an understanding of how to maximize their awareness factors and shift their dimensional consciousness to higher frequencies will remain stuck within the third-dimension duality consciousness. Without preparation, they will be unable to graduate.

Preparation for graduation involves the removal of all third-dimensional programs, imprints, and blocks that have destroyed or damaged an individual's awareness factors. The challenge is to clear all limitations and become receptive by utilizing all available awareness factors. Through belief, intent, and spiritual help, the awareness factors can be restored and drawn into one's consciousness. To a great extent, the awareness factors are restored through your own personal capability of working with your God/Goddess within. As the awareness factors are restored, one has the capability to receive telepathic communications. These messages enter your physical bodies and are stored within the soul. From there, they radiate out to impact every cell in the body. As higher-frequency energies are received and distributed, the whole body begins to vibrate at the higher frequencies.

As these higher frequencies become stabilized, you begin to remember and slowly increase your spiritual light. As a result, you are able to free yourself from the struggles associated with third-dimensional Earth and all of its challenging duality lessons. By remembering, you no longer have to be concerned about past lives, karma, and all of the illusory details and

> **As you raise your consciousness to a certain level, your disguise as a human being is removed, and you become a Spiritual Master.**

false beliefs about the requirements for going to a mystical heaven. You are free to request help from the God/Goddess within and spiritually advance. You have evolved beyond the concept of a *human being*; you have evolved to become a *human doing,* a Spiritual Master.

All along you were, by nature, a creation of God/Goddess, a *human doing* disguised as a *human being.* You just forgot that you are indeed a Spiritual Master who is capable of doing everything needed to graduate and become a resident of the New Earth. As you remember who you are, you no longer have to prove anything to anyone. You are by divine right a Starseed of the new civilization that will inhabit the New Earth. As an aid for you, Jesus said in Luke 11: 9-10 and John 14:12 *Ask and ye shall receive,* and *Greater things will you do than I.*

Know that when you see humans around you resisting change, their decision isn't anyone's fault. A majority of those who plan to continue their third-dimension lessons may have an opportunity to "Wake Up" in a future life. Always keep it in mind that one does not earn the right to go to the New Earth. Your soul will have chosen to guide and direct you along the path which leads you there. Many reading these words will say "I am very interested in graduating and Ascension to the New Earth. "Count me in! I'll see you there." If these are your thoughts then you need to prepare.

Others will be repulsed by these concepts, resist change, and prefer to physically die when their time comes. There are many other choices that involve moving to other planets within the Universe. You will need to contact your Spirit Assistants to become aware of those other choices.

Ascension is not necessarily an accomplishment; it isn't even a process. Ascension is an ever-present knowingness of your magnificent eternal, loving being. This unfolding is always evolving and moving with the flow of evolution. As you keep an open mind to unlimited possibilities, you can become an unlimited possibility thinker. These unlimited possibilities will become your guiding lights, always shining out ahead of you to light your pathway. As you open your mind, you can learn about what is coming and how to prepare for whatever may happen. As you read on, you will discover some potential tools for graduation and Ascension. Ascension is not the end, but the beginning. Going through the Ascension process is when the fun really begins.

Some ask the question, "How should I live my life most effectively to prepare for and go through the graduation and Ascension process?"

One aspect of your preparation is depicted by the Aborigines of Australia. Marlo Morgan, who lived with the Aborigines in Australia and wrote the book *Mutant Message Down Under,* tells of an experience about a group of Aborigines floating on a raft near the coastline of the ocean. Once she made contact with them, she asked why they didn't use paddles to help guide and move the raft in the direction they were headed. They said, "If we used paddles, we might end up some-where other than where we're supposed to be going." They knew the raft would take them to where they needed to go. They trusted the Universal flow of life. Applying that philosophy and the many techniques outlined later in this book can help carry you forward along the most appropriate path.

Shifting consciousness and preparing for the Ascension is like preparing your raft for an unknown journey across the ocean. You and I are preparing our rafts, but we have never taken this raft trip before. Thus we have no previous understanding of how to paddle our rafts towards our goal. We have one option if we are to continue riding on the raft. That is to prepare for the trip and understand that our destination will show up as we approach the shore. The trip involves being open to receiving guidance across the unknown waters. By bringing in more light to guide your raft, you can be assured of safe passage. Your raft will most likely slowly drift in the most appropriate direction. When you try to move too fast (by bringing too much light into your lower third- and fourth-dimensional bodies) you could cause all kinds of damage. You don't need to be overly concerned about hurrying to paddle your raft. Just relax, enjoy the scenery, float along, and know that if you have prepared internally, you will reach the portals (Star Gates), pass through, and arrive on the New Earth.

So as you float along and think about the trip, spirit has a word of caution. If you were to completely remember who you truly are, without adequate preparation, a massive amount of light would enter your location on third-dimension Earth and destroy you. The light of creation is powerful—

> **Be patient with yourself as you prepare for your trip through the portal onto the unknown, parallel New Earth.**

beyond anyone's imagination. If you have failed to cleanse your body of all those 3rd dimensional challenges and that light of creation hits that resistance the body could become so hot it would combust. So be patient as you drift along on your raft. Be patient with yourself as you slowly remember that you are a child of God/Goddess, and that when you ask, the God/Goddess within will regulate the amount of light entering your bodies. You are preparing for something so grand there are not words to describe it. The trip is not out of your reach; you can accomplish it. Just prepare your raft with great care, get in, and let spirit take you towards your goal. A few preparatory procedures for the trip will be discussed later.

Only you can prepare to leave the old Earth by making the *internal shifts in consciousness* that qualify you to pass through the gates to the New Earth. The keeper of the gate will have a complete record of your preparation procedures and the extent to which you have followed these procedures. There is no way to sneak through the Star Gates when the guard is not watching. The process of passage is an individual experience; however, it may have connections to other souls on the same spiritual pathway.

A completely new paradigm (reality realm) must be created for the physical, emotional, and mental bodies to allow them to integrate the higher vibrational frequencies now entering the Earth plane. "Now" is the time to access, integrate, and utilize the infinite amount of assistance available from the Ascended Masters, Extraterrestrials, Archangels, angels, and your own inner spirit I AM Presence (God/Goddess within). Also there are many tools and technologies, brought to Earth by Extraterrestrial sources, available to assist in the embodiment of your divinity. All this support is here to help you transition from third- and fourth-dimensional realities to the fifth- and sixth-dimensional realities.

For additional insights about profound wisdom grounded in ancient knowledge read the English translation of the eight books by Vladimir Megre' (1950). The originals books were in Russian, then translated into twenty languages and sold over ten million copies.

Third-dimension Earth Is Being Up-graded to a Fifth-dimension Earth

Every aspect of life on the old Earth as you have known it will be impacted by the many upcoming dramatic changes. Earth is shifting to a higher frequency. The low-frequency characteristics humans have created and relied upon will disappear. Be prepared by knowing that when physical objects begin to disappear, that is OK. There is no reason to question or become fearful of these disappearances.

The old Earth Creator School was designed to provide an opportunity to create physical illusions such as an automobile. We also created challenges designed with a duality format that involved understanding good vs. evil, health vs. sickness, peace vs. war, and hot vs. cold. Upon the New Earth, these concepts and patterns of duality will be replaced with a new reality called Unity/Christ consciousness. Duality concepts such as evil, sickness, and war will no longer exist. These old duality concepts will not survive the higher frequencies of the fifth dimension.

If you have become stuck in the reincarnation cycles of duality, it should be exciting for you to realize that cycle will come to an end on the New Earth—if you take advantage of your various opportunities, make a choice, and spend time in preparation within your consciousness. When you prepare yourself within and evolve consciously beyond the fourth dimension, then you can Ascend with your physical body intact. As you Ascend, your spirit and body leave this third-dimension plane and, in a sense, you vanish from the perspective of those who remain within the third dimension. By working within to raise your dimensional consciousness, you vibrate at a higher frequency that is invisible to the third-dimensional sensing system. As a fourth- or fifth-dimensional entity, you can see those in the lower dimensions, but they cannot see you.

Prepare spiritually by determining who you truly are, implementing forgiveness, and clearing out all old duality beliefs and programs. Once the blocks are removed, a multitude of new, truthful revelations will flow into your consciousness. This is especially true as humans begin to understand the nature of multidimensional consciousness. According to the Archangel Metatron, posted on www.crystalinks.com, "The Shift," graduation, and Ascension of the physical body to the fifth-dimensional Earth is an event the prophets of the Bible called the second coming.

One pressing question many humans have been asking is, "What is holding back humanity's evolution on Earth, and why have we appeared to be stagnating for so long?"

Adama, the high priest of the fifth-dimensional city of Telos in northern California, gives a partial answer to this question in Telos Volume 1 (2006) by Aurelia Jones.

> *"First, there has been a lack of vigilance and motivation, with too little faith in God/Goddess's promises. A lack of consistency in your resolution to invest enough time and energy in your spiritual development keeps you in a state of spiritual lethargy and in a spiritual negative balance. Your desires for love and Ascension are still in a lukewarm stage. Until it becomes a burning desire in your heart and soul so great that you can no longer live without it, you cannot generate enough love, power, and energy to attain this level of evolution. I will say most of you are suffering from a kind of spiritual laziness. You are all too busy doing rather than becoming. How many of you possess a full understanding why you have chosen to incarnate here at this time?*

How do you respond to Adama's perspective? Are you devoting a good percentage of your time towards spiritual development? Or have you put your spiritual development on hold because you are frequently downright tired? Many humans are trapped in the struggle to keep up with all the challenges required just to survive.

Many on Earth now realize that survival alone has limited value. They are spending more time on their spiritual development. The procedures discussed within this book are a few of the many that can be implemented to help you qualify for graduation and Ascension. All of these procedures involve working with thought forms composed of subtle energy that you create as you align with higher-frequency concepts. Keep in mind that many of these concepts may be true on many levels, but perception of reality is always subject to higher spiritual concepts of awareness that continually change and evolve.

As you make the phase shift to fourth-dimensional consciousness, you will vibrate at a higher frequency. You will still seem physical and visible to yourself, even though you are invisible to others. They are vibrating in the lower-frequency bands. Likewise, your fifth-dimension reality will vibrate at even higher frequencies. Currently, there are many humans who are preparing to Ascend. Spiritual sources indicate that as of July 2008 there are over nine million souls preparing to graduate. Relatively speaking, that is a small percentage: only 0.13 percent of the current seven billion plus souls residing on Earth.

What Leaving the Old Earth and Entering the New Earth Is Like

When "The Shift" is complete after 2012, all humans will be vacating the third-dimension Earth. Earth will no longer support third-dimensional states of consciousness because of dramatic changes in the environment. The old Earth's polluted air will have low oxygen content; there will be a lack of drinkable water; there will be a shortage of food because plants cannot survive; it will be very difficult to travel; and there will be a host of other adverse factors. Most people already sense these changes. Humans are destroying the life-support systems that have helped maintain biological life. To those interested, you can gain some small insight as to the possible changes by viewing the movies *It Could Happen Tomorrow* and *The Future Earth and the CNN documentary* "Planet in Peril. These movies depict violent windstorms (hurricanes, powerful straight winds, and tornados) with flooding, volcanoes with volcanic ash cutting off the sunlight, a possible asteroid collision, tidal waves crossing over the land, melting polar caps and rising sea levels, and massive firestorms that burn off vegetation and build-

> **Realize that when "The Shift" is complete after 2012, all humans will be vacated from third-dimensional Earth.**

ings. The CNN documentary describes how humans are raping the planet and creating potential pandemics.

Many scientists believe a more serious threat is the release and spread of new, destructive, disease-inciting agents (created for biological warfare) that could kill millions because of their damaged immune systems. Any combination of these events could dramatically change the environmental features of the third-dimension Earth, making it difficult to impossible for all physical life forms to survive. Will any of these events take place? Time will tell. However, if they do occur, you will be prepared to accept them.

There will be an end point to the old play, closely followed by a beginning point of the new play. The omega point depicts the end, and the alpha point depicts the new beginning. In between, there is a null point in which nothing exists.

It is highly important for you to understand these three points in terms of their relationship to the changes anticipated to take place on Earth. For example, you may be surprised to know that you don't physically exist all of the time. You are actually blinking on and off many times a second. Your activities are similar to individual picture frames passing through a projector and seeming to move without interruption. All movies and television programs are the projection of individual still frames flashing on and off so fast they appear to be continuous.

Your life is an identical process; it is anything but continuous. In the moment between the omega point and the alpha point, where there is no thing (a null point), there is no manifest reality of any kind. There are an infinite number of these null points where there is only the Creator. This is sometimes called the "void," which one can enter between thoughts. It is a realm of calm and peace. To become aware of the void is very beneficial, since your Source Energy is available there. In the void, you can communicate with the spiritual world and receive guidance. As you practice moving into the void, you will discover an unlimited storehouse of knowledge, much of which can help you prepare for graduation and Ascension.

Note: Only one of you will be created anew on the other side of the null point. As you go through this process, you will begin to see more and more new realities coming into view. These will be new and seem physically real. You will need to accept and gradually understand them. They will become parts of your new reality realm. Many of the items observed may be scary since you have never observed them before. You may also observe multiple snapshots (repeating still pictures) of various items as they gradually come into view. Keep in mind that this is a very important process to go through. One reason for mentioning the appearance of objects you have never have seen before is that when you do sense them, you will realize you are not going crazy. These new items will be a part of your new reality realm. Do exercise caution in looking at or touching these new objects when they first appear, because that activity could damage your consciousness.

As the phase shift continues and you prepare to make the transition, there will be some discomfort, as there is with any birthing process. Keep in mind the joy that comes with any birth. When the struggle associated with the birth is complete, most of the pain will be over.

The New Earth already exists, but you have to align with it for it to manifest for you. The New Earth is here right "Now," but as a third-dimensional consciousness, you cannot see it. Your sensing system is not attuned to those higher frequencies. The closing of the old and preparing for the new is a paradox, or a reciprocal relationship, in which the New Earth calls you and you seek the New Earth. You can expedite the overall transition process by mentally locking into your vision of the New Earth. By locking in, you will create a perceptual field that attracts the New Earth to you.

The New Earth should begin to start stabilizing by the end of 2013. Once that process is complete, the old, third-dimensional Earth will no longer support life as we now recognize it. Without various life-support systems, the third-dimension Earth will enter a cycle of regeneration. Humans will be unable to survive on a regenerating planet. Also, humans whose bodies vibrate at the lower frequencies of the third dimension cannot physically survive the higher frequencies of the New Earth. These humans will have no choice but to leave Earth and incarnate on another third-dimensional planet. This reality may sound harsh. However, that decision was made by the Creators of the Universe when they gave permission for Earth to go through a rejuvenation cycle and for the New Earth to evolve to the fourth- through sixth-dimensional states of consciousness.

As you read on and obtain a glimpse of what the New Earth will be like, there may be a tendency to create a list of expectations. Spirit indicates that you will need to keep those expectations to a minimum. That is, all expectations must be tempered by a conscious ability to be prepared to accept anything and know that you're most appropriate choice will be available.

The vibration you seek is within your consciousness—not "out there" in what you may perceive the New Earth to be like. You will not move into the vibration you wish to have until you release all internal and external factors binding you to the lower frequencies. It really does not matter much what takes place in your external world; it matters what takes place within your internal consciousness. Release all attachments to what could have been, should be, or can be. There will be no need to pack your suitcase for the trip or carry anything with you. Prepare "Now" to leave everything behind on the third-dimension Earth. Temper your expectations of the New Earth, and keep an open mind to all manner of future possibilities. The whole process of graduation and Ascension is a totally new experimental procedure, never before attempted in this Universe. Many of the details will fall into place as each event transpires. On the New Earth, choices will emerge without planning or thinking them out. All activities will take place as a result of receiving guidance from within. You will be guided by the thoughts you receive during each "Now."

* * * * *

2

Human Evolution and Cyclic Nature of Events Occurring on Earth

Creator's Plans for This Universe and Souls in Physical Bodies

According to many sources, including the Spiritual Hierarchy, the Egyptian God Ra, and Edgar Cayce, indicate the Creator essentially got bored and lonely in the distant past, approximately 4.5 billion years ago. The Creator needed something to do; it wasn't feeling complete by experiencing unified consciousness all the time. So it conceptualized the idea of breaking *itself* into parts or Oversouls composed of souls, with a spirit made in the image of the Creator. The Creator knew that the souls within the Oversoul would be able to evolve by their own free will. These souls were given the option to make their own choices and decisions. As a result, each Oversoul would have many individual soul opportunities for many new experiences. Consequently, each soul would experience something that the Creator was not yet able to understand or comprehend.

These individual souls, made in the image of the Creator, are composed of a crystalline structure that is analogous to a quartz crystal. When complete the soul is multidimensional and composed of 617 facets. As a human soul evolves spiritually, the structural features and arrangements of these facets change to register the individual's spiritual evolutionary status. Each individual soul that makes up the Oversoul has its own creative ability and is a Co-Creator with God/Goddess.

Keep in mind the need to take care of your soul. Your soul can become damaged. Its facets can be lost, stolen, or given away. Thus, you need to give frequent attention to keeping your soul together and functionally efficient. This subject would require several books to describe in detail. However, is very important in understanding your spiritual progress and the real you. For additional insights about your soul's features and function, refer to the book *Remarkable Healings* by Shakuntala Modi, MD. *Your Immortal Body of Light* by Mitchell Gibson, MD, and Dr. Gibson's workshops on the human soul are available at <u>www.</u>

tybro.com, Also refer to *Cosmic Insights Into Human Consciousness* by John Hornecker' available at www.Earthscape.net.

The great plan envisioned by oneness Creator was that at the completion of a 4.5-billion-year universal cycle, all of the soul parts that had evolved would come back together in their Oversoul. They would recognize their God/Goddess consciousness, renounce separation, embrace Unity/Christ consciousness, and return to the totality of *Oneness*. The Creator would be enhanced by all the wonders that the fragmented parts had created.

As a part of this Universal plan, the Creators (Elohim) envisioned a planet with harmony and love for all of creation. However, other duality-creating entities (the Interloper's) inserted themselves within the original paradigm and altered its original design. The result was the establishment of duality consciousness, where there is an interaction of the Elohim (benevolent creations) and the Interlopers (aberrant creations).

The benevolent creations have become known as STOs, (Service to Others) and the aberrant creations as STS (Service to Self). These two creations are characteristic of all Extraterrestrials and humans currently residing on all low frequency planets throughout the Universe, including third-dimension Earth. Currently on Earth, each individual's "Method of Operation (MO) is either STO, STS, or a percentage combination of the two. However, that scenario (pattern) is coming to an end as the New Earth is restored to its original destiny as designed by the Elohim. That is, those on the New Earth will exhibit a Method of Operation classified as STO.

The behaviors of those who followed the Interlopers (including the Illuminati) in their selfish desire for power and control will be put to an end. These Interlopers that take on a human appearance have been given a choice concerning their future. Likewise species of animals and plants have been given a choice that many have already made. Specific humans, animals and plants will transfer to the New Earth while others will be leaving to reside upon a planet compatible to their vibratory pattern or state of dimensional consciousness.

Many are concerned when they notice that certain species of plants or animals are leaving. However, spirit indicates that at this point in the evolution of Earth, humans who speak about saving various species or the planet Earth are being arrogant. The Earth can and will survive. After all, Earth has survived for eons through a massive amount of continued abuse. Humans have destroyed the Earth in the past and are again destroying its water, air, and soil through greedy attempts to take without regard for what that taking process does to all life forms. Humans have raped the Earth of its circulatory system (oil), minerals, coal, life-giving mineralized soil, and many other energy patterns. Why? Because humans still lack an understanding of why all these physical features (energy patterns) were placed on Earth in the first place.

Everything that provides for human survival on Earth comes from the Earth. The planet's natural resources are rapidly being depleted. As a result, humans living on Earth have fallen into a pattern where they constantly decline physically, die, and reincarnate in a repetitive pattern. To counteract humanity's abuse of the planet, a wave of change is taking place, orchestrated by the Creators and benevolent Extraterrestrials. These Extraterrestrials have intervened many times in the past and are the reason conditions on Earth can still support life. Extraterrestrials currently have plans to cleanse and rejuvenate third-dimension Earth after humans have vacated it.

Many of the Elohim and Extraterrestrials have incarnated on Earth in human bodies. They are anchoring the energy of change and renewal to facilitate the rejuvenation process. To carry out their responsibilities, it will be necessary to evacuate all of those destined to inhabit the New Earth. Why? It will be much safer and more efficient to remove all biological life before the rejuvenation process. The possibility exists that all graduating evacuees will be taken by Extraterrestrials (in their physical bodies) to a designated interim location, rather than directly to the New Earth. Facilities at this location will help prepare each human graduate to be returned to the New Earth when it is ready to receive its new inhabitants.

One reason the current third-dimension Earth will have difficulty supporting human life is because its soils are rapidly losing their ability to support plant growth. Consequently, a majority of food products grown throughout the world originate from stressed, sick, and diseased plants and animals. Why? Because humans have mined the soils of trace minerals and destroyed the living microorganisms of the soil. These living components originally supplied the plants with minerals and vitamins. The book *Survival of Civilization* by Donald A. Weaver, (1982) with selected papers from John D. Hamaker reveals that life upon Earth cannot survive without a multitude of trace minerals. Plants, animals, and humans become imbalanced and sick when they are deficient in trace minerals and vitamins. Human survival will be impossible due to this factor alone. In the first chapter of the book, *Survival of Civilization*: which is entitled, *Our 100 Percent Junk Food Supply is Destroying Us*: the author provides scientific evidence that most of the world's topsoil has been stripped of its life-giving mineral elements.

Humans in the historic past have destroyed the life-giving soils on Earth several times. Each time, all biological life forms died and were physically cleared from the Earth to facilitate its rejuvenation. Each time this has happened, the Earth has entered a resting period. During this resting period, restoration of the Earth's minerals has taken place. The restoration process frequently involves dramatic temperature changes, tectonic plate displacement of land surfaces, glaciers covering a large portion of the planet, sea levels rise, and other environmental changes essentially make the Earth's surface uninhabitable. For the third-dimension Earth to support life in the future, it must become uninhabitable for a time to restore its ability to support life.

It has been scientifically established that humans are currently destroying the Earth's ability to support life. Every day we witness how these destructive patterns create health challenges. Many of these challenges that appear as diseases are due to stresses induced by a lack of proper nutrition and reduced emotional stability. You can anticipate without question that the majority of humans who fail to graduate (those who are not qualified to be removed from Earth physically) will starve or succumb to a host of dramatic Earth changes and diseases. There should be no fear associated with these potential events.

All souls are eternal and will continue in various forms until the Universal cycle is completed in several million years. Various kinds of Ascension (in spirit or physically) are pathways a soul can take when leaving Earth. These procedures have been prophesied and taught for centuries in every major society on Earth.

Cyclic Patterns in the Universe, Galaxy, and Solar System

There are many different cycles throughout the Universe. For example, a 4.5-billion-year cycle, called the "Day of Brahma" in the Hindu tradition, is the length of a given creation. There is also a 206-million-year cycle in which our Solar System makes one revolution around the Great Central Sun of the Milky Way Galaxy. Another repeating cycle occurs every fifty million years during which, in the past, all life on Earth has been spontaneously destroyed. Thereafter, following an equilibrium period, life returns, generally at a different vibratory frequency. Scientists have been studying these cyclic events for many years. Geologists call this fifty-million-year cycle a "punctuated equilibrium." For example, geologists at UCLA have discovered that the mass extinction of the dinosaurs occurred at the end of one of these Universal cycles. As the cycle came to a close, several chaotic events took place that changed the resonant frequencies of the Solar System. Although the dinosaurs are now physically extinct, their soul essences remain in holograms.

All components of the Universe have been designed to follow specific cyclic patterns. Each of the creations that make up the Universe, such as the Galaxies and Solar Systems, has an individual consciousness. All of these individually created parts are a part of the overall Creator source. A Galaxy such as our Milky Way is a conscious being that creates a design for its components, the stars and their Solar Systems. Stars are aware of the entire range of dimensions and have free will in terms of how they carry out the Galaxy's plan. All planets also have their own consciousness. According to the Edgar Cayce readings, "*each planet has its marching orders from the Divine; only humanity has the free will to defy the will of God*". However, each planet has some say as to how intelligent life evolves within or upon its surface.

Previously, at the end of the Universal cycles of seventy-five thousand and twenty-five-thousand years, some fairly dramatic cosmic events have occurred. As each Solar System is evolving, the structure features of all matter in that system change. Some of these changes are brought about by a spiraling, tornado-like wave that is ejected from its sun. The spiraling coil pushes the planets into spheres of energy that create and maintain a higher vibrational frequency. The spiraling coil wave from the sun has qualities of both radiation and intelligence.

These bursts of spiraling energy from the sun have increased recently and are zapping all creatures on Earth. This increased level of zapping always occurs at the ends of these cycles. Scientists have studied these bursts of energy given off by the sun, but so far have been unable to understand exactly what they are and how they influence the Earth and its living systems.

It is known that as the Earth moves farther from the sun, the number of days in a year increase. During Atlantian times, the calendar year had 360 days. Due to the last polar shift at the end of a twenty-five-thousand-year cycle (the period of Lemuria and Atlantis), the Earth moved farther from the sun, and five days were added to the calendar year. As the Earth moves away from the sun, it also expands in size.

Accumulating evidence indicates that one very dramatic change occurred on Earth at the end of one of these larger cycles. Originally, Earth had one large land mass called Hyperborea. Because of massive volcanic and tectonic plate shifts, that continent broke apart. This resulted in the formation of the Earth's current continents.

This dramatic shift not only changed the physical features of the Earth; it also created a dramatic jump in the evolutionary cycle for its future inhabitants. Some scientists now believe that this shift significantly influenced the evolution of humans on Earth. A shift in the human form, from the Neanderthal to the Cro-Magnon (modern man), occurred as this burst of energy engulfed the Earth and caused the breakup of Hyperborea.

A soul inhabiting a third-dimensional planet generally requires three twenty-five-thousand-year cycles to complete its lessons for graduation onto a fourth- or fifth-dimensional planet. These graduations generally occur at the end of each cycle. Often at the end of a cycle, not all of the human inhabitants qualify to graduate. If the third-dimensional planet on which they resided made the decision to shift to a higher dimensional state of consciousness, then those who failed to graduate must be removed and taken

At the end of a planet's cycle, all life thereon is destroyed. Life returns following an equilibration period.

to another third-dimensional planet to continue their lessons. This whole cyclic procedure does not happen by accident, but is orchestrated by a group of Ascended Celestial Beings who work within the Milky Way Galaxy. These celestial beings are part of a group allied with the Confederation of Planets in service to the One infinite Creator. The Confederation members govern (oversee) a large section of the Milky Way Galaxy and are collectively responsible for managing the transfer of souls from planet to planet.

There are many references and historical records that point out and prove that at the end of a planet's cycle, all life thereon is destroyed. For example, according to an advanced spiritual creation known as Ra, there is within the book, *The Law of One,* www.research.org, the following quote:

> If a third-Density planet has reached the end of a cycle and is about to shift into a fourth-density, then those inhabitants who are not ready to graduate will end up reincarnating on a different third-density planet. This does not happen by accident or simple conscious intention, but rather involves intelligently guided transfer of the souls themselves and of the appropriate genetic material for the creation of physical bodies that will match up with the souls. This planet-hopping process is managed by groups of interplanetary cosmic beings such as Ra, and as star systems are continually moving into different zones of energy throughout the Galaxy, there is always work to be done. From the reference point of Earth, these beings are referred to as angels, celestial beings, ET's, or perhaps the Lords of Karma.

You can ignore any such statement about the nature of reality. However, your beliefs will in no way change the cyclic nature of how the Universe was designed and currently functions. It has been established that at the end of each twenty-five-thousand-year cycle, planets automatically shift in consciousness. In this case, planet Earth has been directed to shift into the fourth- and fifth-dimensional states of consciousness. That move will take place by the simple Laws of physics, whether the inhabitants are ready or not. However, all humans residing on a planet that will go through these cyclic shifts have choices to make. When a planet shifts to fourth- and/or fifth- dimensional states of consciousness, a third-dimension entity cannot live on that planet. Not only will there be no life-support systems, but the DNA of a third-dimensional creation will no longer be supported by a spiraling, tornado-like torsion wave specifically designed for the new DNA characteristics of a fourth- or fifth-dimensional entity. To inhabit the new planet, evolving humans will have to receive new DNA strands. The single-stranded DNA characteristic of the physical body will be replaced with twelve high-frequency strands positioned in several different bodies. Therefore, all inhabitants of planet Earth who are not ready to shift to a higher consciousness will, of necessity, have to leave: since they failed to prepare for graduation, they have no other choice. However, keep in mind that those souls who choose to die and transfer to another third-dimension planet most likely *did not* come to Earth at this time to graduate and Ascend. They planned to die, just as they have in their past lives. Trust that your spirit has designed your experiences according to your divine plan. There is no judgment outside of self. Each soul has the free will to follow its own individual and divine plan.

If you have chosen to die and lack an understanding of the death process, then there is help available. Some individual souls currently residing upon Earth have been called into service to become "Death Walkers," those who can assist someone in the death process. These individuals have the ability to move back and forth from the physical Earth plane to the other side, spirit side of the veil, where spirits are void of dense physical bodies. Death Walkers can help someone die by becoming one with the dying entity and creating a pillar of light to travel upon, helping them move in consciousness. You can ask for the help of a "Death Walker" if and when you become concerned or need help in your transition.

The near-death experience is similar to this process. All of you are quite familiar with near-death experiences as described in many different books. These are individuals who have died, crossed over the veil, and then have come back into their physical bodies.

I went through a near-death experience myself in the late 1970s. Following a trip to Mexico I became very sick and while in the hospital left my physical body. I moved down a tunnel of light then stopped and requested to return with a new contract. With that new contract my connections to Source Energy were upgraded. Since then any time I sense any form of sickness developing, I can just ask for energy adjustments, and health is restored.

Urgent Request for Light Workers to Assist Those in Need

The Earth currently needs individuals who will step forward and assist those souls in need. For example, some need help in regaining the power to heal themselves. Others need help in dying; they need someone to guide them off the Earth plane and into the lower octaves of the fourth dimension. Such help can be considered a gift to that individual requesting help and your opportunity to be of Service to Others (STO). In fact, spirit indicates that this may be one of the greatest gifts you have to offer someone who has chosen to die and pass over. One way you can assist is through the use of sound. Toning, singing, or playing specific relaxing music is often very helpful.

You may also be requested to help those who have already died and have become disincarnates. They left their physical bodies on Earth, but they don't understand where they are or where they are supposed to go. You are all aware that many of these souls have become Earthbound, lost their way, and become attached to some place on Earth. They need help in finding their chosen time line to continue their evolutionary path. You can only help others when they have requested your help. Be careful to avoid interfering with anyone's chosen contract. Many light workers on Earth have been asked to assist disincarnates that come to them for help.

These wandering, disincarnate souls really do appreciate your love and concern in helping them find their preferred path (time line.)

Evolutionary Patterns and Soul Group Adventures on Earth

Soul groups generally evolve together on a specific planet. If they fail to graduate at the end of a cycle, they are kept together and transferred to a new planet as a group. Generally, this procedure has worked quite well, since all souls have free will to make what they consider their best choice. However, in the last seventy-five thousand years a serious challenge has developed. Relatively small groups of humans on different planets have failed to graduate at the end of a twenty-five-thousand year periods. In most cases, those who fail to graduate have been Repeaters on their planet; that is, they failed to graduate after fifty thousand years. Since they again failed to graduate at the end of a second twenty five thousand year cycle, a question arose as to what options they have concerning their continued evolution. In most cases the number of humans within the group of Repeaters was relatively small. It was difficult to justify providing a whole planet for each of the many different small groups of souls. After considerable deliberation about how to solve this problem, Earth was chosen about seventy-five thousand years ago to take in these smaller groups from many parts of the Galaxy. In the history of the Galaxy, this type of experiment is very uncommon. That is, it is very rare to have a planet chosen to accept such a wide diversity of human races originating from so many different planets within the Galaxy. No other planet has such a wide diversity of humans with so many different Galactic backgrounds. Just visualize in your mind the many different races on Earth now. Have you ever wondered why? Each race originated from a different planet. There are various Caucasian groups (Slavic, Mediterranean, and Western European), Oriental (Japanese, Filipinos, and Chinese), the Thai, American Indians, dark-skinned tribes of Africa, native tribes in South America, Eskimos of the colder climates, and others all living in groups on one small planet. All of these human races and tribes previously resided upon different planets before they were given a choice and brought to Earth.

A majority of all human races residing on Earth are Repeaters, those who failed to graduate from their former planets at the end of an evolutionary cycle. All of these races on Earth that originated from different planets within the Galaxy were assigned to third-dimensional Earth to continue their evolution. For example, the Chinese race came from a planet revolving around the star Deneb. Creator Source indicates that the differences between races have a genetic basis and those differences should not be erased. According to the Edgar Cayce readings, these genetic differences are an aspect of the inner character and harmony of the soul.

Keep in mind, these Repeaters came to Earth seventy-five thousand years ago, and most are still here. As outlined within *The Law Of One* books (from Ra), these Repeaters have had chances to graduate at the end of two previous twenty-five-thousand-year cycles. At the end of the first cycle, not one single human graduated from Earth. Normally, 20 percent of the human population graduates at the end of the first cycle; 60 percent graduate of the end of the second cycle (fifty thousand years ago). After fifty thousand years, only 120 humans graduated, and they have stayed on Earth to help those who failed to graduate.

Another contributing factor that can account for many differences in the structural and emotional features of the human body is a scientific procedure called genetic engineering. Many scientists now believe that jumps in the evolutionary features of humans can be correlated with a combining of the genetics of off-planet races with individual humanoids on the planet. These genetic manipulations create a type of hybrid body derived from a cross between different human forms. Many of you are familiar with the genetic crosses made to transfer the Reptilian brain from the Reptilian race into the current physically designed human body. There are many sources and accounts of the potential influence of genetic engineering on the human vehicle. During Atlantian times, many different hybrids were created which, because of their deviant purposes, displeased the Creators.

Here we are seventy-five thousand years later, and a majority of the human population on Earth is unaware that the next graduation is scheduled to occur in the very near future (at the end of the age, somewhere between 2008 and 2014). There are approximately seven billion humans currently on Earth. Extraterrestrial records, continually updated, indicate that currently about 2.5 billion, or less than 25 percent of the human population, has even had a passing thought about preparing to graduate. Why are such a small number ready to graduate? Some possible answers as to why humans have failed to prepare for graduation may be helpful.

First, consider that a majority of Earth inhabitants are totally unaware that graduation is even possible. This opportunity has been withheld by the dark forces in a desire to maintain their slaves. Second, as mentioned, many souls were Repeaters before they were assigned to Earth. This brings to mind four more questions. (1) Why would a Repeater have more difficulty graduating from an Earth school where mixed races reside? (2) Why are there so many human souls currently living on Earth totally unaware of what is taking place? (3) How has the free will given to each soul entered into the failure rate? (4) What influence have the Interlopers and the Illuminati had on slowing spiritual evolution?

The answers to those four questions would take many additional pages; consequently, you have an assignment to find the answers. Those answers could very well help you make sure you graduate at the end of this cycle. Some clues as to why these souls are stuck on Earth are: their attachment to the dramas present, fear of the unknown, the distractions of the Illuminati and Interlopers, and religions keeping secret the requirements and opportunities for graduation.

One possible cause of the lack of incentive to graduate is that the Repeaters have been segregated as a group. If you are aware of what it is like to teach a class of repeaters, segregated because of their reduced mental and emotional capabilities, you may understand what is happening on Earth. In the public school system, individual students with limited learning abilities have been segregated and lumped together in special education classes. I have taught these students in high school and found the task quite difficult. When segregated out, they lack the incentives or stimulation of fellow classmates who have superior mental and emotional capabilities. Thus, now there is an attempt by educators to place these students in a normal class when possible.

God/Goddess and the Creators have been very aware that the experiment of placing many different races of Repeaters on a single planet has failed to solve the challenges of how best to help these Repeaters spiritually evolve. The procedure of moving them to one single planet may have helped solve the problem of what to do with so many small groups. However, it appears that the procedure has created other challenges. These Repeaters have undergone all kinds of spiritual suffering, much of which has made their lives on planet Earth very difficult.

Because of the anticipated number of graduates from third-dimension Earth, a call has gone out throughout the Galaxy and Universe for help. Following a review of Earth's population by the Spiritual Hierarchy and Council of Creators, the decision was made to request and allow an additional one hundred million souls from other planets within the fourth- through fifth and sixth-dimensional states of consciousness to incarnate on Earth. They will assist in the Ascension process. Also many Extraterrestrials from high-frequency planets have come back from the future to incarnate on Earth to be of assistance.

Are you one of those hundred million who came to assist? If so, do you remember what you planned to do? How do you plan to help? Or are you one of the Repeaters, wondering how in the world you can get out of this melting pot called Earth? Have you really discovered who you are and why you are on Earth at this very critical period in history?

If you are a Repeater, and over six billion of Earth's human inhabitants are, then you have a responsibility to help yourself, but you also have a responsibility to help the population of Earth. You will not be called upon to save the world yourself, but you can help yourself, your family, and friends. By the way, Mother Earth will appreciate your help in designing the New Earth by remaining within your physical body during the next few years and connecting with your Source Energy to send out love, joy, and peace to the Earth. Yes, one person can make a difference. This procedure alone could dramatically increase the number of souls who will be able to qualify for graduation and Ascend to the New Earth. Likewise, you can spread the message about what is happening on Earth.

On-going Energetic Changes Related to Universal Cyclic Patterns

As mentioned, as the Solar System arrives at the end of these seventy-five-thousand- and twenty-five-thousand-year galactic cycles, many changes must take place. The Galaxy is changing frequency, and the regions around the Galaxy are becoming more highly charged. This charge is in part absorbed by our sun and radiated to all of the planets. As our Solar System and its planets drift through the Milky Way Galaxy, it passes through these different zones of energy density in cyclic patterns. This density shift also creates intelligent complex torsion waves (twisting, helical, spiral waves), which in turn transform the

DNA structure of life on each planet. As the DNA is altered, existing biological forms go through many different and dramatic changes. Scientists believe that at the end of the previous seventy-five-thousand-year cycle, the human body changed forms, and that change correlated with genetic changes. Archeological discoveries indicate that the human brain significantly increased in size during this period. These more highly evolved forms with a larger brain replaced the older forms with smaller brains. We are again approaching the end of a seventy-five-thousand-year cycle, and many scientists believe we may experience a similar change in our brains. Some channeled information indicates that when this happens, the expanding brain, because of the rigidity of the skull, will have to push upwards through the soft spot of the skull to create a cone-shaped head. Also when this happens, various genetic changes will alter the functionality of hair follicles, and humans will lose their ability to grow hair. Time will tell if these are real probabilities or only possibilities.

As we approach the end of this twenty-five-thousand-year cycle, we are experiencing an intense level of cosmic energy that is having an effect on our DNA and our physical, mental, and emotional bodies. Humans who plan to Ascend will have their DNA upgraded. As you are well aware, graduation is an inside job; individuals make their own changes in consciousness. Those changes in consciousness also change the DNA. As the events associated with "The Shift" take place, an intense level of cosmic energy will arrive on Earth and become available for humanity. This increased energy will assist all individuals in shifting their dimensional consciousness from the third to the fourth, and eventually to the fifth dimension, all a part of the graduation process. So the current shift in consciousness and impending Ascension is a cyclic, Galactic event that has been predicted for centuries and has now been scientifically documented astronomically, archeologically, and geologically.

Here are a few scientific observations that correlate with "The Shift" as discussed by: Wilcock (2006) (1) A dramatic increase in solar activity over the past ten years. Never before in recorded history has the sun released such intense radiation. (2) The moon is developing a gaseous atmosphere called Natrium. (3) Earth's atmosphere contains an increased concentration of hydrogen oxide (HO) gas, a gas previously at very low levels. (4) Global warming is occurring that has nothing to do with carbon dioxide, fluorocarbons, or other air pollutants. The temperature increase on Earth is due to the increased spinning of the Earth's core. (5) Venus's brightness is increasing dramatically. (6) Icecaps are melting on Mars. (7) Earth's icecaps have been reduced by 40 percent in thirty years. The polar icecap crystals must melt in order to release an enormous electromagnetic field. This electromagnetic field is stored within the ice crystals and contains the old codes of planetary resonance. These old codes must be released for the Earth to shift to the higher dimensions. Then, as "The Shift" takes place, a new planetary resonance can be created. (8) Jupiter, the gaseous mass, is changing into a visible tube of ionizing (highly charged) radiation. (9) The magnetic fields of Uranus and Neptune are changing significantly. (10) Voyager 2 found that Uranus and Neptune have had recent pole shifts. (11) Volcanic activity on Earth has increased 500 percent since 1975. (12) Natural disasters (hurricanes, mud slides, typhoons, tidal waves, and tornados) on Earth increased 410 percent between 1963 and 1975, and have continued to increase. (13) Astronomers in 2002 detected a 300 percent increase in the atmospheric pressure on Pluto. (14) The strength of the magnetic field of the sun has increased 230 percent since 1901. (15) The plasma energy around the Solar System (the heliosphere created by the sun) has increased 1,000 percent, indicating the Solar System is moving into a highly charged region of the Galaxy. All of these changes and many more are required for the dimensional shift and resulting increase in the frequency of the Solar System. For more information, read the December 2008 issue of the Sedona Journal of Emergence on Earth changes and other predictions for 2009, and also related messages received in different channelings.

We have all heard that Earth changes will occur in association with "The Shift." In addition, we now understand that many different types of changes are occurring within our Solar System. The Universe, Galaxy, Solar System, and all components of creation are changing. Evidently, what we are observing is conscious energy from all components of creation evolving through an ongoing cyclic process that leads humans towards Unity/Christ consciousness. Keep in mind that every component of creation has consciousness: the sun, trees, and even rocks.

All consciousness is involved in "The Shift" and many components of creation are multidimensional.

When we consider cosmic changes in terms of the upcoming "Shift" and Ascension, we must realize that *all is Energy, and we are more than our physical bodies.* There is no need to be fearful of the dramatic changes that occur at the end of these cycles. As these events take place, we can request and work to shift into a higher state of consciousness. As this shift occurs, the future of our old, physical bodies becomes somewhat irrelevant. As we shift to the higher dimensions, we will take on new, less dense bodies and other significant changes. After Ascension, we will be able to change our bodies' features by thought.

Here are a couple of examples of how these cyclic patterns have influenced life forms on Earth. Geologists studying the Paleozoic era note that the predominant species on Earth was a little crab called Trilobite. At the end of a cycle, these crabs all died, and their group soul evolved into the next stage of evolution; as a result, they entered a new, more advanced form. In like manner, the dinosaurs died. Their souls did not go anywhere; they evolved to incarnate as mammals. As a soul Ascends to inhabit a different body it has, in a sense, graduated. In the evolutionary pattern of creation, this process is called "Soul Graduation." Your soul has gone through several of these evolutionary patterns.

Evolutionary States of Dimensional Consciousness and Graduation

There are at least eight states of dimensional consciousness that all creations must ultimately pass through during their evolutionary pathways. Each dimension has a particular grade or quality of consciousness associated with it. In order to pass from one dimensional state of consciousness to another, an entity interested in progressing must attain and meet some basic qualifications in each dimension before moving upward and graduating.

For example, the third dimension includes the lessons of self-awareness and duality consciousness. The fourth dimension includes the experiences of love and unity of all life, or Unity/Christ consciousness. For a soul to evolve from the third to the fourth dimension, one must shift towards taking on Unity consciousness. This is not just a belief in

Unity/Christ consciousness. The potential graduate must consciously go through the experience of moving from duality consciousness to Unity consciousness. Until that experience of oneness becomes reality, a soul is unprepared to graduate and must continue to incarnate on a third-dimensional planet. That is, each soul assigns to itself, based on its state of dimensional consciousness, a specific planet designed for those experiences the evolving soul requires. Some souls may actually choose a lower-frequency planet for a specific purpose. However, it is impossible for a low-frequency soul to incarnate on a high-frequency planet even under specific conditions. That soul's physical body would be unable to survive because of its incompatibility with its environment.

Each planet has its marching orders and must adhere to them. Earth has recently received its marching orders to shift from the third dimension to the fourth- and fifth- dimensional states of consciousness. Other planets have similar guidelines. However, each planet does have some decision-making powers as to how it will follow those guidelines. Each planet has some influence on the way life forms evolve within its interior and on its surface.

Each planet is also influenced by its position within the Galaxy. Each Galaxy has, throughout its structure, different energy densities and patterns that impact a planet as it moves through the Galaxy. Each Solar System rotates around the center of the Galaxy on a pre-scribed path with very exact cyclic patterns and intervals. At certain points within the Galaxy, spiraling torsion waves occur that transform the DNA of entities living upon the planet as it passes through those points. When this occurs, the genetic codes of the existing biological forms on the planet are altered by the torsion waves. As a result, biological life forms evolve very rapidly and new life forms rapidly replace the older, less developed forms.

Those who remain within the fourth-dimensional state of consciousness, or in the astral plane, will realize that there is still some duality polarization, just like within the third dimension. Those choosing to remain within the fourth dimension have the choice to determine their own agendas as separate entities, whether they are disincarnates, angels, or lower spirit forms. Some of these entities may choose to bypass the opportunity to shift to the fifth-dimensional state of consciousness.

With that choice, they can visit or interact with a third-dimensional reality realm but are restricted from entering a fifth-dimensional reality realm.

According to Ra, the end of this cycle will occur somewhere around December 2012. Planet Earth will have ended the dark portion of the twenty-five-thousand-year cycle and entered into the light portion in 2013. The cycle corresponds to how long it takes the Solar System to pass through a specific energy band (called the Photon Belt) located within the Milky Way Galaxy. For more information, see Wilcock's, *Earth Orbits the Galactic Center (Wilcock, 2006)*.

Every time humanity has passed through these cyclic patterns, it has reached a high level of spiritual development, during the light phase. During the dark phase, humanity falls backward spiritually. In their fallen state, humans have frequently destroyed Earth's environment, making the planet uninhabitable. Humans have again almost reached the point of destroying Earth's environment. Following each destructive period, the planet goes through a recovery period. Then Extraterrestrials monitor the environmental conditions to determine when the planet can become habitable again. Once living conditions become favorable, various life forms and humans can return and proceed to complete another evolutionary cycle.

For those interested, we should be able to learn how to take advantage of the coming light phase and accelerate our spiritual development. However, efforts will be required to control humanity's destructive tendencies. Along these lines, the spiritual realm has instituted a previously unheard-of process designed to prepare our bodies. Some considered this change to be a transmutation towards Ascension. That is, during the period just before "The Shift," the human body will be transformed and renewed, a process currently underway. By examining the experiences of souls who have already gone through this transformation and Ascended, we can hopefully learn from them. They may have some suggestions of things to avoid and other activities that would be beneficial.

Recall that during the end of the last dark cycle on Atlantis, the destruction included dramatic climatic changes as a result of wars that filled the atmosphere with particulate matter and radioactivity. As a result, a large proportion of the animal and human population was destroyed. However, there were some survivors. During and following these destructions, spiritually advanced souls constructed cities inside the Earth and relocated safely away from the surface chaos and uninhabitable atmosphere. There are hundreds of such cities currently inside Earth. A majority of these souls living inside the Earth have Ascended to the fifth-dimensional state of consciousness or above. It could be very beneficial to learn about their previous and current experiences and listen to their advice.

* * * * *

3

Earth's History for the Past Three Hundred Million Years

The Age of This Universe and Human Life Forms in Present

Some evidence indicates that humanoids and related creations have inhabited this Universe for over 950 billion years (as we understand clock time). Records in the Great Central Library, located within the cosmos somewhere, indicate that the schoolroom called Earth (a hollow globe) has had inhabitants residing on its outer and inner surfaces for over five hundred million years. Planet Earth was called a Star Seed, to which external life forms came from several Universes. Some of these life forms combined with each other, generated new life forms, and then left. Thereafter, other Extraterrestrials discovered Earth and set up colonies. Drunvalo Melchiezedek's close advisor, Thoth, indicated that human civilization on Earth dates back five hundred million years. During this historic period, Earth's magnetic poles have shifted five times, most recently during the fall of Atlantis. Ancient records of these events are still housed in the Great Central Library. Apparently, access to that Great Central Library is limited to a majority of humanoids. Also, early records of the Earth have apparently been blocked purposely, since scientists have very limited knowledge of Earth's first 295 million years.

Recent evidence also indicates that the spiritual realm has limited humanity's access to recorded entries within very ancient Akashic records. Thoth, an advanced entity who lived in Egypt, has stated that the Sphinx contains proof that civilizations have resided on Earth for at least 5.5 million years. Thoth has made repeated attempts to access records beyond 5.5 million years ago, but without success. Apparently the ancient memory of planet Earth, stored within the Akashic records, was transferred somewhere, possibly to the Great Central Library for safe-keeping.

Access to the more recent historical records indicates that about 4.5 million years ago, light beings from the land of Mu (within the Dhal

Universe) arrived on Earth and set up communities on the continent of Lemuria. The Lemurian landmass at that time covered what is now essentially the Pacific Ocean and surrounding lands, from India east to California and South America. Shortly after these settlements were established, races from several other star systems such as Sirius, Alpha Centauri, and the Pleiades came to Earth and formed colonies. These colonies were mainly isolated in small villages for many centuries. Over the past two million years, populations of third- and fourth-dimensional humans have cycled through a series of evolutionary steps on Earth. During these intense duality challenges, these societies reached a high spiritual level. But they had difficulty in dealing with ego and negative emotions, and thus an inability to get along with their neighbors. Gradually, some mental understanding about the importance of controlling emotions has developed. Positive emotions must predominate for the sake of survival alone. When the negative emotions predominate, the society essentially collapses, many die, and a few shift into a survival site. Once people discover they are spiritual beings, they are more likely to control their emotions.

During each cycle, a few human inhabitants raised their dimensional consciousness and Ascended to a higher state of reality. These early Earth inhabitants discovered that after they leave their physical bodies (die), they could choose to return to Earth and continue their evolution, or incarnate on another third- to a fourth-dimensional planet.

About one million years ago, there was a thriving third- to fourth-dimensional human race on Mars and some other planets within this Solar System. These humans on Mars became very individualistic and separated themselves from God/Goddess. Then, about two hundred thousand years ago, following the last Lucifer rebellion, those inhabitants on Mars had a shift in consciousness. Remember, Lucifer was one of the most incredible angels that God/Goddess ever made. In fact, he thought that he was as good as God/Goddess. As a result, he separated himself from God/Goddess and convinced about a third of the angels to join him in a rebellion.

In like manner, the Martians became very technical and intellectual. They were very left-brained, with an emphasis on physical creations. They had very little right-brain function. That is, their left brains dominated their right brains. As a result, the logical ego mind took control. Such a human lacks a functional emotional body and has limited understanding of feelings and love. The Martians then created an external Mer-Ka-Ba energy field, as opposed to an internal Mer-Ka-Ba based on love. This externally created Mer-Ka-Ba, along with their materialistic drive, was their demise. As a result, they destroyed Mars's water supply.

Reincarnation Cycles and Humanity's Destructive Tendencies

A related example of how damaging technology can be misused is illustrated by the experiences of an Extraterrestrial race called the Grays. The Grays, descendants of the Martians, known as the Gray-Reticuli, inhabited another planet when they left Mars. They then became a highly evolved technical society. Remember, while on Mars, these souls had limited use of their right brains. Consequently, they lacked any form of emotion or love. Because of atomic radiation on their new planet, this race of Grays lost the capability to reproduce sexually. In an attempt to survive, the Grays created clones of themselves. However, as with any clone, these clones are short-lived, and the Grays realized that their civilization was dying and soon to be lost. In an attempt to find help, they searched various regions throughout this sector of the Milky Way Galaxy for a planet where the people were so engrossed in self-indulgence they could come to the planet and conduct experiments without the general population being aware.

These Grays discovered Earth, negotiated with some United States government officials, and signed an agreement. The agreement allowed them to conduct cloning experiments on U.S. citizens in exchange for their Extraterrestrial technologies. Within this governmental contract, the Grays were given permission to abduct women, impregnate them, and harvest the fetuses for placement in incubators on board their Extraterrestrial vehicles. The objectives of these experiments were to regain their sexual capabilities and emotions. These experiments were in progress for several years before their contract was canceled. It is my understanding that the experiment was relatively successful, and the Grays have now been removed from this sector of the Milky Way Galaxy They moved to a suitable location where they can evolve without interfering with humans on Earth.

During the past three hundred thousand years, the societal cultures of Hyperborea, Pam, OG, Atlantis, and Lemuria experienced physical death and their souls reincarnated time after time. Many humans now on Earth have had past lives in these societies. About forty thousand years ago, living conditions on Earth became very difficult because of air pollution and cold temperatures. As a result, the original Hyperborean culture left the surface of the planet and started building subterranean cities for survival purposes. One of these cities was called Shambhala the Lesser and was located below the Gobi Desert. Some Hyperboreans died and left the Earth, others entered Shambhala, and some migrated to other regions of the Earth. Some of these twelve-foot-tall Hyperboreans still live in an underground city north of the Himalayas in Asia. The original city of Shambhala the Lesser has shifted to a higher frequency. Shambhala the Greater is now a spiritual culture without physical features.

Long before there was life on planet Earth, there was third-dimensional life on the planet Venus, similar to those humans "Now" living on Earth. Currently there are higher-dimensional life forms on most planets in the Solar System, though these planetary conditions are unfavorable for third-dimensional human beings. Currently the only planet adapted to third-dimensional beings in this Solar System is Earth. In the recent past, Venus, Mars, and Maldek (now an asteroid belt) were favorable for third-dimensional humans. Those souls on Venus have Ascended beyond the third dimension. Some of them fused together into an entity called Ra. Ra currently is helping with Earth's Ascension. Ra has been active in this Solar System for the past seventy-five thousand years. When Mars became uninhabitable due to war, Ra helped the Martian souls to reincarnate on Earth. Then, fifty-eight thousand years ago, Ra helped many souls from the Dahl Universe incarnate on Earth.

Several other dramatic changes have taken place on the Earth in the past. Approximately one hundred thousand years ago, there were seven major continents on Earth, including Atlantis, located where the Atlantic Ocean is now. The continent of Lemuria consisted of a large number of islands in the Pacific Ocean area, and in part where Hawaii and New Zealand are now. The larger portions of Atlantis and Lemuria have submerged and no longer exist. Currently there are seven continents on Earth: Asia, Africa, North America, South America, Antarctica, Europe, and Australia.

A hundred thousand years ago, the Earth also had two ice-crystal mantles suspended several thousand feet above its surface. When the mantels existed, life flourished upon all the major continents. This included life on the South Pole. Through a series of events, the ice-crystal mantles fell to the Earth's surface. Following the collapse of the mantles, the far northern and southern regions of Earth gradually began to experience extremely cold temperatures. Also, after the mantles collapsed, the protective features of these mantles were lost. Life was threatened by radioactive particles that entered the Earth's atmosphere from outer space, causing serious bodily injury. As a result, the inhabitants of Hyperborea had to abandon their land of sunshine in the area now called Northern Europe and Asia.

Another significant event occurred about thirty thousand years ago when sociological conflicts developed between the Atlantians and Lemurians. The Lemurians believed that the less evolved cultures on Earth should be left alone to evolve on their own. In contrast, the Atlantians believed that the less evolved cultures should be controlled and live as slaves.

Approximately 12,500 years ago, at the end of the dark phase of that cycle, there were a series of dramatic events on the continents of Atlantis and Lemuria. For example, when the delicate crystal energy system on Atlantis was tuned too high, tremendous explosions occurred. Volcanic activity increased and gigantic Earthquakes occurred, causing tidal waves. Large areas of Earth were devastated. Particulate matter released by the volcanoes blocked out the sun; it became very cold, and crops died. Without food, many died of starvation. Through a series of related energy imbalances, portions of Atlantis submerged into the Atlantic Ocean. Many of Earth's current inhabitants went through these dramatic events and have no interest in repeating them.

Humans now living on Earth could help solve many challenges if they would band together to stop the controllers (the Illuminati, with their political and economic power) from destroying the Earth again. The Illuminati are coming very close to destroying the Earth with their atomic weapons, radiation, and air and water pollution. They have created disease-causing agents spread by scalar wave transmissions, chemical trails containing Mycoplasma, toxic metals, and the High Frequency Active Auroral Research Program (HAARP) in Alaska described by Jerry Smith in the book, *HAARP The Ultimate Weapon of the Conspiracy.* Currently, because of the adverse influence an atomic war would have on the Solar System, Extraterrestrials have deactivated all nuclear devices on Earth. The spiritual realm is also closely monitoring many events planned by the Illuminati and have, on several occasions, interfered to negate these destructive plans. However, spirit needs your help in sending love to those Illuminati who have blown up buildings and caused lasting damage to Earth and its residents.

* * * * * *

4

Carry-Over Beliefs from Atlantis and Lemuria Affecting Humans

Atlantis and Lemuria Destroyed Twenty-five Thousand Years Ago

Some ancient cultures on Earth such as, Titan, Pan, Og, Thule, Hyperborea, Atlantis, and Lemuria reached high levels of spiritual advancement before falling. Where did the Atlantians come from, how did they live, and what happened to them? The Atlantians came to Earth over fifty thousand years ago from the Lyrian star system. Remnants of Atlantis have been discovered within the Bermuda Triangle off the coast of Florida. Hundreds of channelings and scientific expeditions to several areas within the Atlantic Ocean have proven that humans lived within this area. At several locations on the Atlantic Ocean floor there are pyramids, roads, pillars, buildings, canals, and artifacts from Florida to Europe and Africa. One significant discovery has been the submerged roads, pyramids, and building blocks east of Florida. Many have heard of the energy vortex around the Bermuda Triangle that is believed to be related to Atlantis. That vortex is less active now, but in the past is believed to have caused dematerializations and thus the disappearances of humans, boats, and airplanes that have ventured into the Bermuda Triangle.

The Atlantians were also known as the Annunaki, the "tall ones." They were eight to twelve feet tall and had life spans of approximately eight hundred years. Earlier, in Africa, the Annunaki genetically engineered smaller humans as workers for mining gold, farming, construction, and other labor-intensive activities. Those genetic alterations are currently a part of the physical body that our souls currently inhabit on Earth.

The technology in Atlantis was far superior to that which we currently have on Earth. For example, they controlled the weather. They loved to create storms. They set aside areas to observe violent atmospheric disturbances and enjoyed creating volcanic eruptions. For more information search the Edgar Cayce readings, various books, and Web sites about Atlantis.

One crowning accomplishment of the Atlantians was their development of a sophisticated, scientifically based crystal-energy technology. By using crystal refraction, amplification, and storage, they were able to use vital crystal energies for growing plants, propelling their vehicles, healing the body, assembling structures, and even creating matter. They could focus and transmit these crystal energies over great distances through a series of pyramids. Some remnants of these crystal systems have been discovered at several locations on Earth.

The major power source used in Atlantis was reported by Edgar Cayce in his readings. In the readings, The Great Crystal energy was called A Tuaoi Stone. It was a six-sided crystal that was housed in a large, dome-shaped building that opened like a space observatory. When the cover was opened, this crystal received off-planet energy forces, concentrated them, and then transmitted those energies throughout Atlantis. These energies were used for many purposes, such as those mentioned above. Even with their technological capabilities, it is evident that the Atlantians had limited understanding of the power of crystal energies. When greedy individuals wanted more power from the system, they failed to understand how destructive these energies could be when uncontrolled. When the crystal was tuned too high, it activated volcanoes, melted mountains, and caused land masses to sink into the ocean. Ultimately, the greedy desire for power over nature and inability to keep the energy intensity sufficiently low caused the submergence of many portions of Atlantis.

One significant individual, a high priest in the Atlantian Ascension Temple, realized the fate of Atlantis. About 13,500 years ago, this High Priest brought the Ascension Flame from Atlantis to Egypt. In Egypt, he became the pharaoh Amenhotep III, who built the Temple of Luxor. He Ascended in 400 BC and became the Ascended Master, Serapis Bay. Currently, Serapis Bay has dedicated his efforts to helping all those souls on Earth who are interested in preparing for graduation and Ascension.

During the period of Atlantis and Lemuria, intense atomic wars erupted across the Earth, damaging not only Atlantis and Lemuria, but other areas of Earth. Remains from these wars are still evident in the deserts of the world. For example, the Outback in Australia and the Mojave, Gobi, and Sahara deserts are areas where atomic wars were fought. To this day, these atomic wastelands are environmentally unfavorable for plant, animal, and human populations. The radioactive damage and associated disturbances altered the structural features of Earth, causing volcanic eruptions and Earthquakes. As a result, gigantic tidal waves moved up to one thousand miles inland, destroying many cities.

The continents of Atlantis and Lemuria sank into the oceans about thirteen thousand years ago, at the end of a twenty-five-thousand-year cycle. Two thousand years after the sinking, the continents of Earth were still shaking. For several hundred years after the atomic wars, the atmosphere was full of debris; sunlight was insufficient to grow plants, resulting in food shortages. To survive these destructive conditions, some of the more spiritually advanced Atlantians and Lemurians relocated inside the Earth. They still reside there within their youthful, higher-dimensional bodies; many of them have lived in the same body for thousands of years. Many other Atlantians and Lemurians who perished and left their physical bodies have reincarnated in the third dimension and now presently live on the Earth's surface. Some have vivid memories of what happened during the flood and atomic wars. A woman who was fearful of water and unable to take her children swimming vividly remembered drowning during the submergence of Atlantis. Since all experiences occur in the "Now" that fear had to be removed for her to feel safe near water.

Currently there are over 120 subterranean cities within the Earth, some with over one million inhabitants. These cities are inhabited by Hyperboreans, a few Lemurians and Atlantians, and several other off-planet races. Some humanoids living within the Earth have a stature of over twenty feet in height. In fact, spirit sources indicate there are more different races of humans and a greater number of humans living within the interior portions of the Earth than on its surface. A few people reading about the large number of people living within the Earth may have difficulty believing that is possible. That's because those in control have kept that fact a secret. The powers that be don't want you to know about these advanced spiritual societies living within the Earth.

Some of you may be interested to know the United States government has built several secret cities within the Earth. If you have difficulty understanding what is happening upon and within the Earth, I suggest you set aside time each week to study and talk with spirit. Ask for help and understanding what has happened and what is happening on and within Earth. There are many advantages of knowing, since you are connected to all activities on Earth. All of God/Goddess's creations within and upon the Earth are energetically connected.

To better understand the structure of the Earth, astronomers have recently developed technology to measure the mass of a celestial body. When the mass of a planet is compared to the size, the mass turns out to be much smaller than a calculated solid mass. To help explain this observation, astronomers have theorized that these celestial bodies are hollow. The possibility exists that all planets are hollow, thus having a lighter mass than a solid planet would. This theory helps resolve this discrepancy between mass, weight, and size. Some of these original studies were made by studying the Earth's moon. Beyond a doubt, Earth's moon is hollow. A solid moon, because of its weight and rate and of movement around the Earth, would fly out into space. Are there humanoids living on and within the Earth's moon? Go find out if they are there.

In *The Law of One*, Ra says an attempt was made by Extraterrestrial groups to help civilization Ascend eighteen thousand years ago, when Atlantis was an agrarian society. They had to abandon that assistance when the people failed to become aligned to Unity consciousness. Another attempt was made thirteen thousand years ago, shortly before the sinking of Atlantis. Ra then landed in Egypt to assist in their Ascension, but the Egyptians, rather than accept help, proceeded to worship Ra as a God. Again, the Ascension process was canceled. Later, about twelve thousand years ago, Ra returned to help the Egyptians make a dramatic recovery in their spiritual evolution. This was just after the sinking of Atlantis. Six thousand years ago, Ra had the Great Pyramid built in Egypt to help balance the planetary grid. Then the priesthood gradually became corrupt. Ra stood by, waiting to help humanity evolve, but due to the corruption, eventually left.

Ra intervened again in Egypt, around 1365 BC, and worked with the Ascended master Thoth and Akhenaton (Egyptian King) to create a monotheistic religion. Shortly after 1360 BC, Akhenaton was assassinated and the Egyptians reverted to polytheistic religion. As a result, Ra withdrew from Earth for 3,333 years. RA returned in 1968 to help instruct humanity in preparing for graduation. During the 1980s, Ra channeled material for the series of books called *The Law of One*. These books have been published and are available on the Internet. Ra has since left the Earth to carry on other assigned responsibilities.

Atlantian and Lemurian Culture Influence on Beliefs and Life Spans

Since a majority of humans living on Earth have also lived past lives in Atlantis and/or Lemuria, it should be very helpful to know something about these two ancient societies. Both had reached technological levels equal to or exceeding the current societies on Earth. In general, the Lemurians were more spiritually advanced than the Atlantians. If you lived on either continent, you could time travel back along your time line and remember some of your past lives. As you sensed what was happening, you could learn from your previous successes and failures. During the more spiritually advanced times on Lemuria and Atlantis, humans lived for thousands of years. Even today, the human body is designed to live for thousands of years. That fact is scientifically known, since every cell within the human body is renewed every seven years. Since all cells are renewed, all of your body parts could be renewed every seven years.

Why do we fail to live up to our potential life span and die? What causes the physical body to deteriorate so fast? Obviously, there are many possibilities. Some of the following may account for our early physical death: (1) Programmed false beliefs that the body should die before one hundred years of age. This false belief has resulted in DNA changes in our endocrine system. DNA is known to regulate the production of death and rejuvenation hormones. (2) The false belief in an early death is constantly programmed into the consciousness of humans via the communication media. Such programming benefits the medical establishment and pharmaceutical industry and helps support research on human biochemistry. Undertakers and insurance companies benefit from a shortened life span, as do religious groups that set up false beliefs and negative illusions about spirituality and various political systems established to manipulate societies.

Other significant factors are: (3) The destruction of a healthy environment and the poisoning of the food, water, and air supply, as described by John Erb in the book, *The Slow Poisoning of America*, 2003. (4) The constant programming that our society needs to have an enemy to instill fear and be protected from. Fear helps create a host of negative emotions (tension, stress, depression, and anxiety), all of which damage the body's metabolic and immune systems. Many sources of evidence indicate that all diseases have some associated negative emotion that preconditions the body's susceptibility. (5) Science's purposeful creation of disease-inciting agents that attack the physical body, causing early death.

There is also a spiritual reason that the life span has been shortened. As the Ascended Masters and Creators of the Universe observed spiritual evolution on third-dimensional planets, they realized that a shortened life span would allow for more frequent reviews of evolutionary progress. After each review, the spirit will have received a new contract with additional challenges. The purpose of overcoming those new challenges was to accelerate evolution. As you time travel back along your time line, notice how the controllers have limited your spiritual evolution. The controllers' objectives have been to keep their slaves from graduating. Just think ... What if the communication media had been used to educate people about the need to shift their consciousness upward? Possibly, many more souls would have evolved out of the chaos, pain, sickness, suffering, and confusion characteristic of third-dimension consciousness. The Illuminati would have lost many of their slaves if they had knowledge of graduation possibilities. The Illuminati controlled media to this day, continue filling the airwaves and print media with propaganda and illusory beliefs. Because (they say) there is a limited profit motive for marketing spiritual information available, and they would lose control. Guess what? The Illuminati, who have as their primary goal Service To Self, are about to lose their manipulative control over humanity on Earth.

Each time we incarnate on the Earth plane, we come with a contract that describes what we would like to accomplish this incarnation. Our first incarnation on Earth, thousands of years ago, was very dramatic because we experienced emotional separation from Source (God/Goddess). That separation resulted in feelings of abandonment and loneliness. In many humans, that feeling of loneliness still persists. However, by coming to Earth our spirits realized the opportunities available. As a result, we freely choose to meet the challenges as part of our lessons upon a world of duality consciousness, with a goal of learning right from wrong.

Humans "Now" Have Many More Opportunities to Evolve Rapidly

Many spirits have about had it with all these challenges and repeated lessons, lifetime after lifetime for thousands of years on a low frequency planet. Many individuals believe they are ready to graduate and move on to some other reality realm as soon as possible. They are ready for a change. Most are hopeful that the coming changes will bring about a more pleasant, less stressful lifestyle. The newly devised plan by the Counsel of Creators now awaits anyone who is interested and willing to prepare to graduate and Ascend. The choice to physically Ascend is "Now" up to each individual as they strive to complete their third-dimension lessons and prepare their consciousnesses for graduation and Ascension.

As mentioned earlier, only a small of percentage each individual's reality is incarnated on Earth. All humans on Earth have parts of their Oversoul (individual souls) living on other planets. These parallel souls have been evolving just like you have here on Earth. Spirit suggests you have the capability (with training) to visit (through bi-location and time travel) your other soul parts residing on other planets and share each other's experiences. You could learn from them and pool your knowledge to speed up your evolution. In addition, a wealth of information can be obtained from your God/Goddess within, the Ascended Masters, Archangels, Spirit Guides, God/Goddess Bodies, your High Self Spiritual Council, Spiritual Assistants and thousands of other spiritual entities who preceded you in graduating.

In a channeling by Ascended Master Serapis Bay on the Web site of the Lightworkers' Spiritual Network, http://lightworkers.org, Serapis Bay makes the following statements:

Realize beloved ones that never in the history of the Earth have the opportunity for humanity to attain freedom for their glorious Ascension been available. Never has Ascension been offered with so much ease and grace in this wondrous time of preparation for your planet's Ascension. An exceptional window of opportunity is presented to those of humanity who wish to gain their spiritual freedom and who are willing to do whatever it takes to make it happen.

I am not proclaiming that it will be entirely easy for everyone. My promise to you is that I, and the large teams of the Ascension Brotherhood of Luxor and of Telos, stand ready to support and coach, with much love and compassion, those who will seriously commit to their evolution. Yes, many of you will face temporary challenges from time to time, but if you face them with surrender, devotion, joy, and enthusiasm, and the attitude of gratitude for the exceptional opportunity offered to you at this time, be assured that the rest of your path does not have to be difficult.

Long before the continents of Lemuria and Atlantis were submerged, the priests on both continents realized that the destruction was coming. Following the realization that Lemuria was faced with destruction, the priests of Lemuria petitioned the Intergalactic Federation of Planets for permission to build a city inside the Earth. Following approval, the Lemurians built a large city named Telos inside Mount Shasta, an inactive volcano located in Northern California. As of the year 2005, there was a population of over 1.5 million fifth-dimensional conscious souls living in Telos. The Atlantians built a similar city, by the name of Posid, located under the Mato Grosso plains of Brazil, South America. Posid now has a population of 1.3 million. Currently, there are approximately 120 known large cities within the interior of the Earth. Rama, located near Jaipur in India, has a population of over one million. Shonshe, a city beneath the Himalayas near Tibet, has a population of over 750,000. In addition, within the Middle and Inner Earth there are large populations of humanoids from other worlds and Universes with fifth- to seventh-dimensional consciousness.

The Agartha Network that is called "Cities of Light" is located within the inner Earth. It consists of over one hundred subterranean cities, many connected by elaborate, subway-like conveyers. These conveyer tunnels contain vehicles that travel at very high speeds. Thus, inner Earth inhabitants quite frequently visit their neighbors and share many beautiful experiences. Many of these populations are ready and willing to assist their surface brothers and sisters, but only after the surface's inhabitants eliminate their aggressive behavior patterns and shift to Unity/Christ consciousness. Since the inner Earth's inhabitants are technologically superior to the surface inhabitants, they can restrict interferences from the surface dwellers.

These inner-Earth societies have already raised their consciousness to a fifth- or sixth-dimensional state. That is the state of consciousness we surface dwellers are being asked to take on in order to remain upon or inside the New Earth.

Those interested in graduating, Ascending, and remaining upon the New Earth's surface before or after 2012, have many opportunities and choices to make concerning their future path (time line). To graduate, you must pass through some portals (Star Gates) between the dimensions. Those portals between dimensions are well guarded by advanced spiritual beings, and only those who qualify are allowed to pass. Yes, all of your records are readily available for review, and the guards will know who qualifies.

Take Advantage of These Many Opportunities Before "The Shift?"

As we shift to the higher states of dimensional consciousness, we can begin to remember previous "Now" times when we lived under similar conditions. Also, we can follow the guidance of those who have survived and/or retained their memory of Atlantis and Lemuria. Through the joint efforts of the Ascended Masters and Extraterrestrials we can shift to a new reality realm, a pathway to the New Earth. Later we will discuss in more detail the seven required initiations that can take place within the Ascension Temple of Luxor (in Egypt) and/or the Ascension Temple of Telos (in Mount Shasta), along with other helpful disciplinary exercises.

The Ascension Brotherhood has been working for centuries in preparation for this Ascension event. They have continued working to help prepare souls to be ready for the Ascension that begins at the end of the age, between 2008 and 2013. One major part of the Ascension-preparation process takes place within the Ascension Temples. There are seven required initiations within these temples that are available for you and are guided by the Ascension Brotherhood. Those seven temple initiations will be discussed in chapter 19.

So that everyone reading understands, allow me to quote a channeling from Serapis Bay:

"The Candidate for Ascension must meet seven major initiations. And the candidate must successfully pass through the disciplines of the Seven Great Temples."

Hopefully, this statement is clear enough for you to understand. Again, you have a choice to make in your preparation for graduation. It is a process that will require your commitment and dedication.

Everything we detect by our five senses upon the physical Earth is, in reality, an illusion. It only has some sense of existence because of our conscious perceptions within. Conscious perception holds the illusion in place. Illusions are constantly changing as the result of the collective consciousness shifts. As consciousness shifts, these changes are recorded within our DNA, which in turn influences our well-being.

The Earth's physical features change as the consciousness of the human population changes. The shifting of tectonic plates creates mountains. Some land masses sink and others rise, based in part on the consciousness of humanity. Evidence is also surfacing from different sources that portions of the inner Earth have been repositioned due to shifts in consciousness. In addition scientists have known for many years that consciousness influences weather patterns.

Within the Earth, advanced technologies allow the inhabitants to drill tunnels and hollow out large areas for various purposes. There are similar tunneling machines currently used by U. S. government agencies to make tunnels, liquefy rock and pressurize it against a vertical surface to support the rock above the chambers.

Humans involved in spiritual activities can shift their dimensional consciousness to continually evolve to new reality realms. These activities have been in progress for thousands of centuries on millions of planets and will continue into infinity. Hopefully, you will be open-minded enough to realize the value of shifting your consciousness to higher dimensions. There you can interact with Extraterrestrial societies in different Universes. Once you take on "Light Body" status and move into Unity/Christ consciousness, you will be able to communicate telepathically with societies in many other Universes. As a result, you can more accurately convey the meaning of your thought forms, travel to any destination within your Mer-Ka-Ba's field, use bi-location, phase shift to another physical form, create anything you desire, and experience Heaven on Earth.

Those who are sensitive to the current energy changes realize that we are approaching one of the most dramatic changes in the history of the Earth. Obviously, these changes did not start in the nineteenth or twentieth century, but have been ongoing for a very long time. Most humans on Earth are currently searching for more peaceful solutions to conflicts and ways to heal all the damage to the planet Earth. The spiritual realm has heard these calls for assistance. As a result, several things have recently happened. For example, in 2002, the Creators of this Universe opened seven major gateways, sub-gateways, and portals to allow an increase in the spiritual energy flowing onto the Earth's surface. Many other new energies have been and are currently being directed towards Earth to help facilitate "The Shift."

The continued flow of these energies has assisted the consciousness of humans to regain their multidimensional characteristics. For several centuries, humans have been anticipating a movement towards a new reality realm. That new realm will follow the "Great Shift" in consciousness sometimes called "The Shift of The Ages." Many ancient predictions are coming true as heavenly events help prepare the way for a new reality realm. This new realm is being accelerated by the new energies directed towards Earth by the Creators of the Universe and from the Great Central Sun.

In early December 2007 we were informed by spirit that the preliminary stages of Ascension have been speeded up, and we are "Now" experiencing new Ascension events. However, each person is responsible for their thoughts and

Remember, you are not a victim; you are a Creator. You can help create humanity's new reality realm on the New Earth.

thus each individual is to participate by using their Creator skills. Always remember: you are not a victim; you are a Creator. You no longer have an option to just stand by and watch; you have a choice to do something—to help create humanity's new reality realm and prepare for your arrival on the fifth-dimensional New Earth.

To assist in your Ascension efforts, the spirit realm has recently provided you a new, upgraded hologram called the "Ascension Hologram." This new hologram will assist you in clearing all karma and other energies that could interfere with creating your new body parts. To facilitate the many required clearings and rejuvenations, light workers have requested that all energetic patterns be cleared and balanced. We must have an adequate energy flow—an optimal energy transfer from the Creator Source—to create and maintain these new body parts. Many other changes are constantly occurring, such as the passage through the Photon Belt. Dimensional doorways were opened in December 2007 that moved the Solar System into a region of the Galaxy where many believe we have become astrologically positioned for both the New Heaven and New Earth. These energies are available to help you tangibly manifest your desires. Spirit indicates that the completion of all aspects of the New Earth will be a gradual process that will take a hundred years or more to complete. Will you stay around to go through "The Shift" and witness all of the excitement as the New Earth takes form?

* * * * * *

5

Shifting Your Dimensional State of Consciousness to Higher Levels

States of Dimensional Consciousness and Multidimensionality

The cyclic nature of events occurring on Earth is tied to the dimensional state of consciousness as described by Ra. The spirit called Ra is a "Social Memory Complex who evolved through the third, fourth, and fifth-dimensional states of consciousness on the planet Venus. Ra is currently in a sixth-dimensional state of consciousness. He advises that all Spiritual Creations must evolve through eight densities or dimensions. As a review, outlined below are paraphased descriptions of the dimensions through which we evolve, as described by Ra.

First-dimensional Consciousness
   The first dimension is composed of the basic building blocks of physical creations. It primarily consists of the four basic elements of the Earth: minerals, air, fire, and water. The fire and air (wind) act upon the minerals and water. Once acted upon, the minerals and water become building blocks for the creation of second- and third-dimensional creations. All of the microbes, plants, animals, and humans have, as their basic building blocks, water and minerals.

Second-dimensional Consciousness
   The second dimension includes all of the lower-frequency biological creations, such as the elements, microbes, bacteria, some animals, and plants. These parts of the evolutionary fabric have evolved to their current structural features after 4.6 billion years of energetic change. Each of these second-dimension entities were designed and created to help maintain the higher-frequency third-dimensional creations.

Third-dimensional Consciousness
   The major entities that make up the third dimension are those humanoids with self-awareness and self-consciousness. Humans have

been assigned as the keepers of the third dimension. These humanoids have two distinctive features: **(1)** they exhibit both rational and **(2)** intuitive thinking. The purpose of the third-dimensional physical body is to help each individual soul to evolve and become more compassionate in its relationships with all other components of creation. Soul growth is accomplished by learning how to maneuver through various duality concepts to overcome fear, pain, suffering, and physical death. In third-dimensional consciousness, the catalyst is pain. Your character has essentially been shaped by your pain, and you're seeking a process of overcoming pain. It is all required for the fullness of your experience. Once we learn who we are, move to become compassionate, and become love, we can move out of third dimension and into the higher states of dimensional consciousness. The typical time for repeated incarnations that result in qualifications for graduation from the third dimension is seventy-five thousand years.

Fourth-dimensional Consciousness

The fourth dimension is the non-physical kingdom of archetypes, guides, and angels. As humans move here, they achieve the ability to understand compassion and create harmony through group consensus. Individual differences are obvious. Some polarity still exists; however, the catalyst is love. The experiences of each entity are available to the whole, since everyone can know what others are thinking. This is where the soul experiences the love and unity of life called Unity/Christ consciousness. The pure light of creation and love pass through the Oversoul and can be viewed as essences. Each Oversoul exists to explore a particular essence. However, all Oversouls are simultaneously exploring their own essences. Since all Oversouls are united in Unity/Christ consciousness they are connected. All Oversouls have the potential for interacting with many different essences. This process will provide a rich basis for many different experiences. As a result, you will become more of who you really are.

In the higher realms of the fourth dimension you can travel without machines. You don't need food, and you can change your body form by thought. The typical time for one incarnation in fourth dimension is ninety thousand years. The Annunaki Extraterrestrials are keepers of the fourth dimension.

Fifth-dimensional Consciousness

Fifth-dimensional consciousness centers on love and creativity. The lessons of compassion learned within the fourth dimension lead to a whole new reality in the fifth dimension. Here, wisdom and focused intent create instant manifestations. You can dissolve one creation and manifest another quickly, since you can control time. You can create a new house at will. Aging, confusion, and disease are things of the past. The keepers are the Pleiadians, who are quite involved in assisting with Earth's Ascension.

Sixth-dimensional Consciousness

Within the sixth dimension, there are expressions of the spirit in a form of light and love. There are challenges here, since this density includes the consciousness of morphogenetic fields and sacred geometry. The etheric terrain is quite different. There is never a reason to become bored; there is great diversity within the sixth dimension. Here you become your own teacher and can experience solitude. The keepers are the Sirians.

Seventh-dimensional Consciousness

The seventh dimension encompasses the Galactic highways of light. The completed soul realizes its potential as a Creator and realizes that it has evolved towards becoming One with the original Creator again. Here, one's skills are perfected as one works with the Master Teachers. The evolving soul becomes one with all, having no previous memory, no past or future, and no identity. It exists within the All. One becomes an agent of service to all of creation where virtue surpasses intelligence. The keepers are the Andromedans.

Eighth-dimensional Consciousnesses

Within the eighth dimension, The "Light Body" returns to infinity, and the soul becomes a Universal traveler. According to Ra, there is a mystery here in the eighth dimension that cannot be put into words. Here you become aware of all past events, throughout millions of experiences you've had as you have evolved throughout the Universes, on your path to Oneness. You will be able to understand where you have been, you're current state of affairs, where you are headed, and your potential spiritual evolution.

This review of our past history will be essential. After all, we have incarnated on many planets within the Universe for many thousands of lifetimes. The objective will be to examine and bring together the events we've experienced in all of our dimensional states of consciousness. This encompasses dimensional states of consciousness that extend well over two hundred thousand years. The keepers of this region are from Orion.

Ninth-dimensional Consciousness

The ninth dimension ties into the Galactic Center of the Milky Way Galaxy the Great Nothingness. Many consider the Galactic Center as "A Black Hole" where the great being Tzolk'in resides. Tzolk'in is the Spiritual being that created the Mayan calendar, a guide designed to assist Earth's evolutionary cycles.

Tenth-dimensional Consciousness

The tenth dimension is used by spiritual entities trying to find their way throughout the many Universes within Creation. Lower-frequency souls—humans, for example—cannot move from the ninth-dimensional consciousness to the tenth; they are not linear. Nor can you, as a human creation. You are restricted from having access to the tenth dimension.

Eleventh-dimensional Consciousness

The eleventh dimension is that state of consciousness in which the Archangels function throughout the multitude of Universes. Humans cannot participate in eleventh-dimensional consciousness. This dimension is the source of angelic creations that have periodically incarnated in physical bodies on Earth.

You Are a Multidimensional Creation That Desires Change

The Pleiadians indicate that since you are a multidimensional creation, it is important that you review, understand, and work within the first eight dimensional states of consciousness by 2012. The recently published book, *Alchemy of Nine Dimensions* by Barbara Hand Clow (as channeled from the Pleiadians), should help you understand how to work through these dimensional states of consciousness.

"The Shift" in Relation to Living "Now" and Multidimensionality

What is occurring "Now" on Earth and within the Milky Way Galaxy could have only happened following a series of events lined up throughout the Universe to allow for "The Shift." This is an event for which many humans have been preparing for many lifetimes. Many outer and inner voices have been asking for you to make changes in your life so you are prepared for the coming dramatic changes on Earth. Some have followed the instructions provided; others have continued living life as usual. Everyone on Earth is faced with many different choices. You can (1) hang on to the old, existing energy patterns and continue as usual; (2) complete your assignment on Earth and return to your home planet; (3) clear out all of those low-frequency duality energies and prepare for Ascension; (4) die and move within the fourth dimension for rest; or (5) choose another path of the many available.

To Ascend, you will have to purge all of the lower emotions and prepare to shift from duality consciousness into Unity/Christ consciousness. If you have not been living by spiritual principles, then the time to make the necessary changes is very short. Within three to four years, decision time will have passed within this cyclic period. To those on a spiritual path who choose to Ascend, continue clearing old patterns and take on new, high-frequency patterns that automatically assist you in the process.

Planet Earth has chosen to take on these new, high-frequency patterns and is in the process of shifting its vibratory rate upward to receive energies from the intergalactic core, The Great Central Sun, the Solar System's sun, and other sources. Everything is energy, and all forms of energy have certain vibratory rates or frequencies. The Earth and all natural physical matter on Earth are increasing in frequency. This is called a phase shift or "The Shift." The vibratory rate characteristic of the third-dimension planet Earth is giving way to the higher frequencies of a fourth- and fifth-dimensional Earth (called Gaia or Terra). As a result of this phase shift, the patterns of life, perceptions, and ideas we have become accustomed to for thousands of years are dramatically changing. Your internal wiring related to emotions and mental capabilities has been relatively dysfunctional on the third-dimensional Earth for quite awhile. Now as you prepare for Ascension, your energy circuits are being repaired and Vital life forces will start to flow through your bodies with more efficiency, improving your emotional and mental capabilities.

You have the opportunity to know that every time you look at something or think about something, that *something* is inside you. You exist as a part of what's out there but what you really know occurs within? Because all of the illusions out there in your external world are sensed, analyzed, and stored inside your consciousness. As your consciousness changes, those illusory creations disappear.

As we progress towards "The Shift" in consciousness, things out there are going to get very intense and confusing. To avoid being pulled into these events, you will need to remain in a state of Unity consciousness with everything that unfolds within. If you are pulled in by those outside illusions, you could feel threatened, believe you are separate from All-That-Is, and become fearful of those events out there. When this happens, your energies could congeal instead of flowing, and you will be unable to respond appropriately. To feel threatened brings in fear and gridlock. It is much easier to be in a constant state of acceptance and/or love when you have eliminated any type of gridlock.

The world around you is on a collision course with oblivion and will pass away within the next few years. The old world that is passing away does not need you to supply it energy. That is, you are not needed to help save Earth. You are needed to help create the New Earth. Therefore, direct your energy towards creating the New Earth. The old play within the Earth amphitheater, the drama you hear about on television and see around you, are in the closing scenes. That old play is supposed to close. A new, different play will soon come into view. As the old play ceases, all of the scenery and props are being replaced with a whole new design. All the emotions and excitement of the old play must be cleared and everything on the planet purified to make way for the new. All the rules you were taught and may have accepted are null and void for making the journey to the New Earth. The process of clearing the old play is not helped by resistance on your part. It is helped by your allowing the process to unfold as the amphitheater is preparing for the new reality realm, the New Earth. Any resistance you create will only make the confusion and chaos more intense. Every thought designed to retain the old, duality programmed rules and regulations will require a matching energy to overcome those holding energies. A tremendous waste of energy is required to balance out this negative resistance.

Your task is to let go and let God/Goddess take care of the process of change. You are the only one responsible for you; everyone else has their own responsibilities. This does not mean you cannot help another when asked. Everyone must take personal responsibility and let go of their past in order for the transition (Ascension) process to proceed smoothly. You must be calm in the midst of the storm as we approach "The Shift." Tune out all the noise and confusion. Wean yourself away from the communication media as soon as possible. Most of the events reported within the communication media are exaggerated and dramatized over and over again to keep you caught up in the drama. Create a sanctuary within yourself that you can go into consciously to find out what you truly need to know and how to find solitude during the storm.

To accept the enormous amount of change going on, you will need to rely upon the DNA codes previously established by your Oversoul to help you make the appropriate choices. The secret is to make every effort possible to remain in Unity/Christ consciousness with everything around you. One very helpful approach is to utilize the realization that you are a part of God/Goddess, "I Am, That I Am, a component of "All-That-Is, a part of Unity/Christ consciousness. Unity/Christ consciousness means that you are a part of everything. It is helpful to constantly observe things around you using "I am" statements: I am that tree, I am that car, and I am that person. Realize you are a part of everything. All of creation is one within you. All of creation is a part of All-That-

Is (Creator Source Energy) expressed in different forms with different frequencies. You are a part of All-That-Is. Recognize that you are to become One with All-That-Is, That type of consciousness functions within the higher frequencies and will assist your Ascension process.

Your consciousness has been moving towards Unity/Christ consciousness for some time. As you clear all the lower-dimensional thought forms from thousands of previous lifetimes, you will open up new channels of understanding. All of these lower-frequency thought forms stored within your physical, mental and emotional bodies can limit your spiritual growth. Following these clearings, you will become more sensitive to perceiving all the new realities. Also, as you simplify your third-dimensional activities, you will be more prepared for having your current needs satisfied with a minimum amount of Earthly requirements. You can begin "Now" to mentally detach yourself from all the clothes, dishes, equipment, tools, and *things* that fill your home. Rid yourself of these items; they will have no value upon the fifth-dimensional New Earth. None of these *things* can be taken with you to the New Earth. Practice finding pleasure in all the natural things around you, those items close to where you live. Your goal should be to live fully in the "Now" with no concern for the past or the future. Begin believing that everything you need, want, or desire will be available right where you are "Now" and during every future "Now" moment of your new life on the New Earth. Your expression and essence will take on new meaning as you practice and implement Unity/Christ consciousness in your everyday activities.

The Power of "Now" and Passage through the Star Gates

The Ascension process is an accumulative process that involves two major components. There is a physical change in the subatomic particles that make up the body, and a spiritual component related to a shift in your consciousness and ways of perceiving reality. Both accumulative processes are taking place at the same time and are interrelated. Always keep in mind that consciousness has a direct effect on the physical and genetic features of all your energy bodies. That is, there is no way to separate the physical body from consciousness, a fact science and the medical establishments have been slow to comprehend. Consciousness is the basis or matrix out of which all physical matter emerges. Your consciousness is a portion of the infinite mind (All-That-Is) from which you secure your creative capabilities.

Once you have crossed over and anchored your awareness within the fourth-dimensional consciousness, you will have an expanded awareness of everything that is happening. You will have completed what you came to Earth this time to accomplish. Just beyond that accomplishment, a portal will open to an entirely new set of possibilities. From the fourth dimension you can shift through another portal (Star Gate) into the fifth dimension, where peace, joy, and love predominate. Within the fifth dimension, the veils will have been removed and you will be in full and continuous communion with the mind of the Creator. You will then be able to affect, alter, and create material reality from the place of infinite blessing. You will become aware that you have always been a co-Creator- with God/Goddess. You will come into full consciousness and merge with the mind of the Creators. These are the future experiences you are moving towards and into right "Now."

To know means to become aware of your feelings about the rightness or wrongness of any situation based on listening to and following the guidance from the thoughts of your God/Goddess within. One key is to stay rooted and centered where you are in the present moment, rather than in the past (where you have been) or in the future (where you are going). There is no need to be overly concerned about what happened in the past or what might happen in the future. Make your choices in the "Now." Quiet the body before deciding to proceed in making a choice. Cut through the cords of memory and interrupt the inner voices by saying out loud, "That was then; this is "Now." "Feel the "Now." Bring your attention into the "Now" and say out loud, "Now." right "Now." Then—*boom*—you are in the present moment. Cultivate the practice of living in the "Now." Live each moment as the only moment you have available. Continue to study *The Power of "Now"* by Eckhart Tolle.

If for any reason you become upset, wait until calm returns to make your " Now" choice. The objective is to find purpose and direction within the best choice you can make. Your goal is to make a choice that is in harmony with guidance from God/Goddess and synchronized with Unity/Christ consciousness. To accomplish that goal, create a habit of feeling into a situation when it presents itself. Be aware, then center yourself and feel what your inner sensing system is telling you. A feeling of tightening or pressure is a *No*. A feeling of expansion and release is a *Yes*. In other words, use your feelings to help you know and understand what your best choice is "Now." That is, sorting out, within the "Now" the most desirable of all choices available. Do not proceed until you have a clear answer to the most appropriate choice. Nothing is so important it cannot wait for a clear understanding of what the best choice is. A realization will come, and you will know what to do at this "Now," since in reality there is no time other than the "Now." This is what life will be like on the New Earth. Get used to living in the "Now" and making your choices there in the "Now." "Now" is the time to start practicing how to live in the "Now" the only place you can create anything. "Now" is all you ever really have.

There may come an experience when you will need to make rapid choices in the "Now." In order to make sure these choices will be the most appropriate, it is time to start practicing. Continue to make sure you have cleared out all of the clutter in your life. Any clutter could slow your choice-making process. As you gradually shift in consciousness, you will have full awareness of everyone else and thus no need for books or the Internet. To assist in your consciousness shift, begin as soon as possible to create a habit of quieting your mind and listening to the still, small voice within for guidance. Then, no matter what is taking place around you *out there*, inside you will have peace and quiet, knowing that all is in divine order. If you can remain detached from the confusion, you can then feel and remain calm as you stand and look over the broad, beautiful landscape. You will then be isolated from events and others around you. Even within a noisy crowd, it is possible to detach yourself enough to be calm and have a sense of safety.

One technique to quiet the mind and emotions is to listen to the silence within you. There is no need to get caught up in the emotions that take you out of your calm center, where silence resides. If you are still engaging in third-dimensional duality behaviors, Spirit suggests you discontinue those patterns as soon as possible. Clear all past life experiences that inhibit or slow your spiritual progress. The third-dimensional world around you is becoming quite precarious and somewhat chaotic as all the old patterns are being phased out. As everything tumbles down around you, you will detect confusion and notice irrational behavior on the part of those who failed to prepare for the upcoming events. Those unprepared will attempt to find something to hang on to. Some may become desperate and angry when those in whom they put their trust fail to meet their expectations. They will realize there is really no one to solve the complex problems that society has created. Events in society have gone too far for making meaningful corrections. It's becoming quite evident that many parts of society will appear to spin out of control. When this happens, let the peace of the Creator become your peace. Let go and let God/Goddess within guide. Let others do the same for themselves. The deepening conflicts within the third-dimensional state of consciousness will have come to an end on planet Earth in the near future. Once "The Shift" is complete, all false duality beliefs, illusions and confusion will be cleared away.

Helpful Suggestions to Facilitate the Ascension Process

Facilitating the Ascension process requires that you maintain a healthy body by supplying it adequate water for hydration, optimize your pH, consume supplemental minerals and vitamins as co-factors for all metabolic reactions, and add electrolytes to help carry various electrical charges throughout the physical body. There is also a need to maintain adequate iodine for thyroid function, silicon for restructuring cells, and iron for the blood's transport of oxygen. Use pendulum dowsing frequently to monitor and keep in balance all these and other health-related energy patterns.

If you thought the Ascension was going to be a single event, spirit indicates you will need to adjust your thinking process. Ascension is more like a series of ongoing events that all flow along together in sequence to create a process. Thus, Ascension is a process that never ends. Ascension cannot be an individual event, because spiritual evolution is a continuous process. The spiritual journey continues forever. The journey of experiences never ends; it will continue after each veil falls. Therefore, it will be very helpful for you to realize that there is no ending in sight for you. You will go on eternally because you are a part of the Creator that goes on eternally. Ascension is a long series of many, many events over millions and billions of years. It can be called an evolutionary spiritual process.

Those who have been preparing for graduation have been clearing thousands of adverse energies accumulated periodically over thousands of previous lifetimes. Those on the Ascension path have reworked many of their energy-flow patterns by removing energy blocks, optimizing the flow of over forty-four different energies grouped together as the *"Available Energy Complex."* This complex has a power code of (10-3-5-5- 4-8-4-2- 1-9-6-7). Repeating this power code in a sequence for nine times out loud can increase your available energy. By optimizing your available energy complex, your well-being and balance can be restored. However, these clearings and energy adjustments are only the beginning of a long process that has just begun. Many, many illusory challenges still remain to be brought into balance. Humans planning to Ascend will need to continue to clear thousands of adverse energies that have blocked their energy-flow patterns and thus slowed their spiritual evolution.

As new, high-frequency energies became available (many started arriving in 1982), humanity began a lengthy program to integrate these new energies into their bodies, bodily systems, and body parts. As the Ascension process continues, other new high-frequency energies will arrive from off-planet to assist. The power code above is integrating these new, required energies so that the above power code that contained forty-four different energies now has over sixty-four different energies. Between 1994 and 2004, those on the Ascension path continued to clear out blocks and adjusted hundreds of energy-flow patterns (holograms, axiatonal lines, prana tube, internal and external chakras, meridians, various grids, core star, slip strings, brain strings, etc), all designed to help optimize energy flow through all bodies. These changes have helped shift our bodily energies into new reality realms. In 2005 and 2006, many fine-tuned their electrical systems, balanced their polarities, filtered their blood and lymph systems, optimized hydration, and maintained an optimum pH. Again in 2006, spirit emphasized the importance of obtaining adequate nutrients, minerals, vitamins, and electrolytes. The year 2007 (9 for completion) was a year of monumental change, fine-tuning, and completion of previously designed experiments. As a result of these efforts, in November 2007 some individuals were shifting their consciousness to higher frequencies. All of these events were in preparation for a host of new experiments and helpful adjustments in 2008.

The year 2008, numerically a *one* year, has been and will be a new beginning for many. This will be a period when many prepare for the second wave of Ascension, as predicated. Also during 2008 we will have a golden opportunity, one we have been waiting to experience for thousands of years. We can "Now" transform our bodies, creating new bodies. A whole new sequence of Redesigning, Repatterning, Rejuvenation, and Restructuring has begun as a means of altering our bodies. For example, we recently discovered that our body overlays have been severely damaged. As a result, many were having difficulty remaining attached to their physical bodies. Then we discovered that these individuals had attached "Grieving-Beings" draining their energies. These Grieving-Being thought forms are created during and following traumatic events in someone's past history. They have since been dissipated and/or transmuted to beneficial energies. Many other transformations are occurring, many of which are now on automatic pilot since we have an inability to understand what they are and how to deal with them. Many are beyond anyone's human imagination. We do know that they have all been designed to help change our future reality realm. Also, they will help humanity adjust to the new environmental features of the New Earth.

For example, when we receive a request for the repair of a body part, we now have an option to request the creation of a new body part. Spirit has provided us with the ability to visually create an ideal holographic image (etheric mold of a body part), with intent, and then superimpose that imaging over the part needing repair. This procedure is discussed in detail later.

To successfully carry out all these experiments, and many others proposed, spirit has requested that you keep an open mind, believe anything is possible, and be ready to accept all possible changes. You will need to be open to hearing about all of the ever-changing events around you without becoming mentally or emotionally disturbed. You can then realize that the upcoming changes are for the good of all. You can also integrate the new transforming energies arriving on Earth by focusing your attention on creating a vision of what you want to be and what you want to accomplish in 2008, 2009, and 2010 and beyond. Create a vision; imagine what you would like. Use positive thought forms to create visions that have future beneficial purposes. Avoid all negative thoughts. Thoughts are the foundation on which manifestations materialize.

One very important transforming tool is discussed in detail within the book *The Amazing Power of Deliberate Intent: Living the Art of Allowing*, by Ester and Jerry Hicks. This book is based on the teachings of Abraham, voiced by Ester. The use of focused intent can help speed up transformations within your life and within the lives of others around you. Dr. Wayne Dyer, in his book *The Power of Intention*, shares a profound understanding of how each person possesses the infinite potential and power to co-create anything through intention. The power of intent provides you with a procedure whereby you can focus your attention through deliberate, conscious action to receive and/or carry out exactly what you want to accomplish. Spirit emphasizes the need to become constantly aware of your thoughts. As you shift to higher states of dimensional consciousness, what you think will manifest much more rapidly in 2009 and beyond.

Focused intent can start with your free will to make a choice. One very important choice is to live in harmony within yourself, then in harmony with other humans and all components of nature. By continuously concentrating on positive thought forms (love, peace, joy, patience, and harmony), they become your reality. Seize upon the opportunity to bring health, freedom, and prosperity into your everyday activities. Always focus on what you *do* want. What you focus your thoughts and intent upon is what you get. Remove all thoughts about what you *don't* want. Your subconscious mind cannot differentiate your wants and don't wants. The subconscious creates all your focused intents equally efficiently. Think about, visualize, and verbalize only those thoughts you would like to create. Use focused intent to bring each though form into your reality. These processes are what Creator school is all about. Learn to un-create your old realities and create your new reality realm as you chart your own future.

Several important concepts about what to ask for come up daily. The concept of "ask and receive" requires knowing what to ask for.

These concepts and knowing the question can help you maintain your energy and well-being. You will need to monitor these items with accurate pendulum dowsing to make sure that each one is the most appropriate for every "Now" experience. For example, each individual should have an overlay energy pattern around all your energy bodies. The overlay and your aura should extend out from your bodies a certain distance. The optimum distance for women is thirty to fifty feet; for men, forty to sixty feet. If it is too close or too far out, your energy becomes imbalanced and needs to be adjusted. Use pendulum dowsing to make sure your overlay is properly positioned. When properly positioned, energy from outside the body flows more efficiently through the overlay to the meridians and chakras. While making this request, it is also important to balance the external and internal chakra systems. This request should include all 14,600 chakras which make up the total energy-flow patterns of the physical body.

For good health, your body needs deep sleep (delta brain wave frequency of less than two cycles per second) for at least one hundred minutes per night. Anything less indicates you are failing to rejuvenate your body to its optimum functional energy level at night. Those tired and aching feelings may indicate you lack the proper amount of delta-wave sleep. Sleep time alone may not supply the proper amount of delta time. Ask your Spiritual Assistants to insure you receive the proper type of sleep for physical body rejuvenation. Continued loss of delta time can cause a host of physical, mental, and emotional imbalances.

In addition, for protection from outside forces, your Buddhic Web located between your Etheric and Astral bodies, needs to be efficiently maintained. The magnetic features of the Buddhic Web provide the astral body protection against malefic (destructive) entities attempting to disrupt your vital life forces. This Buddhic Web, unknown to most people on Earth, is the most protective energy field available. Refer to the book *Spirit and Matter: New Horizons for Medicine*, by Dr. Jose Lacerda de Azevedo, MD, in Brazil for many important insights for helping create a balanced energy system.

Make sure all your lower twenty-four energy bodies are turned on and operating at the highest or most appropriate frequency possible. Your second spiritual energy body, when turned on, can be requested to help balance all other bodies. Frequently ask your High Self Spiritual Council and/or God/Goddess within to raise the frequency of each body to its most appropriate level, and to bring them all into balance with each other. When all energy bodies are brought into balance, the process of shifting to the higher states of dimensional consciousness will be much more efficient and stabilized. For your physical body to Ascend to the new Earth, all of your energy bodies will need to be balanced and harmonized with each other.

The human energy system is a multidimensional creation that simultaneously vibrates at many different frequencies. As a part of the Ascension process, you are on a magical mystery tour that has never before occurred on planet Earth. All of the tour events are being guided from higher spiritual levels; you don't have to figure them out. Actually, the web of events is so complex it is beyond our current human comprehension, so don't even try. Many are on automatic pilot, orchestrated by a multitude of Spiritual Assistants. Just lean back, relax, do Prana Breathing, sink into your experience of multiple realities, and enjoy the tour to a whole New Earth.

* * * * *

6

Making the Choice to Ascend with Your Physical Body

Preparing for the End Times Mentally and Emotionally

A majority of Earth's inhabitants now believe they are "Now" living in the End Times. Many are asking what this really means. Accumulating evidence indicates that humanity is approaching the new millennium, or Golden Age. As a result, humans will have an opportunity to free themselves from the destructive and challenging duality patterns so prevalent on Earth.

Even those in positions of control and power apparently believe that the End Times pose a serious threat to life on Earth's surface. For the past fifty years, the largest construction project in the known history of the human race has been under way. A large number of underground bases and cities have been built at a cost of trillions of dollars. For obvious reasons, these projects have been kept secret. If the recently released reports of their construction are true, why are they being built? These activities appear to indicate there is a real threat to life on the Earth's surface, otherwise why all this financial outlay and effort to build facilities inside the Earth? For those interested in obtaining more information, do your own research on this subject. You can time travel into the past and future to study the MJ-12 project and many other related projects.

As End Times approach, many believe that planetary changes like Earthquakes and Volcanic eruptions will become more severe and occur more frequently. As these changes occur, many will be required to quickly make new choices. Each person has free will to accept or reject the coming changes. Many will be so entrenched in the old illusions and false beliefs they will actually reject the opportunities to make new choices. Some will even deny the possibility that these events could happen, even though they are detailed in the communications' media.

There have been many examples of this form of behavior in the past. Because of previous beliefs, humans may be unable to sense or

89

accept what they have read, heard, or seen. As a result, they will simply ignore the current events and continue with their daily routines as if nothing of importance is occurring. Some will continue to function on automatic pilot, forgetting about spiritual matters. Some may need to ask the question, "Am I, or should I be, sensitive to current events?" If I were to become aware of events around me, what difference would that make?"

An example of this inability to accept is depicted by the story of an event that took place off the coast of a South Pacific island. Several European ships arrived near the island and dropped anchor. The aborigine tribe living on the island totally ignored the presence of the ships. They had never seen anything like ships before. They had no previous experience on which to judge what was there, so the ships were invisible to them.

Perhaps you can recall an experience when you were unable to use your logical mind to see what was occurring. This happens because what is occurring *out there* can only be real when sensed within. Without a reference experience of what appears to be out there, the vision cannot be processed mentally. In reality, there *is* nothing out there. Everything occurs within, since that is where the sensing system resides.

A similar situation is about to take place on Earth. Are you studying and preparing to understand the coming events on the old Earth and the New Earth? Will you be ready to interpret, see, know within, and accept what is right in front of your eyes? To be ready will require letting go of karma, false beliefs, discordant programs, grieving beings, illusions, attaching spirits, and many other blocking energies. Spirit indicates we need to clear all adverse experiences from thousands of lifetimes, even those that Mother Earth has absorbed. Mother Earth is no longer interested in storing your adverse experiences; because she is also going through a cleansing. Make a request to your Spiritual Assistants to remove all undesirable experiences and recycle them through a black hole so they can be restructured. Be very alert and cautious as these experiences re-surface. Make sure they are transmuted or uncreated and flow out away from all of your energy systems. Let them go as soon as possible, because what you think about and voice you create and/or magnify.

During the process of clearing, and/or removing process you may realize that since, in reality, there is no time, you may be reliving these past experiences. Because of the intense charge of these memories, there is a very high possibility that they can currently manifest in one of your bodies. Therefore, you should work with your Spiritual Assistants to transmute, un-create, phase shift, and/or clear all adverse experiences immediately—as soon as they come into consciousness or start to manifest somewhere in your body. Your goal should be to clear out all the completed challenges and restore your bodies to their originally designed state of perfection. Also be aware that many past-life experiences caused damage to the body when they originally occurred. Some of that damage may still persist and needs to be repaired. So continue to call upon your spiritual helpers and various Creators to repair or replace damaged body systems, parts, and organs. For example, when Mycoplasma invades a physical body cell they alter the RNA and DNA creating Artificial Encodements. Request your Spiritual Encodement Technician remove these Artificial Encodements and repair all Natural Encodements. For better understanding carefully study the book, *Change Your Encodements, Your DNA, Your Life,* by Cathy Chapman, 2005.

There is also the issue of linear time in terms of the waves of Ascension. The first wave has been initiated; the second wave will occur in December 2008. This means that clearing and damage repair for those in the first- and second-Ascension waves will occur while they are still in their physical bodies. In the third wave of Ascension, souls may be required to be placed within the healing chambers on board Extraterrestrial vehicles to complete their clearings and attunements. The third wave must be prepared with help from the Extraterrestrials for transfer to the New Earth. This option is available because of the element of clock time. There is limited time to complete all the clearings and attunements needed before the third wave Ascends.

If you are in the third wave of Ascension you should make every effort possible to keep all of your bodies in a healthy state. This is especially true of the physical, mental, and emotional bodies. In order for you to be taken on board these Extraterrestrial vehicles, you will need to be beamed up into an awaiting spacecraft. Once on board, you will be placed in a special chamber to help shift your consciousness to a point where you can be transferred to a Midway Station for additional adjustments as you await transfer to the New Earth. Keep in mind that those individuals within the first two waves should have completed their preparation *before* evacuation takes place. The field generals, those humans who have volunteered to assist in the Ascension process, will also have to be prepared before evacuation—or before they depart for their home planets. A majority of these field generals will be present for a brief period as assistants. Many of them will not be going to the Midway Station or to the New Earth. They have many other choices, responsibilities, and destinations.

Many of the upcoming changes in consciousness will be so new that many humans will tend to reject them on the basis that what they sense is illogical and scientifically impossible. Acceptance will be more difficult within some groups and races because of their belief systems. People with a western Caucasian background and a strong connection to the Atlantian mindset may be challenged. The Atlantians developed the philosophy that they were each a separate ego entity. This philosophy, containing various aspects of duality, was based on the belief of a struggle of good against evil. Many with this belief have taken on a Service to Self (STS) philosophy. These individuals have discovered their truth and would like for you to buy into it. They have been termed the warrior types. One 2008 presidential candidate is a good example of a warrior type. Many of these warriors have a tendency to become religious and judgmental. Their belief was and frequently continues to be, *Those others out there are the evil ones, and we are the righteous ones.* That philosophy and doctrine has been based on the assumption that -- *I have the answers. If you don't believe what I believe, you are evil, and you need to be saved. If you reject my way of salvation, that is justification for your demise.*

This doctrine has continually been promoted on Earth by religious groups controlled by infiltrating dark forces, many of which are Interlopers, for over twelve thousand years. These thought forms have created fear and caused most wars on Earth. These false doctrines have also created a separation of humans from God/Goddess within. Many members of fundamental religious groups (world-wide) believe in a God/Goddess *out there*, as opposed to the God/Goddess within themselves. Many conservative fundamentalists are having difficulty accepting the challenges required for Ascension preparation. Because of their conservative mindsets, they are unable to accept the many changes. Unless they clear all their false beliefs, they may fail to meet the qualifications to pass through the Star Gates to higher dimensions.

The keepers of the Star Gates will review everyone's records and behavior patterns as they approach the gates and decide if they are qualified to pass through. If their records are incomplete, they will be unable to safely make it through "The Shift" and take their physical bodies with them. They will have chosen an alternative pathway for leaving Earth previous to or during "The Shift." After "The Shift," everything will be left behind on old, third-dimension planet Earth. Third-dimension Earth will be cleared for cleanup and rejuvenation. Everyone on the Earth's surface will be gone from the present planet, through one path (time line) or another.

If you could compare notes, you would discover that different people will experience different things. You will gradually visualize your path and/or destination more clearly as "The Shift" approaches. Likewise, others will be able to visualize a similar or different destination. All will be accommodated in line with a continuity that correlates with their perceived reality. Individuals will, by their own thoughts, help create their perceived realities. You will need to concentrate on your path, not the path of someone else. If you have chosen the time line that leads to the New Earth, you can then follow that path. If you have chosen to follow the path of the deceivers, then that is your path. If you have chosen to do nothing in selecting a path, you can physically die, just as in your past lives, and transition your spirit to the lower levels of the fourth-dimensional state of consciousness. Once there, you can make a choice about what path to take. Again, your beliefs and thoughts about your choice will help bring that choice into manifestation.

Those who have made a God/Goddess of science may also have difficulty graduating. Their belief systems are based on their perceived reality as understood by the five physical senses. Many scientists have a reality based on the world they physically sense; the unseen is essentially an unknown illusion. Some individuals who have made science their God/Goddess believe that anything the physical, conscious senses are unable to detect does not exist.

Humans have many different sensing systems. One such system

is the internal sensing system used during dreams. All of the experiences recorded in dreams by the inner sensing system primarily function within the subconscious and super-conscious realities of mind, and they correlate with the outer five senses. Other experiences, such as time travel, bi-location, shape-shifting, out-of-body experiences, remote viewing, and talking with God/Goddess or spirits are just as real as those recorded by the five physical senses.

All human spirits and their associated souls have been created in the image of God/Goddess, thus they are all equal. They are one in spirit, so God/Goddess dwells within all components of Creation. Since we are "One" in Spirit, there is no place for separation and a dominating, self-centered ego. To qualify for Ascension, each human must control the ego in order to evolve towards Unity/Christ consciousness.

Choices You Make "Now" Will Determine Your Futures

During 2008 and beyond, you will continually have the opportunity to make choices that will create and chart your destiny for thousands of years into the future. It is the destiny of the Earth to return to the fifth-dimensional consciousness called the New Earth. Comparatively speaking, when you graduate, you can experience prosperity and beauty and live in a place

> **Everyone can choose. You have the option to Ascend any time you are ready.**

where everyone shares equally in the bountiful supplies the New Earth provides. Realize that the year 2012 is fast approaching and appears to be a possible opening when *"The Shift" occurs and mass Ascensions take place. Those humans who have awakened from their deep sleep and made appropriate preparations can Ascend at any time.* No one has to wait to be a part of the mass Ascension at the end of the age. You can Ascend any time you are ready.

The full planetary evolution for Earth will occur over the two-thousand-year illusionary period from 2012 to 4012. Earth is currently preparing her "Light Body;" that should be well under way by 2012. Thus, Earth will be making her Ascension into the Light soon. Mother

Earth welcomes anyone to join her. To join the New Earth, you will be required to complete the twelve steps of "Light Body" activation outlined in Section IV.

Through positive thoughts with focused intent, you can choose to raise your consciousness and prepare your Light Bodies for "The Shift" and graduation. You are destined to reside upon a part of the multidimensional Earth called the fourth- to fifth-dimensional state of consciousness. After "The Shift," you will learn how to use the Photon energy from the Photon Belt and prana to maintain your body.

As you focus on some choices outlined within this book, choose those that feel right for you. Then make the decision to implement them to help achieve your goals. You can then enjoy every upcoming experience during 2009 and beyond. Through these exciting experiences, you can reap the rewards of health, happiness, and peace of mind.

A complete understanding of these upcoming events and changes, for those interested in Ascending, are beyond any human's mental comprehension. However, as we look around, we realize that the third-dimensional world is in the process of dying. Regardless of whether we comprehend it or not, "The Shift" will occur in the near future that is when God/Goddess, Universal Consciousness, and humans have prepared for these dramatic changes sufficiently. In order to help you prepare, there are many Ascension books and channelings posted on the Internet. I suggest you seek guidance from within, follow your intuition, use discernment, and search for helpful suggestions.

Each time in the past when Mother Earth cycled through to a new level of consciousness, the Creator, in Its infinite love and wisdom, allowed most humans to experience physical death and return to the spirit realm of the fourth dimension. The spirit and soul were separated from the physical body, which remained on Earth. During previous shifts, ice ages, atomic wars, and Earth changes, a majority of humans simply died. Their spirits left their physical bodies and returned to one of the overtones of the fourth dimension.

This time, the Creator has allowed for a dramatic change in the process of making the transition. Many of these changes have been approved and are being implemented. As stated earlier, those who are prepared can go through "The Shift" and take their physical bodies to the New Earth.

To create this possibility, you will have to request that your Spiritual Assistants transmute your physical body (vehicle) into etheric energy. These newly altered physical components, in their etheric forms, become closely attached to the spirit and soul and create a "Light Body." You will still have a physical body; however, it will be larger and considerably less dense.

Let's briefly go over some parts of the Ascension process so you will be able to ask the appropriate questions of your Spiritual Assistants. The physical form, as you know, it is composed of air, water, and Earth minerals. As mentioned, when an *un-Ascended* individual physically dies on Earth, the spirit Ascends without absorbing the substances of the Earth body. The physical body remains on Earth following death. Humans "Now" have the option to request that the Earth elements (air, water, and minerals) that make up their physical body be purified spiritually. Once they become completely purified and permeated by spirit, they are converted to etheric substances that lack physicality. Thus, in order to Ascend and take your physical body with you, you must purify all components of the physical body so that they can become etheric substances. When these Earth elements are transformed into etheric energy, they become closely attached to your spirit body. When ready, your spirit and soul simply transport you—spirit and physical body as one component energy unit—to your chosen destination. The physical-body Ascension can only occur after you have prepared. That is, you have made a choice and prepared to take your physical body with you. No one will Ascend with a physical body without having made the choice to do so.

The many conscious experiences that will take place during this Ascension event are so dramatically wonderful there are few words to describe them. Then, once you arrive within the higher state of dimensional consciousness on the New Earth, you may say, "Wow, what a place!" Some characteristics of the New Earth are well known and will be discussed later. Other characteristics are being designed by spiritual entities, and many will be created by Ascending spirits like you.

The challenge all humans have is that the physical Ascension experience will be very new. We humans living on Earth have never remained alive (while incarnated) and taken our physical bodies with us to the other side during a shift in consciousness.

To help you gain a perspective of how many humans are aware of the coming changes, spirit has provided the following. Slightly over one third of the humans on Earth (2.5 billion out of 7 billion, or 35 percent) are actually thinking about preparing to go through "The Shift" and physically Ascend. There are many possible pathways for those who do not choose to Ascend. Some are obvious, while others are still in the planning stage; all individual pathways are dependent upon the individual's spiritual status. One thing is for certain: each spirit on Earth is eternal and will continue on its evolutionary path somewhere—on this fifth dimensional planet, or on another planet in another Universe—after leaving third-dimension Earth.

Even the Spiritual Hierarchy, God/Goddess and other Spiritual entities do not know what will actually happen during "The Shift." The Creators have made it clear that many events occurring during "The Shift" are up to humanity; each person will have an influence on what happens. Humanity is in the process of creating the upcoming events. All you can do "Now" is continue making preparations to shift your dimensional consciousness to the most appropriate level, activate your "Light Body," and upgrade your Love Body with the help of your God/Goddess within and Spiritual helpers. The spiritual realm has been preparing and practicing for "The Shift" for many years and is ready to help you. Based on pendulum dowsing, this

> **Humanity is creating the upcoming events. All you can do "Now" is continue making preparations to shift your consciousness**

book is 95 percent accurate. It is not perfect, but it contains many helpful suggestions. There are other books and Web sites that provide suggestions and give you a glimpse of some of the upcoming events with the same level of accuracy.

Many souls now on Earth knew that during their current incarnation, third-dimension Earth was going to reach the end of a 12,500-year period and come close to being destroyed. The continuing abuse and destruction of Mother Earth has become quite evident. During this historical period, many humans have incarnated this time on Earth in anticipation of "The Shift" and possible graduation. Our higher selves realized that we would have an opportunity to experience dramatic changes and take advantage of the yet-unknown multidimensional features of New Earth. But even before incarnating, we realized that we must make adequate preparations for these coming events. As noted above, many will opt out of going through "The Shift" and prefer another pathway (time line). This is evidenced by the large number of people dying and leaving the physical Earth in the last few years. The rate at which people are dying has been prophesied to accelerate as we approach 2012. Humans who realize that they need to complete their third-dimension lessons can choose another pathway (time line). They can physically die, incarnate on another low-frequency planet, and Ascend in a future life. Or, if they have prepared to Ascend, they could die, move to the higher overtones of the fourth dimension, and Ascend from there.

To help humanity understand, the Ascended Master El Morya has given a spiritual perspective about upcoming events. There are many similar channelings on the Internet and in books. From a previous channeling by El Morya he states:

> *That material gives you an idea of how life was originally meant to be expressed on this planet. It also gives you a glimpse of the direction the Earth is taking for the future of humanity. What is ahead for humanity is so wondrous; it simply cannot be described in a book. The whole plan cannot be revealed at this time, either.*

Ascension can be an individual experience or a group experience. As mentioned earlier, millions of souls came to Earth for this incarnation to go through a new experience of taking their physical bodies with them when they leave third-dimension Earth. There have been trillions of other souls, in spirit, trying to obtain permission to be here for the transition. Because of the crowded conditions and limited life support on Earth, the majority of their requests have been rejected. Those who have been approved and currently reside on Earth need to "Wake Up," remember to prepare their bodies. Many humans have been working for years to Ascend, and they plan to Ascend as soon as possible. In fact, many do Ascend every day. Pendulum dowsing indicates that eleven percent of the missing persons reported in the news media have recently Ascended. Many others not reported as missing have also Ascended.

The upcoming changes will be experienced by every soul on Earth. As the End Times draw closer, most everyone will realize that Earth will never be the same. Even those in the deepest sleep will be aware of their need to move off the Earth. The events leading up to this shock wave are mild in comparison to what will happen during the sorting process. The process of sorting out individual souls on different time lines has been relatively slow and tame up until now. Once "The Shift" kicks into high gear, millions of people will die, and those Ascending will just disappear. Those individuals in different realities aligned to different time lines will split off from each other. Each soul or group of souls will proceed down its chosen path and journey towards its future destination.

We are in the midst of what can best be described as humanity's final examination prior to graduation. We are passing through the piv-otal point of a twenty-five-year process that began in 1987 and will be in high gear between 2010 and 2013. Once various individuals have passed the exam, the next step for those who plan to Ascend to the New Earth is to obtain approval to pass through the Star Gates between the third-, fourth-, and fifth-dimensional states of consciousness. During this twenty-five-year period, as mentioned, each soul that has chosen the time line that leads to the New Earth and has prepared will have an opportunity to Ascend. Some ask what will happen to those souls on the Ascension time line that missed the first opportunities and find themselves in Bardo, between lives in the fourth dimension. All souls in Bardo who qualify for Ascension will have several choices, just like those within their physical bodies. They can continue their evolution on another third-dimension planet; they can create a new body and Ascend to the New Earth; or they can choose to return to their home planet.

Everyone's destination depends on their soul status, spiritual quali-fications, and chosen time line. The journey for each soul is unique and unfolds differently according to the individual's own distinctive pathway. Thus, the time required to complete all of the Ascension re-quirements will vary for each individual. Most souls who have tuned into Universal Consciousness indicate that Mother Earth will Ascend between 2009 and 2013. Many humans are anxious to Ascend with the Earth. Regardless of when you Ascend, Mother Earth is waiting for your arrival. For more detailed information about spiritual evolution review *The Law of One, Books one, two, and three,* channeled from the advanced spiritual composite Ra during the 1980s.

Reality in Third, Fourth, and Fifth Dimensional Illusions

Since all physicality is illusory, then where is reality? Each individual decides and creates his own reality. Others may ask for your opinions about what you think is real, but those are only opinions, not reality. When you share, you can state that these are your opinions as you currently understand them with your limited abilities. Then others can accept or reject your current opinions or views without judgment. No human can understand true reality. However everyone has chosen their own personal reality.

Spirit indicates *that when you are right, there is no need to acclaim it. If you are wrong, then you can pray and ask for forgiveness.* Nor are you here to control anyone else, or to control upcoming events on Earth. We can request that the most appropriate outcomes occur, and leave the control to Universal consciousness. Your goal should be to understand who you are, let go of your past illusions and false beliefs, and let go of the delusion that you are separate

> **Ascension preparation: the best approach is to accept everything, even though you cannot understand what's happening.**

from God/Goddess. You can then apply the suggestions received from your still, small voice within and use that knowledge to live in synchronicity in the "Now." As you quiet the mind, you will be ready to receive guidance from the heart and the still, small voice within. As part of your responsibility, you will be required to accept all upcoming events and divine will, for the good of the whole. Your best approach is to accept everything, even though you cannot understand why it is happening.

Thus, as dramatic changes occur on Earth, you can avoid entering into a state of shock or denial. You have prepared your consciousness for upcoming events and are ready to accept whatever happens. For those Ascending, you will be moving out of duality consciousness into Unity/Christ consciousness. There will be no *good* or *bad* duality concepts; everything will just be as it is. One helpful objective is to dissociate one's self from all personal and planetary delusions and illusions of the old Earth. Then, as you request help in shifting your consciousness to the higher frequencies, the pathway is clear to accept many new, accurate beliefs. These new beliefs will be parts of your new Unity/Christ consciousness.

It is the responsibility of humans on Earth to help create the New Earth as you want it to be. Start "Now" by dreaming about your visions of Heaven on Earth and how you would like your life to be. Be very specific, and don't hesitate to include all the wondrous details. You are one of the co-creators with God/Goddess. The new Earth is waiting for your creative contributions. No one knows the details of what will happen to create our new bodies and the New Earth, partially because humanity is in the process of creating the details. The complexity of the whole process is beyond the comprehension of the human mind and its limited consciousness.

Some individuals have a challenge concerning Ascension because of the process. Many humans have instilled a belief system that they must physically die. An unconscious fear of death or a lack of understanding that a person can Ascend without experiencing death are both false beliefs. These false beliefs need clearing to help maintain a healthy body. Keep in mind that anything we fear, resist, or judge, we attract into our experience.

* * * * * *

Section II: Factors Influencing the Future of Humanity

7

Avoiding Fear, Accepting Change, Time, and Earth's Magnetic Field

One Major Task is to Avoid Fear and Accept Change without Question

When reading *You Can Avoid Physical Death*, by all means, let your fears go and choose to experience understanding and enlightenment. In reality, fear only exists as a figment of your imagination carried over from your past. The fear was created and transferred to your mind from your left brain, since the right brain knows no fear. The challenge is to be willing to accept the greatness of "The Shift," a process that no life form has ever experienced, while living within a physical body on a planet.

You may observe individuals running around hither and yon trying to understand what is happening. As these events take place, realize that you will be safe when you decide to be safe. Also realize that some things you will read within this book could take time to understand. As various events unfold in your life, you will be aware, prepared, and ready to accept the changes taking place. I pray that you will accept what is happening, feel safe, and choose to see the greatness and joy of having an opportunity to go through all the upcoming experiences.

Fear is part of the duality concept and is primarily a warning message. Fear is generated in the left brain as an attention-getter. Fear involves a relay of messages stored within your left brain. Following a logical analysis of various situations, these messages are stored in the left brain. They are then transferred from the left brain to your conscious mind. Your right brain's intuitive senses know no fear. Your left brain would like for you to understand that the fear message it is sending to your conscious mind is a caution. The left brain's message is: *As I analyze these situations, I see that they have led to pain in the past. Therefore, be cautious and alert. The fear I am creating and you are picking up* on is an opportunity for you to use love to heal the situation. You can also use love to clear out all excess fear.

The ongoing evolutionary process termed "The Shift" will change everything on the old Earth and bring into being the New Earth. To go through "The Shift" and come out on the New Earth will require a shift in consciousness that involves a high degree of dedicated ac-

> **Will you wait until your survival is threatened before you act? It may be too late to prepare then.**

ceptance and patience with all upcoming events. Obviously, the first step is to become aware and "Wake Up" up to what is happening daily. For some to "Wake Up" Mother Earth may have to create a traumatic event to get their attention. Only when their survival is directly threatened do some humans take action to change their way of life. But when they do "Wake Up," they change very quickly.

If you want to clean your body by taking a bath, you prepare yourself, take off your clothes, and get wet. In the same way, if you want to go to New Earth free yourself from sickness, pain, and suffering, and be prepared and embrace any change without question.

All evidence indicates "The Shift" is a real phenomenon that is taking place and will accelerate in the very near future. "The Shift" is a change that is both internal (within you) and external (upon the Earth). All of these changes will involve energetically accepting new approaches to living. A large percentage of each individual's preparation for graduation and Ascension will include interior changes within the mental and emotional bodies. By clearing out any resistance to change, preparation will become easier and much more efficient.

The original divine plan for humanity on Earth was to multiply, experience limitation, and become separate from everything, including God/Goddess. In order to carry out the divine plan, we had to get lost, drop down to a low state of dimensional consciousness, and then see if we could find our way back. It is "Now" time to "Wake Up," remember our magnificence, realize that we are beings of love and light, and find our way back. As you "Wake Up," you can tune in to all aspects of "The Shift" and realize that these events will lead you on your way back. You can then join the planet Earth in its transformation, enjoy the new experiences, and progress spiritually.

As we approach "The Shift," we can anticipate various climatic and physical changes on third-dimensional Earth. For example, many believe that a pole shift will occur. In close association with the pole shift, the Earth may stop spinning and reverse its direction of rotation. Then there is the possibility that as the Photon Belt approaches, the Earth will experience a period of darkness. Regardless of what happens, we need to be prepared consciously to accept change. According to the Master Kirael, a channeled message through Kahu Fred Sterling, www.Kirael.com.states that:

> *The current shift is atypical. Usually, the force of Creation, in all its wisdom, removes all advanced life from the surface, resets the planet, and then allows another evolutionary journey to unfold. This is what transpired at the end of both Lemuria and Atlantis. With the current shift, the dramatic physical transformation of the planet will occur with humanity still onboard.*

One helpful procedure for use in the coming days will be to maintain a high level of love energy. The power code for love is built with a combination of the number nine for *Completion* and the number five for *Love*. When a power code is visualized and voiced, that thought form is intensified and can be directed towards a target object or person. The "Power Code for Complete Love is (9-9-9-9-9-9-9-9 and 5-5-5-5-5-5-5). Verbally repeat the number sequence without dashes as many times as necessary. Use pendulum dowsing to measure the love energy before and after repeating the "Power Code. Love energy can cancel hate and fear and heal everything that you direct that energy towards.

Keep in mind that fear is not the opposite of love; hate is the opposite of love. Love is the focal point of acceptance; hate is the focal point of denial. Fear is like an alarm system. It seems like fear is to be avoided, but this is not so. Some fear is present to tell us where we need to shine Light and Love on something that needs balancing. Thus, fear can serve as a trigger mechanism for providing an opportunity to love more. If any fear arises during "The Shift," flood it with Light and Love.

> **Key understanding:**
> **Fear is not the opposite of love;**
> **Hate is the opposite of love.**

A shifting of the Earth's magnetic poles has happened in the past. Drunvalo Melchizedek mentions that Thoth, his close advisor, indicated that human civilization on Earth dates back five hundred million years. Refer to *the two books, Ancient Secrets of the Flower of Life,* Volume 1 and Volume 2, by Drunvalo Melchizedek. During this period, the Earth's magnetic poles shifted five times, most recently during the submergence of Atlantis. Scientific evidence also indicates that the Earth's magnetic poles have changed five times. Core samples of the Earth, when magnetically analyzed, reveal changes in the magnetic orientation of the samples' electromagnetic features. During these Shifts, the Earth's magnetic field changed, and this was recorded within the electromagnetic orientation of sensitive molecules within the core samples. The molecular orientations of the sensitive molecules changed directions in correlation with changes in the magnetic field of the Earth. There is one thing we can say for certain: based on history and science, at some point in the future, the magnetic poles of the Earth will change. Some scientists think *the magnetic poles will take up new positions in the future, as they have in the past.*

Many scientists, history books, channelings, prophesy, and Internet discussions agree that the Earth's frequency and magnetic field intensity are currently changing. The Earth's Schumann resonance frequency is increasing, and its magnetic field strength is decreasing. For more details, review the books, *Awakening to the Zero Point* and *Walking Between the Worlds* by Gregg Braden. In *Awakening to the Zero Point*, Braden discusses the scientific evidence that the Earth is passing through the Photon Belt; the resonant frequency of Earth is increasing; the magnetic field strength is decreasing; the Earth's rotation rate is slowing; and clock time is collapsing. Many individuals are aware of these changes and their importance.

The Nature of Clock Time, Its Illusory Features, and Real Spiritual Time

Most humans sense that the length of the twenty-four hour day is physically shortening. Although clock time appears to maintain a twenty-four-hour day, actual physical activity time has shortened to approximately fifteen hours and continues to decrease. Following "The Shift," available activity time will approach zero. As we evolve into the higher dimensions, there will be no clock time.

Time was created within the third-dimensional state of consciousness and is really an illusion, just as space or distance is an illusion. Within the third-dimensional state of consciousness, clock time was created for our spirits to experience physicality and all the associated limitations, such as being separate. Illusory time gave us a reference

> **In order to experience clock time and duality, the reality realm of time on Earth was slowed down.**

point, a perspective of progression, and a sense of self so we could focus on an event. To accomplish this illusory creation of clock time, the reality realm frequency was *slowed down* so we could experience the gradual unfolding of growth. We were then able to use our senses to experience the process of Creation as it unfolded.

That process has been altered, and *the reality-realm frequency will continue to increase.* In the more spiritual levels of dimensional consciousness, there will be no need to concern ourselves with time and space. These changes and many more are in preparation for "The Shift" and man's Ascension to the New Earth.

These changes in time are very important. Thus, as time permits it will be very helpful for you to study about real time. We are not referring to clock time. Real Time is a wavelength of light, a measurable period, or, more accurately, a progression of reality realm energy. This increase is correlated with the required shift in dimensional consciousness that allows humans to graduate and Ascend to the New Earth.

Time was also created as something that could be bought, sold, and traded in this world of survival. Time is used to manipulate life's activities for a purpose. As an example, the Gregorian calendar was designed by a man disconnected from the Earth and divine concepts. The Gregorian calendar does not define anything real. It does not even mimic obvious progressions that exist scientifically, cosmically, or

> **Real time is a wavelength of Light, a progression of reality realm energy.**

spiritually anywhere in the Universe. This false, male-dominated, illusory perception of clock time, as outlined in the Gregorian calendar, is strictly linear and is based on cause and effect. As a result, humans have become trapped within a two-dimensional, perceptional illusion of linear time. This false belief needs to be removed from consciousness.

To those who have chosen to Ascend, as you become more and more aware of your eternal beingness, you accelerate your frequency and move beyond the grasp of time and its influence. The old version of linear time is obsolete. By allowing the balance of male with female and left- brain with right-brain aspects of reality within your consciousness, time energy becomes circular, with no end and no beginning. The female aspect of time supports accelerated growth. Then the energy of time becomes what you want it to be. It is your servant. You are no longer under the control of the male-dominated aspect of linear time. You become the controller of time when you evolve to take your physical body to the New Earth. Thus, the importance of bringing your reality realm of time into balance—a balance of your male (left brain) and female (right brain)—in preparation for a new cyclic pattern that prepares you for graduation and Ascension.

Ascension and evolvement into "Light Body" status are beyond the limitations of time and space. Love is the key component of Service to Others (STO) orientation. Love will help you Ascend beyond the concepts of past and future into the "NOW," a main feature of the fifth dimension. Love is always

> **When you live in the "Now," beyond time, you become a force of love greater than anything you can imagine.**

true and real in the moment; it is beyond time. When you live in the "Now," beyond time, you become a force of love greater than anything you can imagine. You are to be in control of time. *When you live within the "Now" and within love, you have moved into a new reality realm of no-time, a characteristic of the New Earth.* These concepts depend upon your perceptions and understandings of what is real for you. You create your reality by what you think. You can be in control of illusory time and realize it was a gift in the third dimension. By your thoughts, you can create heaven (harmony) for yourself, or you can create hell (discord).

Real time is a type of energy and has no direct relationship with clock time. There is a way out of the trap called clock time. As we evolve to where there is no clock time (zero time) and begin to understand time energy, we can gain control of that energy and use it for our benefit.

The ability to use clock time for your benefit will be determined by where you come from, who you are, why you are, and your awareness of illusory time and space. That ability to use time will also be influenced by how your energy system relates to the incoming wavelengths of light energy. If you give your power over to time, it will influence you one way. As you shift away from the illusion of clock time, the entrapments will have no affect on you. You will be freed from that state of conscious and illusory reality that is called clock time. As you prepare to Ascend, you will be required to comprehend time from a spiritual perspective.

Everything that happens in the world of physicality is first set up in the non-physical, spiritual world. That is, the subconscious world dictates the primary order of events. Within the spiritual world, we are under the hierarchy of the divine, our spiritual friends in high places. However, realize that we are also divine creations that have projected ourselves into these physical bodies. Thus we choose to be controlled by clock time within the physical world. Now with "The Shift," we will have an opportunity to release ourselves from this entrapment and control time energy.

Planet Earth is Ascending, and many humans are Ascending with Earth. Prior to this event, the Earth and humans were condensing and contracting. As we Ascend, we will be spreading and expanding. The acceleration of time energy has come with this expansion and, as a result, helped prepare those interested in obtaining "Light Body" status. Clock time will become less real as you manifest more and more of your divinity in order to move into "Light Body" status. Time energy is accelerating with or without humanity's help. You have a choice to accept the eternalness of your being and latch on to the incoming waves of time energy. Then, as you flow with these new, accelerated energies, your life will be accepting and implanting the reality of your soul's eternalness.

Yes, you can choose to reject everything you just read and let energy time flow on by without acceptance. Spirit indicates that if you have rejected these concepts of time, you are unprepared for passing through "The Shift." Up to this point in your life, you were unaware of an opportunity to evolve spiritually and thereby transition to the New Earth. An understanding of time could help you "Wake Up," leave the world of duality, and Ascend.

When you accept these incoming energies, you are preparing to move to the New Earth. When you reject the many opportunities these new energies provide, you have chosen to move to another planet. Don't forget, if you reject these new, high-frequency energies, your low-frequency, third-dimensional body will not tolerate the high-frequency, fifth-dimensional energies on the New Earth.

I have been recently informed by spirit that those who choose to reject these new energies may have a choice as to which new planet they are transferred to. Some of those choices have already become available; others are in the planning stage. Extraterrestrial drone ships are being sent throughout the Universe to locate inhabitable planetary systems for those who choose not to Ascend. The Extraterrestrial survey team's first choices are suitable planets where a society has been eradicated by its previous misuse of energy. Following a recovery period, that planet may now be ready for inhabitation. The survey team's task is to determine the frequency of each planet and if the environmental conditions are favorable to receive and support human inhabitants.

Other planets of choice include those where societies have become so self-indulgent that the inhabitants pay little attention to things not directly affecting their private worlds. This was the characteristic features of planet Earth when the Extraterrestrial Grays were allowed to conduct cloning experiments within the United States. Many humans on Earth were so engrossed in their daily activities that they were totally unaware of how many women were used to create baby clones for the Zeta Rectulian Grays. There may be other planets where the society is so engrossed in their private lives you could incarnate there and they would be unaware of your presence. That is, you could choose to incarnate on such a planet if space is available.

You have a free choice, based on desire; to create what you consider is the most appropriate lesson for your spiritual evolution. Yesterday is history; tomorrow is a mystery; and today is a gift; that's why "Now" is called the present. For additional insights, review the many postings on the Web sites www.zakairan.com, www. ascensionmastery.com, and www.cybertrails.com. However, your most accurate insights are received directly from your God/Goddess within.

Reality of Earth's Changing Magnetic Field, and Memory Retention

Some helpful sources of information are present within the records of the Mayan civilization. The Mayan calendar was aligned to the Earth and the cosmos and has a spiritual foundation from which to understand reality. By understanding the Mayan calendar, you can gain a greater understanding of reality. The Mayans were very advanced spiritually, and many of them Ascended together into a higher state of dimensional consciousness many years ago.

These records indicate that every realty realm of consciousness on all dimensional levels has its own specific time-energy reference. The progression of entities residing in each reality realm have based their evolution on that time-energy reference. Time energy is not only within the consciousness of humans but within the structure of their chromosomes. As humans shift in consciousness from third to fifth dimension, they surpass the capabilities of the light-time reality realm and must alter their chromosomes to facilitate a new Light-Body reality realm. These different states are called consciousness time zones. In order to accommodate these changes, the geomagnetic fields of the Earth are being altered. As we Ascend and take on "Light Body" status, we will enter the New Earth's consciousness time zone and become part of the New Earth's civilization of Light energy.

When we review our evolution, we realize that we have been trapped in a time warp. This self-imposed time warp has helped create our reincarnation cycles. As we go through "The Shift," we will be capable of releasing ourselves from this illusory time warp. We will then be freed from the duality world of polarity, reincarnation, darkness and light, and all other associated challenges. Consequently, following "The Shift," traditional reincarnation cycles will become an illusion of the past. You can live as long as you prefer in an ageless body on the New

Earth. Those illusions within Earth's third-dimension school had value. They served as an important challenge for our evolution.

In higher-dimensional reality realms, life in relation to time is an eternal unfoldment where everything that we used to consider to be happening "Now," the past, the present, and the future becomes one. The overall process has been defined as taking on "Light Body" status. Once this is accomplished, there will be no need for the many bodies we have had. We will have new, lightweight bodies with untold capabilities. We will approach Ascended Master status.

You and I can gain many additional understandings from the channelings of Master Djwhal Khul on the Web site: www.masterdk.com. On this Web site there is a question-and-answer section. For example, the following question was asked: Master Khul, what effect will this magnetic shift have on humans and animals?

His answer:

> Earth eventually stops spinning, hangs for a short while, and then begins to spin in the opposite direction. When the Earth starts spinning again, many things will be different. For example, the prevailing trade winds will reverse from west to east; the sun will rise in the west and set in the east. The North Pole, which is now positively charged, will become the South Pole, which is now negatively charged, so that after the reversal, the North Pole becomes negatively charged and the South Pole becomes positively charged.
>
> With regard to consciousness, the most potent time would be in the hang time between when the planet stopped rotating from east to west and begins rotating from west to east. During that time, there would be no magnetic field around the Earth. In that brief time span (roughly two to seven days); there would literally be no history for Earth.

From these comments we can assume, based on Master Khul's analysis, there would be no memory of past events. All memory would be released, because a magnetic field is required to store memory. Without the Earth's magnetic field, no memories could be stored during "The

Shift." During previous shifts of the Earth's magnetic poles, evolving souls lost their memories. When they reincarnated, they started their new lives consciously with a clean slate.

However, you "Now" have the option to retain your memory by creating your personal protective magnetic field. That field can be created when you purposely create a Mer-Ka-Ba. The procedure for creating a Mer-Ka-Ba will be discussed later, in Chapter 10.

A recent example illustrates how the loss of the magnetic field influences humans. Russians scientists reported that during the early days of their space program, when their cosmonauts were out of the Earth's geomagnetic field for more than two weeks, they lost their memories and went literally crazy. The Russians have since developed equipment to create an artificial magnetic field to protect their cosmonauts in space.

Spirit indicates that because of help from the Extraterrestrials and changes in human consciousness, there is a high probability that this hang time, (the lack of Earth's magnetic field) may be reduced somewhat. No one knows for sure how long the exact hang time will be.

We can assume that humans who currently lack a Mer-Ka-Ba "Light Body" would lose their memories and no longer know who they are. So what difference would the Mer-Ka-Ba make? The three tetrahedrons that make up Mer-Ka-Ba have two that spin (one clockwise; the other counter-clockwise) and one that is stationary. The two spinning tetrahedrons create a magnetic field around the human body. That Mer-Ka-Ba-generated magnetic field can help protect your memory from collapsing.

Other important questions are: How long will it take before the absence of the Earth's magnetic field causes human memory loss? How long will the Earth be without a magnetic field? If the hang time is less than two days, then possibly some memory would be retained. If the Mer-Ka-Ba is working, then a large percentage of one's memory would be retained regardless of the hang time. Thus, we need to make sure our Mer-Ka-Ba's are working and pray that our Spiritual Assistants intervene to limit the hang time or maintain a sufficiently strong magnetic field around the Earth so that humans retain their memories.

To continue quoting Master Khul on www.masterdk.com:

> The Great Shift, 2001: The upside of this is that such an experience would have the potential to completely wipe the slate clean. -- There would be no

unhealthy repeating patterns; there would be no way to repeat past mistakes. --.The down side would reside in those who become fearful, thinking that without their past they must not now exist. There could be some pandemonium, I suppose, and perhaps some would, in effect, go insane, but since that goes on all the time to some degree, I don't think it is of particular significance.

Set your sights on enlightenment, and determine to see through any fear that arises. Seen in this manner, such an experience would be very exciting, indeed. "If this event indeed comes about (and it is more likely at this point in time then it has been for any time in the past 15,000 years), greet it with your very best self, you should face such an experience as you would any other important experience in your life; show up, pay attention, give it your best effort, and don't be too attached to the outcome.

Obviously, knowing of this possibility, it would be beneficial to prepare for the time when the Earth stops spinning. When it stops, the "Photon Belt will have absorbed all the light from the sun and the Earth will be in darkness. Think about the need to prepare, and ask God/Goddess within what to do. For possible choices, check out the information on various Web sites such as   www.ascensionmastery. com, www.survivalcenter.com, and www.kirael.com. Those in control of their lives can shift their consciousness to a higher state, enjoy the Ascension process, and look forward to enjoying living on the New Earth. The important thing to consider is that following "The Shift," you will have an opportunity to experience yourself in a reality realm of Unity/Christ consciousness.

Workshop notes from Drunvalo Melchizedek on the *Flower of Life* and Mer-Ka-Ba activation procedures, also considered the potential pole shift. Quoting Drunvalo Melchizedek:

There will be a pole shift ....We may find that the environment, even though the poles may shift, may not be nearly as violent as we think. It could actually be a very beautiful experience. My feeling on this may go against what a lot of people think. There are many people saying go out and dig holes in the ground, put lots and lots of food in, and guns and munitions and hold on for the worse. But really what you are preparing for is that time right before the pole shift. Because when the poles shift, we will go through an electromagnetic no zone for about three and a half days, and then, after that time we will be on a totally different Dimensional level of the Earth. Then anything that is happening on this third Dimension level will make no difference. That is, a preparation prior to the time when all the systems, the social and the financial systems, and all kinds of things break down. And it will be normal for these systems to break down. Scientists will see in the magnetic field a direct correlation with the events occurring on Earth.

When the magnetic poles of the Earth move to new locations, human consciousness has an opportunity to shift into the fourth-dimensional state of consciousness. The end of each twenty-five-thousand-year cycle throughout the past history of the Earth has been characterized by worldwide confusion before chaos. It has been a period where most people go insane. Social, financial, and political systems collapse and the planet is plunged into total chaos. Generally, this period of chaos occurs on all planets

> **Notification:**
> **The transition began several years ago. You will have some clock time between 2008 and 2012 to prepare spiritually for "The Shift", graduation, and Ascension.**

going through "The Shift." During past shifts, the chaos lasted for three to twenty-four months and primarily occurred prior to the actual pole shift. This interval of time is called the transition period, or sometimes the Tribulation. If "The Shift" were to occur in the latter part of 2012 or early in 2013, this would mean that we can anticipate that the transition period would be in full swing sometime in 2010. Actually, preliminary stages of the transition period have already begun: we just haven't experienced the more traumatic events yet. Study the many postings on the Web site www.2012.com.au for more details. With any Web site posting, use pendulum dowsing in consultation with Universal Consciousness to determine the accuracy of the information presented. An alternative is to use discernment and listen to the still, small voices within for guidance.

As you mentally make preparations for Ascension, ask to receive a better understanding of why God/Goddess and the Creators of this Universe approved a different kind of Shift at the end of this twenty-five-thousand-year cycle on planet Earth. A shift of this kind has never before occurred in the history of this Universe. No being, however spiritually evolved, knows what will actually happen as "The Shift" takes place.

Between the years of 2008 and 2012, everything you do *physically* to prepare for "The Shift" on Earth will be of limited value (with some exceptions). All the third-dimensional illusions you have created as part of the duality lessons on the old Earth need to disappear from your conscious perceptions. If you have stored up food or money or bought material goods, they will disappear. You will not need them anyway. Hoarding material goods is totally unrealistic. Some may doubt these events will occur. The question is -- will your doubt change an evolu-tionary pattern that has been put in place by the Creators of this Universe? We all real-ize thoughts are very power-ful, but is every thought cre-ated powerful enough to

> **Important note:**
> **Continue many of your normal daily activities, since they are a part of your current contract.**

change the course of history? Only time will tell how the thoughts of the collective consciousness will manifest and influence "The Shift." There is a message from spirit that could be important for you to con-sider. There may be a tendency to cease many physical, mental, and emotional activities as you anticipate "The Shift." Why continue your normal activities when many of the results of those activities will disap-pear and have no lasting value? All of your activities are a part of your contract you agreed upon before coming to Earth. These activities are a part of your lessons and opportunities for soul growth. So why waste these valuable experiences during the time frame between 2008 and

2013 or up until "The Shift" takes place? Yes, make preparations to Ascend, but also maintain those contractual activities that enhance your soul growth.

Once you have completed all your preparations and received approval to pass through the Star Gate portals, you will be propelled into the fourth- and fifth-dimensional reality realm. As a result, there will be a significant need on your part to make many adjustments in your beliefs and behavior patterns. During the historical period between the years of 2008 and 2013, all evidence indicates that everyone on planet Earth will go through significant changes in their lives. This includes those who woke up earlier and are prepared to Ascend, those who woke up just in time to graduate, and those who are still asleep.

According to my twenty-five years of research and messages from many spiritual beings, these predicted changes will occur. It will not be the end of civilization but a beginning. Some evidence indicates that your physical preparation may help a little bit at the beginning of the transition period. For example, it would be wise to maintain a healthy body, practice prana breathing, enjoy living, commune with nature, and take time to relax, exercise, and share with others. Then practice how to be more effective in Service To Others (STO), a pattern characteristic of the fifth dimension. Many around you could benefit from your kindness and service when they ask for assistance.

The most significant preparation you can make, in order to create a smooth transition, is to work diligently to make internal changes within your consciousness. The key is to know who you are, (a spirit part of God/Goddess) how much love you have for self and all of creation, your quality of character, how open your heart is, and to what degree you have synchronized your consciousness with the God/Goddess within. As the world you have known changes, the only thing you can count on is your consciousness. Your love for and patience with self and others will pay great dividends.

Because of the limited amount of time you have left to prepare for graduation, the best approach is to consciously prepare mentally, emotionally, and spiritually. Once you have prepared internally, then go within and ask God/Goddess how to prepare physically. Determine how you will obtain water, food, and shelter before "The Shift." Yes, there may be water and food shortages. Hoarding is not the answer. The most appropriate answers come from God/Goddess within.

Therefore, the question is: "What can you, as a spirit and soul, do to prepare yourself for Ascension? Presumably, if you came to Earth to spiritually advance your soul and take on "Light Body" status, you need to prepare. We were endowed with the capability to become one with Creator Source and God/Goddess. Thus we have a responsibility to call upon the God/Goddess within to guide our activities. By listening to the voice of God/Goddess within, we can establish objectives and goals that can assist us. We are striving toward some level of perfection that appears to be out of reach but do-able in terms of advancing our souls' growth. As we discipline ourselves and implement Service To Others (STO), our souls evolve, and God/Goddess evolves. Remember, God/Goddess evolves through his/her creative parts; all human souls are parts of God/Goddess. Let's contemplate and be thankful for the many opportunities we have had as we traveled along our spiritual paths, helping God/Goddess to evolve.

Spirit indicates there are changes within that will survive the loss of the magnetic field and our memory storage systems. Changes within are real, that component part of us created by God/Goddess, called the Spirit and Soul are permanent. Everything else is an illusion that we have created on Earth for our challenging lessons. To retain as much memory as possible, make sure your Mer-Ka-Ba "Light Body's" magnetic field is properly positioned and spinning appropriately every day. Another important personal responsibility is to make sure all of your 617 soul facets are present, properly positioned, and synchronized with each other. This will require accurate pendulum dowsing to measure the number of facets present and their degree of synchronization. When you detect a need to recover, clean up, install, and synchronize missing soul facets, request help from your Spiritual Assistants. Hopefully, the above suggestions emphasize the need to go within and change your consciousness.

* * * * *

8

The Photon Belt and Its Influence on Earth and Human Evolution

The governments and other groups in control on planet Earth have largely withheld information from the public about the Photon Belt and its relation to "The Shift." If you are unfamiliar with the Photon Belt and why it's such a secret, I suggest you do some research. If you plan to graduate and move to the New Earth, then when you arrive upon the New Earth the Photon Belt's energy will be one of your major energy sources. For a more complete description of the doughnut (torrid)-shaped Photon Belt located within the Milky Way Galaxy refer to the book *You Are Becoming a Galactic Human* by Virginia Essene and Sheldon Nidle. Be cautious as you learn about the Photon Belt because of false and misleading information disseminated by those who are attempting to slow your spiritual evolution. Some consciously mislead by promoting self-proclaimed knowledge that is false; while others mislead because of their lack of understanding.

There is a sequential, repetitive cycle of events within the Milky Way Galaxy. All stars and their planets within this Galaxy rotate around the great central sun, Alcyone, located within the Pleiadian Star System, a region in space where our Solar System is located. The rotational period of twenty-five thousand years has repeating, cyclic periods of dark and light, or periods of different states of consciousness. As our Solar System first entered the vortex of the Photon Belt in May 1998, we came to the end of a 12,500-year dark period. We now have begun a new 12,500-year light period. Our Solar System is gradually coming under the influence of the Photon Belt light.

The Photon Belt is a massive region in space containing a high concentration of photons. Science defines a photon as *a particle of energy representing a quantum of light or electromagnetic radiation.* The individual photon carries a frequency signature; however, it lacks mass. The Photon Belt consists of twelve gigantic vortexes of intense celestial bands of light, each with a structural frequency. When Earth first entered the Photon Belt, these incoming frequencies started out as short bursts of radiation. Every day now, photons are bombarding the Earth with more intensity and consistency. There is no turning back; Earth will move through the Photon Belt. There is no other choice; this event is part of a grand, cyclic pattern.

To prepare for the energy of the Photon Belt and to utilize the available photons, Kirael, channeling through Kahu Fred Sterling in a book, *The Great Shift*, 2001, provides this possible scenario:

> Imagine for the moment a world in which a sudden heavy chill begins to permeate the air, a chill unlike anything you have ever experienced, a chill that touches your bones. As you look around, everyone appears to be getting sleepy. No matter where you might be, people get less and less restless. Some people are smiling, but many have a look of fear in their eyes. The sun in the middle of the day begins dimming, until suddenly there is no sun at all. Welcome to the three days of darkness. Many will decide then that this is not the journey they desire to take and will move on to other arenas. You can choose to be afraid or you can choose to face the adventure. Hear me clearly. You will need to be awake, you will need to be alert, you will need to know what your journey must be, and you have to participate in that journey in a moment's notice. It will happen that quickly.
>
> The question is always asked, which has no answer, is: Master Kirael, please tell us what day this will happen so we might prepare. What are you going to do, get flashlights? That will not help you because batteries will not work post-shift. What are you going to do, fill up your car with gasoline? Don't worry about that either. When your numbers are great enough, you will expand yourselves through the belts of the photon energy, and a new world will begin. Until that time you will just have to keep preparing.

As the Solar System and Earth revolve around the Great Central Sun, Alcyone, Earth will enter the Photon Belt completely sometime around 2012 and remain there for over two thousand years. This event will be extremely important as a means of helping bring into consciousness the many changes that are to take place in the next two thousand years. These energies are designed to assist star systems and their components in making shifts in consciousness. Within the Photon Belt, the veils between the different dimensions become increasingly thin or nonexistent. Each state of dimensional consciousness can be correlated with these different frequencies. These frequencies also help define the different vibratory rates of the photon.

The last time Earth passed through the Photon Belt was when Atlantis and Lemuria were at their height of spiritual development. Historical records indicate that this event occurred before the time when the continent of Lemuria sank into the Pacific Ocean. However, that was not the cause of Lemuria's destruction.

Those who resist the Photon Belt light and coming changes will not be able to make it through the twelve gigantic vortexes. According to the Ascended Masters, many will choose to vacate their physical bodies (die) rather than let go of their third-dimensional illusions. They will prefer to hold on to their fears, false beliefs, and personal agendas. Many will also lack the discipline to prepare themselves and go through the graduation steps. Thus it is obvious that each person has a free will. There is never a judgment about the choices made. Each soul evolves according to its chosen path (time line).

Entrance into the Photon Belt will assist in preparing planet Earth and all its inhabitants to Ascend into the fourth and fifth dimensions. Historically, though, transitions into and out of the Photon Belt have been characterized by radical weather patterns and dramatic Earth changes. Some of these transitional events have already begun. They will gradually increase in the next few years. Humans need to prepare for any of these possible happenings without fear. Also, passing safely through these light energies means you have aligned your energy-pattern frequencies so that they are compatible with the energy-pattern frequencies of the Photon Belt. Preparations for "The Shift" have been ongoing by a host of Spiritual entities for many years. The Spiritual Hierarchy and Extraterrestrial groups have made several adjustments in the Solar System's energy patterns in preparation for the arrival of the Photon Belt.

However, humans who plan to graduate will need help in making internal alignments in their consciousness. Deep within, you are aware of your need to prepare and your need for spiritual help. In fact, many people have been preparing for years. Efforts have also been initiated to help protect your biological systems from psychological overload and emotional distress. There are multitudes of Spiritual Assistants that can help assist you in your preparations. However, you need to ask and do your part. No one else can live your life for you. Other humans and Spiritual Assistants can help you help yourself. Our experiences indicate that Spiritual Assistant and other helpers can proceed to complete 77 percent of your requested changes. The remaining 23 percent is your responsibility. That is, you will need to know the questions to ask and make some personal effort to remove various imbalances and adjust energy flow patterns.

There are groups of individuals and "Light Workers all over the world making preparations. There are thousands of books and channelings about how to prepare for these upcoming events. The Christian Bible mentions the three days of darkness, and many religious people throughout the world also believe strongly in the importance of preparing for the future.

In order to take advantage of these intense photon energies arriving on Earth, you need to prepare your physical, mental, and emotional bodies by shifting your consciousness from the third to the fourth dimension. To prepare, you need to "be here "Now." The objective is for you to gain mastery over the polarized duality of the third dimension. You will need to become more aware of your third-dimensional consciousness. When you shift into the fourth-dimensional state of consciousness you will be shifting into a new reality realm with less material density and limited duality. This fourth dimension is the reality realm of archetypes, guides, and all kinds of spiritual entities. As you prepare to shift to the fourth dimension, just ask for assistance and follow the still, small voices within "Now." Ask and ye shall receive, based on your belief and intent.

Before we approach the following chapter, Spirit indicates you should be aware of a very recent message sent by the Extraterrestrial Arcturians, www.cybertrails.com. Their message is: *During 2012, do not plan to take long trips in any kind of vehicle.*

You can interpret that message any way you choose. They have presented this message for a purpose; hopefully, someone will obtain more details. If you find out, let others know what you discover. Many are well aware that if you were driving across desolate West Texas and "The Shift" arrived, your car would stall on the side of the road and you would fall asleep. When you awaken after three days, your car will stay right there on the road because the new energies present after "The Shift" will not allow mechanical engines to function. Accurate pendulum dowsing, directed towards Universal Consciousness, indicates that this scenario concerning the inability of mechanical engines to function is 95 percent accurate.

* * * * *

9

Ascended Masters' and Extraterrestrials' Assistance for Earth's Ascension

Many humans are fascinated with the concept of Extraterrestrials, UFOs, and the government cover-up concerning the presence of Extraterrestrials. Consider the possibility that this fascination is because they (and you) are Extraterrestrials. There is secrecy about Extraterrestrials because the reality is that all humans on Earth originated from other planets. This knowledge would alter the history books and shake up the plans of the Illuminati. Yes, planet Earth has been invaded by aliens many, many times in the past. You are one of those alien invaders. Many Extraterrestrials continue to come and go, disguised to look just like humans, every day.

Is this your best dream come true? Have you always felt that your home was on some other planet? Or does this instill fear in you to know that you are surrounded by Extraterrestrials? Realize that the physical bodies of all humans on Earth have been genetically engineered to combine various genetic features of different Extraterrestrials. For example, humans have a functional Reptilian brain.

Even though most humans have heard of UFOs and millions of others believe Extraterrestrial are present, there are many sleepy, unaware humans who still doubt their existence. Bashar's channeled via Darryl Anka (www.bashar.org), about Extraterrestrials follows:

Question: "Can you tell us a specific time frame for the general and public acceptance and understanding of the UFO phenomenon?"

Answer: "By your year 2012–2013 there will be quite a lot of information. By 2029 almost everyone on the planet will be aware of Extraterrestrials no later than 2037 everyone will not only be aware, but the vibrational resonance of Earth will become a part of the Association of Worlds."

Extraterrestrials from Andromeda have indicated that the human life form was created in the Lyrian system. Humanoids that possess Nordic features have lived on many different planets within this Universe for approximately forty million years.

As you scan the Internet and read books and magazines, you may see articles about first contact from the Extraterrestrials. A majority of all Extraterrestrial ships—even the Mother Ships, hundreds of miles in diameter—are vibrating at frequencies above what human vision can detect. These intergalactic vehicles are obviously thought forms that lack the material density we are accustomed to on Earth. They are created and controlled by thought. These thought-created vehicles can change dimensions for certain purposes. From a third-dimensional perspective, these vehicles change dimensions, become less physical, and disappear from view on a radar screen. Without a physical, third-dimension structure to reflect back radar pulses, they become invisible.

> **Extraterrestrials from off-planet are here now, awaiting "The Shift" and New Earth.**

Most of the UFOs which have physically landed on the third-dimension Earth were made by entities from low-frequency planets or created by government contractors on Earth. These vehicles are primarily constructed on the basis of external Mer-Ka-Ba technology. Some of the UFOs have been a part of the Lucifer Rebellion. These more ancient types of physical Extraterrestrial vehicles are being replaced with more elaborate vehicles capable of traveling throughout many Universes. Even those created on Earth are being upgraded constantly.

The spiritually designed Mer-Ka-Ba ships of light are created by Love and Light via thought within the fifth dimension or higher. Large numbers of Intergalactic ships of light have been and continue to land on the higher dimensions of multidimensional planet Earth. In fact, there are so many of these vehicles on and around Earth, they are challenged to find room to park. So if you are waiting for these Extraterrestrial ships to land so you can go on board, you should first transition to a higher dimensional state of consciousness, where you can see them. They can then descend in consciousness, but you must first make an effort to Ascend in order to meet and communicate with them telepathically. The large Mother Ships, the size of planetary moons, must remain at a certain distance from the Solar System in order to avoid disrupting various energy fields around the planets. So if you see a UFO, realize that most often, the vehicles with the colored, blinking lights have been manufactured on Earth through the use of external Mer-Ka-Ba technology. In other cases, these vehicles have been created by Extraterrestrial entities residing on other low-frequency planets.

There are limitless numbers and types of Extraterrestrial beings on limitless numbers of planets in limitless overtones of the various dimensional states of consciousness. Many look similar to humans, or like those depicted on *Star Trek*. Many have human bodily features, such as those from the Pleiades, while others have varied humanoid features. Of course there are many other types of Extraterrestrials, for example, the insectoids, reptoids, and dinoids. We very seldom observe these other forms on third-dimension Earth. Most of them exist within higher states of dimensional consciousness; they are invisible to third- and fourth-dimensional humans on Earth. Most highly evolved Extraterrestrials are unable to survive on a low-frequency planet like Earth for any length of time. Or they are restricted from landing on Earth in order to limit the possibility that they might inadvertently interfere with a soul's spiritual evolution.

A short list of Extraterrestrials that have visited Earth includes the Lyrans, Vegans, Pleiadians, Procyonians, Orions, Draconians, Zephelium, Sirians, Zeta Reticuli, Alpha centurions', Arcturians, Reptilians, Reptoids, various Grays, Rectulians, Zionites, Athenians, and Andromedians.

Most everyone is familiar with the contracts between our government and the Gray/Zeta/Reticuli race signed several years ago when the Grays asked to experiment with humans in an attempt to create a hybrid race. In that contract, our government was given various technologies in exchange for permitting the Grays to carry out their experiments. In the Subtle Energy Research program we had an individual Research Associate who volunteered to participate in these experiments.

Very recent information concerning the results from these experiments indicates that the Zeta/Reticuli successfully created their desired hybrid. When you time travel into the future, you can confer with the Gray/Zeta/Reticuli in another reality realm and learn about their resulting hybrids. This new hybrid race has been called the Essasani. They have regained their sexual capabilities and their ability to experience emotions. In addition, a report from the Intergalactic Federation of Planets indicates that these Extraterrestrial Essasanis are enlightened.

You may wonder why the Grays were interested in surviving their damaged planet and regaining their emotions and sexual reproductive capabilities. It becomes fairly obvious that they had an interest in continuing their spiritual evolution and transition to the fifth-dimensional states of consciousness at the end of this current seventy-five-thousand-year cycle. Remember, the *next shift* of many other third-dimensional planets within this Universe to a fifth-dimensional consciousness will occur twenty-five thousand years after 2012. They realized the upcoming opportunity in 2012 and were preparing to evolve as soon as possible.

The fifth dimension is a plane of existence where unconditional love and complete oneness exist. In several religious groups, this place is called an unknown Heaven. That belief will supposedly take you to Heaven or an alternative Hell. These concepts are illusory beliefs created by those who have attempted to control humans and create fear. In reality, spirit indicates that when a human dies on Earth—when the spirit and soul leave the physical body—the soul has several choices. To a great extent, your conscious beliefs determine where you end up. If you believe in a Heaven or Hell, then that is what you create and where you go. Some choose to remain on Earth and become Earth bound spirits (e.g. ghosts). Other humans, who choose to move toward the Light, generally move into the middle overtones of the fourth dimension. Within those overtones, called Bardo, the Edger Cayce readings indicate there are several options. First, souls are counseled, have a life overview, and are given options to choose from. Some may rest for awhile. Some choose to remain within the reincarnation cycle and continue a new life on a third-dimension planet. Some may choose to go to a higher-frequency planet (such as Venus in this Solar System), their home planet, or to another planet in this Universe. Wherever a soul goes, it will receive a new contract for guidance along its spiritual path.

When the soul goes to the lower fourth-dimensional overtones, that soul can choose to Ascend and transition out of the reincarnation cycle. However, for that soul to Ascend to the fourth- and fifth-dimension New Earth or another fifth-dimensional planet, it must have prepared internally, mentally, and emotionally. Any soul Ascending must take on love and "Light Body" status and shift into Christ (Unity) Consciousness, as discussed in future chapters.

To gain a partial understanding of Universal Law concerning graduation and Ascension from a planet, you may benefit from studying an experiment by the U.S. military. Several years ago, the military set up a time-travel experiment to move a ship and its crew from the third dimension to the invisible fourth and fifth dimensions. The Philadelphia and Montauk experiments were scientific experiments designed to make objects invisible by changing their frequency. Those experiments were conducted by some of the top scientists in the world. Some may consider the Philadelphia experiment a failure, partly because of considerable loss of life. Also, the military ship docked in the Philadelphia harbor with the electronic equipment required for "The Shift" became lost as it time-traveled to different locations on Earth. When it has showed up, efforts have been made to recover the bodies of those who died.

For those interested, there are many sources of information on these and related experiments. In terms of understanding dimensional shifts, these experiments had some degree of success. However, there are Universal Laws that govern humanity's ability to shift dimensions. Those attempted scientific procedures did not consider the importance of human consciousness in relation to frequency changes and Universal Laws.

In order to prepare for Earth's Ascension and the Ascension of many humans, a Planetary Transition Team has been sent to Earth to be of assistance. Some reading this book are members of this team. You have come to Earth in human form at this specific time for the purpose of helping to make the transition from third dimension to the fourth- and fifth-dimension New Earth as smooth as possible. Most transition team members are from another high-frequency planet, another reality realm in the Universe, or another time frame along a different time line. Regardless of where you're from, you took on a physical human body and "Now" have some responsibilities. You are an advanced spirit having a human experience. You are one of many Extraterrestrials who recently incarnated. Spirit indicates that about six million Extraterrestrials and fifty thousand angels have taken on physical human bodies in the past fifty-five years. They are all here to help.

Several Extraterrestrial groups are helping from off-planet through channeling. A group of Extraterrestrials from Arcturus frequently channels through David K. Miller. Their up-to-date channelings are published in the *Sedona Journal of Emergence* each month. Also, the books *Connecting with the Arcturians* and *Teachings from the Sacred Triangle* (volumes 1 and 2) can help you prepare for Ascension. You may also take advantage of the healing chambers on board the larger Extraterrestrial vehicles from Arcturus. Just ask your High Self Spiritual Council to take you to the healing chambers while you sleep at night. Do this as often as you like. Many participating Research Associates have benefited from the balances they received in these chambers.

Many Extraterrestrials have come with some very dramatic plans to help Earth survive and shift in consciousness. These plans have created fear in members of the Illuminati, who have maintained control of the human population for thousands of years. Many of these controllers are "Now" resigned to the fact that their days are numbered. Some have chosen a spiritual path, joined the Light forces, and are preparing to Ascend. Others are holding on to their positions of power as long as they can.

Various members of the Galactic Federation have set up Web sites and programs designed to assist Earth and its inhabitants. For example, the Sirian Council appointed Sheldon Nidle as its representative on Earth. In the book *You Are Becoming a Galactic Human* by Virginia Essene and Sheldon Nidle, the Sirians provide details about Earth's history and humanity's destiny. Review the Websites: www.galacticfriends.com, www.awakening-healing.com, and www.dimensionaltransitions.com for helpful insights.

In 2005, the Creators of the Universe became aware of the potential of a global war on Earth because of the impatience and impulsiveness purposely created within the consciousness of third- dimension humans. These behavior patterns did not originate on Earth, but were channeled down from the higher dimensions to fourth-dimension operatives and seeded into the consciousness of third-dimension entities. In order to limit possible excessive destruction, the Extraterrestrials intervened. Thus, the Ascension process may have to be accelerated. You will be able to detect possible changes in plans by noting sensations that feel like there is a state of emergency. Your physical body may feel like you are in a rapidly moving vehicle that is going beyond its normal rate of speed. These feelings are caused by a rapid increase in frequency and an associated energy-enhancing shift in the physical body. The objective is to prepare your physical body so that it can safely be taken on board an Extraterrestrial ship if and when environmental conditions on Earth become unbearable.

Each person is being attended to for calming purposes. However, you can make things easier by choosing to ride the wave of change calmly and without resistance. Detach from the drama and turn your attention to calming yourself. The stimulus created by the activities of the manipulators to intensify the drama is increasing daily. If you don't detach from the drama, you could get caught

> **Detach from the drama and coming chaos by stepping back and allowing negative thought forms to sweep on by you.**

up in the swirling thought forms and get sucked down into the chaos. The Creators recommend you step back and let the flood of negative thought forms sweep past you entirely.

Every human on Earth is tracked individually. For those who plan to graduate, the Spiritual Hierarchy wants to insure that you will be able to handle the acceleration in progress and on board the ships. Once on board, you will be processed and attended to. Obviously, all plans are based on a set of probabilities that are subject to procedural changes. No one knows the exact plans. However, if and when the lifting begins, you will be informed of the procedures to follow. Maintain mental communication with the Ashtar Galactic Command and/or the Intergalactic Federation of Planets to receive your instructions and guidelines. Use discernment when listening to any message. Their messages will always be full of hope, positive affirmations of unity, and reverence for God/Goddess.

Remember, the Intergalactic Federation of Planets and the Ashtar Galactic Command has a sufficient number of Extraterrestrial vehicles available to quickly evacuate those who qualify to be beamed up, if and when the need arises. They will be ready at a moment's notice when physical life on Earth becomes threatened.

However, with the help of God/Goddess, the Ascended Masters, the Extraterrestrials, and many Light Workers, we are sitting pretty. It's now becoming evident that planet Earth may not have to rock and roll severely enough to shake humans off her back. No entity or spirit knows for sure exactly what will happen during "The Shift"

> **No entity or spirit knows for sure exactly what will happen during "The Shift and Ascension process**

and the Ascension process. When it happens, we will know. The objective is to be prepared, whenever and whatever happens.

We mention these facts about the "Hosts of Heaven because there are other Extraterrestrial civilizations interested in intimidation, inserting implants, abductions, and various types of mental control. Any entities that instill any form of fear, depression, or menace are to be avoided.

For those interested in the characteristics of the many different ships currently used by these Intergalactic groups, refer to the Web site www.ashtarcommand.net and pull up the section entitled "The Command Ships of The Ashtar Command- Mer-ka-bah Flaming Chariots of Adonai. The large Mother Ships are about one hundred miles in diameter and twelve stories high. They can accept third-dimensional beings and adjust their frequencies to that of the ship. There is also a much larger Midway Station (called "Share") orbiting the Earth. It can easily house twenty enormous Mother Ships. The relatively smaller shuttle and scout ships are up to twenty miles in diameter. They are used for evacuation purposes and temporary housing before transfer to the larger ships. Keep in mind that for safety purposes, most physical bodies are carried in their sleep state. Obviously, some humans may be lifted in a waking state. If for any reason rejuvenation of the physical body is required, that will be carried out on the Mother Ships by thousands of highly qualified staff members to insure safety.

Another group helping Earth is the "Elven." The Elven (the elves), who lived in Lemuria and Atlantis fifty thousand years ago, recently returned to assist in humanity's Ascension process. They are available to anyone who requests their assistance and are willing to share their ideas with you. They will not interfere with your journey; however, they will remain as long as they are needed. They know that you are in command of your future journey. The elves function within another plane of consciousness, just like the angels do.

Some people would like you to believe that the Elven and angel worlds do not exist. It is possible they have never experienced their presence. Or, with their limited eyesight, they may lack the ability to see these entities vibrating at higher frequencies. Sensitive individuals can feel the presence of elves because they radiate an intense love. If you would make a concerted effort to see, feel, or touch the elves, and meet them in consciousness, they would appreciate your interest. They need your recognition and appreciation because they are a little taken aback concerning humanity's slowness to accept their presence. Journey with your spirit body and visit their beautiful world. Your angels will help you time travel to their state of dimensional consciousness, where you can meet. They are so filled with light and love that the only way you can make meaningful contact with them is to shift to their state of dimensional consciousness and become immersed in love yourself.

It is interesting to realize that the Japanese society has a very close relationship with the Elvens (elves). This is why their society is advancing more rapidly (spiritually) compared to other societies on Earth. The Elven have sensed, and are very pleased, that humans on Earth are moving away from religion and toward becoming more spiritually minded.

* * * * *

10

Importance of the Mer-Ka-Ba Energy Field
around the Human Body

For many purposes, the human body should be surrounded by several geometric energy fields. There is a prana field near the surface of the physical body generated by the chakra/meridian energy flow. There is also an egg-shaped field extending several feet from the body called the aura, which is generated by your thoughts and feelings. There should also be a Buddhic net (magnetic energy field), located between and protecting your etheric and astral bodies. There should be an energy grid surrounding the body that is connected to the acupuncture points, through which spiritual energy enters. There is another energy field called the "overlay" that helps maintain the integrity of all energy bodies and their associated energy patterns. All of these organized, geometric energy fields create what has been called the human "Light -Body," in part because together, they emit light energy of varying colors.

Another very important energy field that should be created by individual consciousness and placed around the human body is a field of light called the Mer-Ka-Ba. Up to this point in history, the Mer-Ka-Ba does not usually form automatically. However, recent evidence indicates that if you raise your dimensional consciousness to some as-yet-undefined energy level, the Mer-Ka-Ba may form spontaneously. Many believe that when you prepare to Ascend to the fourth dimension of this planet, you will know how to create your own private Mer-Ka-Ba. The Mer-Ka-Ba is made with three star tetrahedrons. These tetrahedrons extend out from the eight original "God/Goddess" cells located in the center of the body.

Note: *If you have been on Earth or a related planet for at least thirteen thousand years, your Mer-Ka-Ba energy field has probably become dormant.*

Eighty-four percent of all humans on Earth have been on third-dimensional planets for over thirteen thousand years. If you came to Earth more recently, you may have a functional Mer-Ka-Ba. Most humans have lived thousands of lifetimes on Earth, frequently changing nationality, and sexual orientation in order to help create sexual and spiritual balance within.

Three star tetrahedrons (interlocking, sacred geometric forms) make up the Mer-Ka-Ba. Together they appear as a three-dimensional structure that can be contained within a cube. If you are unfamiliar with the Mer-Ka-Ba, it would be very helpful to have an accurate three-dimensional diagram of these star-tetrahedrons to help you visualize its shape. This will give you a better understanding of how to structure your own Mer-Ka-Ba. You could buy one, or construct one following the directions outlined in *The Ancient Secret of the Flower of Life: Volume 2* by Drunvalo Melchizedek. This book also provides a detailed description of the breathing exercises used to create a Mer-Ka-Ba energy field within and around your body. The object of using these exercises is to create an internally designed, three-dimensional Mer-Ka-Ba. Once you have created your Mer-Ka-Ba and continue its maintenance, it should become a permanent "Light Body" that can assist you in a multitude of ways. Some key starting points to consider when creating a Mer-Ka-Ba are:

1. When you visualize your three tetrahedrons (that make up the Star Tetrahedron), make sure your body is mentally positioned in the center of the geometric forms.

2. It would be helpful to visualize the relative size of the star tetrahedrons by stretching out your arms. The tetrahedron should encompass an area the size of the space between the middle fingers of your outstretched arms (slightly taller than your height). Another alternative is to build a star tetrahedron and get inside it.

3. If you have an opportunity, it would be most helpful to take a Mer-Ka-Ba workshop. With the help of your God/Goddess you can locate someone skilled in helping you create your personal permanent Mer-Ka-Ba.

4. To cover all the details about constructing a Mer-Ka-Ba would require a large number of additional pages. Because of the limited space in this book, please take a Mer-Ka-Ba workshop, buy one of the books describing the procedure and follow the instructions, or go to one of these Web sites: www.floweroflife.org, www.wingmakers.co.nz, or www.holisticwebs.com. They all have helpful suggestions and specific references.

Regardless of where you find help to create your Mer-Ka-Ba, make sure your source of help or guidance is approved by spiritually advanced Light Beings. The appropriate method to create a Mer-Ka-Ba is to use love and/or your emotional body and left brain to create a living energy field in and around your body. Your Mer-Ka-Ba will be an extremely important spiritual reality vehicle for your experiences in the higher dimensions.

A warning: When you create an external Mer-Ka-Ba with your ego mind, you utilize and magnify the logical right brain to create that Mer-Ka-Ba. Using only the theoretical right brain to create your Mer-Ka-Ba omits a balance that the left brain's dedication and internal love energy can provide. This ego-mind-directed, technical procedure can create an external Mer-Ka-Ba that is a possible path towards destructive energies. An internal Mer-Ka-Ba, centered on the prana tube that is created using spiritual principles, has many beneficial properties.

> **Check your Mer-Ka-Ba "Light Body" daily to ensure that it is correctly positioned, balanced, and spinning properly.**

Every day, make sure your Mer-Ka-Ba is spinning properly, balanced, and in fine working order. You may need your Mer-Ka-Ba for several reasons in the very near future. Use accurate pendulum dowsing to check you're Mer-Ka-Ba as often as required.

If you don't have a Mer-Ka-Ba and don't even know what one is, then you need to do some homework. When you maintain a functional Mer-Ka-Ba, you will be able to retain your memory, avoid the physical death process, and pass through the Star Gate to the higher dimensions with total awareness. *Remember to create and maintain your Mer-Ka-Ba as soon as possible.*

* * * * *

11

Who or What Is God/Goddess? The Eternally Evolving Creation

Many humans on Earth have been purposely misled about what the term "God/Goddess" means. Therefore, I asked my High Self Spiritual Council to help me understand this term God/Goddess. I was immediately directed to the Web site www.God/Goddesschannel.com. To my amazement, this Web site has many important write-ups that pendulum dowsing shows to be 97 percent accurate. Until recently, the term God has applied to the three *masculine* members of the divine family: Spirit, Father, and Heart. There is a fourth member, however, that has been overlooked for far too long. That is the feminine part of deity: the Mother or Goddess.

God says on this Web site www.God/Goddesschannel.com:

> While I am referred to as God, and worshiped as God … the truth is that I am only one part of God/Goddess, one part of the whole gestalt responsible for causing and sustaining Creation. The other essential half of Deity is the Great Mother or Goddess, the cosmic womb of creation…. She is the one I love, and to whom I owe my existence in manifestation. It is she who opens and holds the space that contains my Light. She is the magnetic field of being within whom my color and hues take form. Her essence is magnetic, drawing, holding, supporting, and nurturing. The Mother's energy is both subtle and powerful … emotional, feeling, and grounding
>
> Until recently my messenger, prophets, and channelers have ignored the importance and even the existence of the Mother aspect, the Goddess. The mother has her own voice, and hers is quite different than mine. You cannot hear her voice in your mind. You can only know her essence and hear her voice through feeling her inside of you. Hers is the language

of emotions, movement and sounding. And like mine, the Mother's voice can be most truly felt and heard … only inside of you.

The most important understanding I can convey about myself is that I AM Evolving. This understanding is crucial if you are to know me as I AM, and not as I was. I have revealed myself to humans on many occasions. Each time I have done so in terms of the people receiving me so they could understand. Each time I have revealed myself, it was as I was, at that time. Because I am evolving, I am changing. And because humanity is evolving, you are changing. You are "Now" much more ready to accept the role of host to our presence here on Earth.

Although the Mother and I have created this Universe and everything within it, there is a larger Universe and another level of Deity beyond us. Our local Universe is one of several separate Creations … each of these were created by an original offspring of your divine Grandparents. Just as I have a relationship in which I am constantly present within you … Pure Original Spirit I call Grandfather is always present within Me… Although Grandfather did not create this Universe, he and the Original Grandmother created the conditions that made it possible for Mother and Me to create it.

From these comments, we should understand that the Creator is more accurately called God/Goddess as two parts of *one*. Others use the terms Abba/Amma or Mother/Father to honor these aspects of the Creator.

The new language of Heaven is moving away from making distinctions between Deity and human beings. Gone also are Thee and Thou and the other archaic forms of the second person in addressing God/Goddess. We prefer an informal Hello God/Goddess or Hello Mother as a greeting. The mother and I wish for you to find us within yourself, and this will be easier with a more level field of linguistic relating.

The Web site www.God/Goddesschannel.com has a good approach you can use to lessen spiritual tension as you drive along on your journey to prepare for graduation and Ascension. In "Driving Your Vehicle (Body) by Turning Backwards to Face Past Creations," God/Goddess states:

> My intention is that you find me within yourself and express or channel my Truth into the world, should you choose. To this end, I want to share with you more of who I am and the way I experience Creation. From my perspective I am deep within you, a traveler on a journey through Creation. I am simultaneously everywhere in everything and aware of all things and all of their relationships. From your perspective I am moving through Creation in the same way you are moving through linear time. I am just a little ahead of you, creating each new moment as it emerges through me ... and in each moment the Universe is created anew.
>
> A useful metaphor is that we have been on a long bus trip through Creation. Like the bus you drive through your own life, I am the driver of a larger bus and you are aboard. Throughout all of time I have been sending messages to you ... inviting you to come up from the back of the bus and visit with me here by the wheel. Now you can do that more easily ... more than ever before. Let's visit ... as we get comfortable with each other I'll show you how I drive. Perhaps we will even find a new way of driving together.
>
> As you make your way toward the front of the bus you will notice more synchronicity and deeper meaning in events. I must tell you the road immediately ahead is quite bumpy, and it may also feel a little like a roller coaster. The secret here is not to stay rigid in your seat.... You will want to be light on your feet and move

with the changes so you can stay in balance ... The easiest and quickest way to do this is to release your judgments.

If you would like to learn a better way of driving, I'll share a secret and show you how I am positioned here at the front of the bus. I am facing backward. Yes I drive backwards. What is ahead is un-manifested, it is the Void. Ahead of me there is nothing. Behind me is everything, all of Creation. If I were facing forward I would not be able to see anything, I'd be staring into the Void. Facing backward, however, I experience all of Creation streaming out behind like the wake of the swan, or the flow of a river.... As I evolve through time, Creation evolves with me.... Facing backward as I am has several advantages. First, you more easily stay centered in the present moment. Second, you find the grace in the flow of Creation and move toward the center of it. Third, you resonate more closely with me, making it easier for us to communicate.... Fourth, you get a good practice for driving your bus the way it was meant to be driven.

Facing forward has disadvantages. First, it prevents one from participating in Creation, which is always happening here in the present moment. Second, looking toward the future sends energy out ahead that creates resistance to the flow of existence, taking one away from what is and making life more difficult. Third, looking to the future prevents one from appreciation and using what is and what has been.

There is much to harvest from the past, you can reel it all in and make it your own. Where you are "Now" is the present moment. This is the farthest into the future anyone has ever been, including me. There is an extremely important quality that you will develop as you practice driving backwards. That quality is allowing yourself to *trust*.

By driving backwards we can bring ourselves back from the future. Our culture has taught us to look forward and plan ahead. Emphasis has been placed on doing things to help make the future safer and more abundant. This philosophy assumes that we are not already fortunate and safe. The concepts of fear, harm, and a lack of material goods have been driving our culture's conditioned obsession. Remember, becoming fully present in the eternal "Now" is the aim of spiritual practice, graduation, and Ascension.

For helpful suggestions, go back and study in detail the book *A New Earth* by Eckhart Tolle. Apply those truths to your life. When you turn away from the future (drive backwards), you can very quickly return to the present moment. Even though you are driving backwards, you are still moving forward, but you see all the past memory banks more clearly. You can then notice and analyze what has worked and what hasn't worked. You can also observe how others have managed their lives in similar circumstances. You will "Now" have a more complete picture to obtain guidance about what to do in the present moment, here and "Now." The present moment is all there is. The future is a mental fabrication; it's made up of illusions of what might be. Just think of all the energy you waste by driving forward.

That's not to say that the future doesn't have value and require some energy. However, excessive thought about the future wastes valuable energy. Some planning for the future is helpful for upcoming events and in planning things to do on Earth currently. This practical use of planning for the future is not the issue here. The challenge we have is to avoid dwelling in the future and becoming fixated on it, as if our thinking and worrying about it will somehow improve the future. The key is to catch yourself whenever you spend excessive time thinking about the future. When this happens, turn around and drive backwards. Then release all judgments about what might happen and about whether everything was highly organized and done in an orderly pattern.

Doing things right is often less important than maintaining your health and well-being. Here are a few signs of dwelling in the future: (1) When anxiety or worry comes up, realize those feelings occur when the future is uncertain. (2) Notice when fears arise about what may or may not happen. (3) Any feeling of uneasiness will indicate you are in the future again. (4) When you realize you are doing a lot of thinking and planning minute details about a future event. (5) You realize you have an almost senseless ego drive to control things.

Driving backwards, trusting yourself and the Universe following along with the flow of things, and listening to your intuitions and inner guidance can make life so much more pleasant. Trusting in the goodness and guidance from the God/Goddess within and turning away from expectations and disappointments will go a long way toward helping you stop punishing yourself. Driving backwards can also help eliminate anxiety, fear, tension, worry, and stress. There is much more on the Web site www.God/Goddesschannel.com that may be helpful as your drive backwards towards the New Earth.

* * * * *

Section III: Spiritual Evolution Creative Potential

12

Factors to Consider in Preparation for Graduation and Ascension

The Ascension process is an internal spiritual journey tied to the choices related to your understanding of your multidimensional realities. To Ascend, one must sustain a series of vibrational frequencies within the consciousness of soul and spirit. Relying upon anything outside of self to Ascend is a denial of the God/Goddess within. The human consciousness hologram was designed to maintain the various bodies together as a unit. There are several external factors that are useful in making the process more efficient and pleasant, but many of these are not required.

Many in the past have limited their Ascension capabilities because they relied upon external factors. They thought that some external factor or factors based on scientific technologies would help them Ascend. Those individuals who worked so hard for many years to create Ascension devices gradually realized how futile their efforts were. Some of these attempts resulted in harm to the environment and harm to the human bodies involved. Your Ascension efforts should focus on internal factors as discussed in Section IV.

There are many examples of how humans have misused technology. For example, the Martians consciously created an external Mer-Ka-Ba as opposed to an internal Mer-Ka-Ba. They were unable to control its intense energies; as a result, they destroyed the life-providing features of Mars. By destroying most of the water on Mars, they created a desert landscape. Water is the key component of living systems, since it is the conductive medium through which a life force called prana is carried to each cell. Space program probes to Mars indicate the presence of ancient buildings and some water on its surface; however, the planet's third dimension is still uninhabitable.

In a similar way, the highly technical Atlantians created a massive, external system of collecting crystal energy and distributing it throughout their continent. This external energy system was so powerful that when tuned too intensely, it actually melted mountains, created volcanoes, and was in part responsible for the sinking of the Atlantian continent.

Factors That Reduce One's Ability to Move through the Star Gates

There are Universal Laws that govern the process of Ascension. All physical creations present on Earth must increase in frequency to Ascend. This includes the Earth, humans, plants, animals, and other creations. The question is, then, how can you increase your frequency?

Following are some examples of factors that influence your ability to raise your frequency:

1. Your Method of Operation Will Influence Your Graduation Scores

Your method of operation (MO) in terms of whether you are directing your efforts towards Service to Self (STS) or Service to Others (STO) is very important. Those of the STS - MO show their true motives by always wanting something for themselves. Their primary goals and agendas are self-first, regardless of what happens to those around them. The STS behavior pattern is of the warrior type, characteristic of those who are judgmental and caught up in the duality consciousness of separation.

By contrast, in the STO - MO, one's primary goal in life is to be of assistance to others in a way that does not infringe upon an individual's free will and lessons of choice. Thus the STO - MO helps create a philosophy of life that moves you towards Unity/Christ consciousness.

Before working with others, it would be best to know their Methods of Operation (MO). Determine to what degree they function in the STS and STO modes before entering into an agreement? Always ask for spiritual help when working with someone else. Find out who and what the relationship will serve. Are all involved parties being helped, or is one party benefiting out of proportion to the others within the relationship? By the fruits of their labor ye shall know them—not by what they say or write, but by their actions. Go within your consciousness to determine another's STO and STS – MOs—

without any judgment attached. Check for the presence of negative thought forms, negative attachments, or adverse presences within the work environment. Individuals controlled by the Interlopers are to be avoided; they primarily have STS - MO. When you gain your spiritual confidence, you can work with your Spiritual Assistants to remove the Interlopers or other undesirable entities. This form of service can help an individual gain back an STO - MO.

These concepts are important because as you prepare for graduation, your MO will, of necessity, need to be classified within the STO category. Duality concepts (STS) will need to be removed from consciousness when Unity/Christ consciousness (STO) prevails. This means gaining complete control of your *ego's* tendency toward self-centeredness and its acceptance of guidance from negative thought forms. No negative thought forms will be allowed on the New Earth.

2. Excess Use of Electronic Equipment Will Damage Your Health and Potential New Body

Excess utilization of electronic equipment such as cell phones, televisions, the Internet, high voltage transmission lines, video games, microwaves, radios, and hair driers can damage the body's electrical system. Much of this electronic equipment has been designed, promoted, and sold without due consideration of the health of those who purchase and use the equipment. It sometimes appears this is intentionally designed to create stress within the human body. Yes, these devices do appear to have some desirable and useful purposes. However, realize they have created one of the most electromagnetically polluted planets in the Milky Way Galaxy. Electromagnetic pollution is just as dangerous as or more so than chemical pollution within the environment. Excess use of electrical equipment can damage the brain and body's electrical system, a proven scientific reality purposely ignored by members of society who market these electrical devices.

You can gain some understanding of how the electromagnetic damage to the brain and nervous system is expressed in society by noting the destructive behavior patterns of some individuals as reported in the news media. Scientific studies have indicated that individuals exposed to electromagnetic fields have nerve damage and other imbalances which render them susceptible to external programming. There is subliminal programming within video games, movies, and television programs. A subliminal program is merely a hidden, projected energy pattern that can be implanted in one's consciousness and is generally designed to elicit a predictable response. The objective is to influence people without their being aware of the installed program. All programmed subliminal forms stored within one's consciousness will need to be cleared before Ascension.

3. Avoid Reading Materials of Questionable Value That Can Stress the Nervous System

Spending excess time reading books, newspapers, magazines, and any other written material containing useless information puts stress on the nervous system and blunts the mind and spirit. Materials that discuss crime, sports, violence, sexual deviants, fighting, and war can cause serious mental harm. These subjects are designed to divert your attention away from your spiritual path. Avoid reading materials that are based on false beliefs and old illusions that have long since lost their spiritual value. Read materials that the God/Goddess within recommends. Seek out new, more efficient beliefs from the still, small voice within. Then use *accurate* pendulum dowsing to check the value of each item of reading material you consider picking up, especially material channeled from untested spiritual sources.

4. Attending Many Lectures, Workshops, and Worship Services Can Be Counterproductive

Attending an excessive number of lectures and workshops or following guidance from some religious leaders touted to know "The Way", can be counterproductive. There is value in learning from others. However, much of their material is based on limited and false beliefs that can slow spiritual growth and Ascension. Use of accurate pendulum dowsing, discernment, and intuition can help you select those workshops, teachers, and ministers with helpful spiritual information.

5. Staying Busy Is an Escape Mechanism Designed by Ego to Slow Spiritual Growth

Staying busy all the time takes away from meditation time, relaxation time, and just enjoying communing with nature. Here are some activities that can hold back one's capability to Ascend: accumulating useless physical items; spending excess time grooming yourself or cleaning your car or home; cooking big meals with limited nutritional value; excess driving back and forth through town (cruising) because of limited planning; excessive participation in sports and related group activities; an addiction to shopping; any kind of busy work; and working at jobs with limited spiritual value.

6. Improper Construction of the Mer-Ka-Ba Will Fail To Provide Your Needed Protection

Improper construction and use of the Mer-Ka-Ba and improper use of the Mer-Ka-Ba can be very harmful. The Mer-Ka-Ba is a very helpful "Light Body" which needs to be properly constructed and maintained daily. At the higher states of dimensional consciousness, the Mer-Ka-Ba will serve many useful purposes. For more information about how to properly prepare you're Mer-Ka-Ba "Light Body" refer to Chapter 10.

7. Avoid Consuming All Natural and Man-made Drugs That Destroy the Human Bodies.

Consuming any natural or manufactured drug that destroys any portion of the brain or nervous system or damages any part of the body is counterproductive. This includes the use of illegal, mind-altering drugs and medically prescribed drugs designed to cover up disease symptoms. Also, avoid all toxic, poisonous chemicals and stimulants such as caffeine, Aspartame, propylene glycol, nicotine, Nutra Sweet, and monosodium glutamate (MSG). Avoid a host of other food additives such as preservatives, coloring dyes, and flavoring agents—all used, with no concern for public health—to market dubious, low-quality, processed food products with minimal nutritional value.

8. Brain-wave-Altering Music and Flashing Pictures Can Damage the Brain

Listening to brain-wave-altering music and/or the constant flashing of pictures on a video screen can alter your brain-wave frequency. These communication media techniques are designed to make the mind more receptive to advertisements and propaganda promoted by multinational corporations and the Illuminati. Loud music can damage the eardrums and some nerves within the brain. In fact, loud music has been demonstrated to be so destructive that it can kill plants. Loud, low-frequency noises such as boom boxes are designed to damage the body. Note: many types of music are beneficial to the body. Some music actually quiets the brain and improves plant growth. There are also certain combinations of frequencies that can assist in raising one's consciousness, such as Hemi-Sync tones.

9. Everything in Creation is Constantly Changing, Even the Concepts in This Book

The information in this book must also shift in consciousness. That is, everything must constantly change in order to be in alignment with future, higher states of dimensional consciousness. It will be very important for you to update and add new insights to the concepts you are reading about and applying to your life. The secret in life is to always keep an open mind, look for new ideas and ways of understanding, and use discernment in all of your educational and spiritual activities.

Factors Useful But Not Mandatory for Moving through the Star Gate

1. Consume High-frequency Foods That Are Compatible with a High-frequency Body

The consumption of high-frequency foods can help improve one's health, an important criterion for moving into the higher states of dimensional consciousness. We have frequently discussed the importance of consuming high-frequency, unprocessed foods, that is, fresh fruits and vegetables that have been juiced. Avoid consuming low-frequency, processed foods and fried and flame-blackened meats that become poisonous when heated excessively or burned. Also, avoid all irradiated foods and foods cooked in a microwave because of the destruction of prana life force within the treated item.

2. Participate in Activities That Are Peaceful and Relaxing to Your Body and Mind

Participate in all kinds of activities that create a peaceful state of mind. This could include taking a walk in nature and communing with the plants and nature spirits; listening to quiet, relaxing music; watching the clouds; walking or swimming outside in fresh air; prana breathing; taking relaxing baths in clean water; visiting a lake or ocean shore to commune with the water and receive its health-giving energies; sitting in the sun to absorb its life-giving energy; and meditating by quieting the mind and listening to the still, small voice within.

3. A Belief That You Qualify to Enter Heaven Will Not Be Sufficient to Meet the Standards to Pass through the Star Gates to the New Earth

Just believing that it would be desirable to live in "heaven" on a planet that has a higher vibrational frequency will not satisfy all Ascension requirements. However, belief can help you create thought forms that help change your consciousness so it vibrates at a frequency compatible with established requirements. Realize that in order to live on the New Earth, you need to believe and adjust your frequencies to become compatible with your desired visions. *Believing alone is insufficient to meet Ascension requirements.* As the planet Earth evolves through the fourth dimension into the fifth dimension, changes within your consciousness will be required in order for you to be compatible with those frequencies.

4. Use Your Clock Time Wisely as You Prepare for Graduation and Ascension

It will be important to determine what tasks should be carried out to assist in your spiritual evolution. However, as mentioned before, there is no need to be always doing something so you don't waste time. Time is never wasted. Since in reality there is no time, you have an eternity to do what you find most helpful. There is no need to be rushing around, trying to complete a task that creates stress and tension. Set up a schedule where you have free time to do nothing but relax and enjoy just being you. Remember, clock time is collapsing, thus you have less time to work. List and prioritize your activities, eliminating many of them.

5. It's Highly Important to Avoid All Kinds of Fear

Allowing any kind of fear to take control of your energy bodies will dramatically damage your bodies and interfere with your DNA and metabolism. There is nothing to fear except fear itself. This includes any kind of stress, tension, anxiety, trauma, depression, escapism, anger, hate, greed, guilt, worry, jealousy, or intolerance. Replace all negative emotions with love, patience, kindness, joy, consideration, and helpfulness. The more you work to gain control of your emotional body, the more likely you will be able to avoid all emotionally disturbing events.

6. Removal of Third-dimensional Duality Programs and Imprints from Consciousness

To make room for fourth- and fifth-dimensional consciousness it is important to remove everything recorded in your energy bodies that could in any way interfere with maintaining your new bodies and body parts. The objective is to clear all factors that have no value within your future new reality realm. Those factors that could actually slow your evolutionary progress need to be cleared. Decide what you want your future world to be based on, and clear out everything else. You will observe that many things within your consciousness that have been covered up are and will be revealed for clearing.

7. Clear All Subconscious Programming Designed to Create Dramatic Earth Changes

Because previous shifts in consciousness have been associated with dramatic Earth changes, many humans have programmed in their consciousness that these events will occur again. Some individuals currently hold on to various dire predictions with undesirable consequences. They can become self-fulfilling prophecies. Thus, avoid thinking about predications of Earthquakes, floods, famines, a shift of the planet's axis, or other disastrous events. Obviously, these events can occur as Mother Earth cleanses herself. However, there is never a need to fear or worry about these possible events. Thinking about them and worrying will help bring them into reality. In fact, when several people concentrate on any event, they help bring that event into reality. Go within, ask what is true for your world, and adjust your activities accordingly. It is your energy that will determine where you are during "The Shift" and how you will experience the transformation.

8. Open Your Consciousness to Receive Revitalizing Energies Arriving From Off-Planet

Take advantage of various energies arriving on Earth to assist in the Ascension process, for example, the arrival of crystalline light in the form of gamma-ray bursts from black holes. This crystalline light has a higher frequency than white light. Request that your Spiritual Assistants integrate this light into your new, high-frequency bodies. Take advantage of the available ray of Ascension originating from the helix of the platinum ray and crystalline gold. In addition, the rays from palladium, rhodium, and pristine quartz can assist in the Ascension-preparation process.

9. A Reminder to Prepare for Your Graduation and Ascension without Anticipation

Keep in mind that there is no need to anticipate your Ascension. There will be a scheduled time for every individual to Ascend. If you need to inform a relative or friend that you are planning to Ascend, do so as diplomatically as possible, without ego or judgment. When your Ascension preparation is complete, you will have the ability to change form to suit the circumstances. That is, as circumstances change, you can change to flow with them, even changing your form if that is desired. You will be very adapted to your circumstances *via your thoughts* throughout the many stages of the Ascension process, always listen for guidance from within. Everything will take place in its perfect time and sequence. It is all being carried out by multitudes of very advanced Spiritual Assistants. Nothing coming into view will be boring, especially after you pass through the veils and Star Gates.

* * * * * *

13

Changes Brought About by the Pole Shift and the Photon Belt

To gain a partial understanding of events associated with "The Shift," we need to go back to approximately eighteen months before "The Shift." Events taking place during this period are triggered by a decrease in the intensity of the geomagnetic field around the Earth.

We have previously discussed some of the possible events that may occur with "The Shift." We also understand that the events may be less severe than in previous times. However, it is your responsibility is to be prepared for any future event. Based on historical records, there is evidence that if and when the poles shift, some people may start to lose their memories and many social systems may begin to collapse. Many changes will be required in preparation for the New Earth. These changes are a cleansing process; undesirable thought patterns need to be removed.

The stock market may crash, fuel for automobiles may be limited, electrical power may be interrupted, governments may become non-functional, martial Law may be invoked, and food may be in short supply. It will be best to accept any of these possible events without fear.

If you are prepared and can remain calm through the twelve months leading up to "The Shift," the next period to be wary of is the day before "The Shift." Native American tribes have made the following suggestion in some workshops:

> When you intuitively sense that "The Shift" is about to occur: go inside your ancient pueblo built of natural materials, pull the curtains, do not look outside, and pray. To look outside could cause fear, which is the last thing you would want to do. Why go within a house made of natural materials? During and just after "The Shift" all unnatural manufactured materials will disappear from Earth.

Some materials relatively close to the natural state, such as wood and glass, may persist for awhile. This means portions of your car will disintegrate and be unstable. Your house may be unusable because of the many artificial materials incorporated within its structure. A pueblo house made of mud, straw, sand, stones, and wood will remain intact.

As the third and fourth dimensions overlap and merge together, many third-dimensional creations will disappear, and fourth-dimensional creations will begin to appear. Drunvalo Melchizedek (www.floweroflife.org) and many others recommend that you do not touch these objects when they first appear. These objects may have shapes and colors you

> After "The Shift", don't touch newly created objects because they will raise your vibrations too quickly.

have never seen before, and you may be curious as to what they are. Drunvalo's suggestion is:

> "My strong suggestion to you is, don't touch one of these objects. If you do, it will instantly pull you into the fourth Dimension at an accelerated rate. It would be easier and best if you avoid moving that fast.... Therefore it would be best to be in nature when this happens, but if you cannot be, and then it is the will of God/Goddess. I would not worry about this. I am only informing you so that you will understand as "The Shift" begins."

Indications are that there is nothing anyone can say or do to fully prepare humans for all the changes that will take place leading up to, during, and just after "The Shift." Kirael, a master guide that channels through Kahu Fred Sterling in Hawaii, has a large volume of published information about '"The Shift." Refer to Kirael's books and the Web site www.kirael.com for more helpful insights. Quoting from Kirael:

> "In the actual shift process, Tara sees light workers in the process of awakening from their deep sleep during the three days of darkness. She also sees that the world will appear unsuitable for human life if viewed through physical eyes. People will have difficulty standing upright because gravity has been altered. Each cell in the human

system will have expanded its matrix energy. Its density will have diminished by 30 percent. This will create a situation of imbalance which can be brought into alignment only through thought. Your awakening into fourth Dimensional state of consciousness will require a comprehensive realignment of the way everything is experienced.

The first time you sneeze in the fourth Dimension you will send your body reeling across the room. This will be because your body will no longer be functioning on oxygen. By third Dimension habit, you will inhale a large breath prior to this action and then expel it in a grand push. The difference is that along with your deep breath, you will also have inhaled an extremely large amount of prana into your system. This is because oxygen will be combined with prana in the fourth Dimension to physically lighten the body system.... this energy will overtake you, while the gravitational resistance you are accustomed to will be nonexistent. So across the room you go."

"The Shift" will be considered the most wonderful transformation in recorded history. After "The Shift," humans will get to continue creating Heaven on Earth. Science has been slow to help provide understanding about "The Shift." Science tends to shelter itself inside the safe harbor of materialism. By excluding the spiritual, subtle-energy aspects of creation, the scientific community has slowed humanity's spiritual development and understanding of the fundamental Laws of creation. Also science's lack of understanding of the etheric or subtle energy fields that shape physical reality has significantly slowed man's evolution. Scientific understanding of the design of creation has been primarily based on observable physical manifestations. Emerging quantum sciences indicate that consciousness is directly related to all physical illusory realities.

For example, located on the surface of the third-dimension human body are seven major chakras, or energy vortexes, that channel spiritual energy into the body. Inside are additional chakras that channel that energy to the proper location. The health of each organ adjacent to a chakra is related to the functional efficiency of that chakra. The medical profession has ignored these very important energy centers, partially because they cannot physically see etheric chakras. Also, there is Within the third-dimensional state of consciousness, clock time was created for our spirits to experience physicality and all the associated limitations, such as being separate. Illusory time gave us a reference point, a perspective of progression, and a sense of self so we could focus on an event. To accomplish this illusory creation of clock time, the reality realm frequency was *slowed down* so we could experience the gradual unfolding of growth. We were then able to use our senses to experience the process of Creation as it unfolded. That process has been altered, and *the reality-realm frequency will continue to increase.* fear in many professionals that this knowledge could damage the multibil-lion-dollar business of the medical and drug cartels. When the physical body was created, these vortexes were created to sustain the associated organs. The health of each organ is directly correlated with its associated external and internal chakras. Make sure your chakras are spinning properly and harmonized.

During and following "The Shift," the seven chakras will become unified into one major chakra. Everything the body needs energetically will be filtered through this unified chakra, to be located within the heart region. The love-based energy of the unified chakra will flow through the heart. *Be aware that this new, unified chakra needs to be fine-tuned every day to help assist in your change in consciousness.* Spirit recommends you utilize the following procedure at some

> **During and following "The Shift," the seven major chakras will be unified into one major chakra that should be attuned every day.**

predetermined time of the day to help you to remember to fine-tune all of your chakras and begin working with your future unified heart chakra.

Begin by getting into a comfortable, relaxed position. Deepen your breathing, and breathe prana and photon-light energy down and up through your prana tube into the heart chakra. On each out-breath, visualize your heart chakra becoming larger, opening and expanding it in all directions to create an enlarging sphere. As you expand this sphere, include each succeeding pair of your chakras as you breathe in and out: third and fifth, second and sixth; first and seventh; eighth and your knees; ninth and your ankles; and tenth with your feet chakras. Your unified chakra should "Now" be a golden sphere about twenty to fifty feet in diameter. The expansion of your unified chakra will also help stabilize your multidimensional state of consciousness. Visualize your golden sphere extending and expanding out to include the eleventh chakra (soul level), the twelfth chakra (Christ level), the thirteenth chakra (the "I-Am" Presence), and the fourteenth chakra (Source). Maintain this sphere and extend your aura out around your physical body for approximately thirty to fifty feet.

Having visualized and created this golden sphere, you will have established a foundational energy pattern to assist you in becoming a Love-based creation, as opposed to a fear-based creation. You can become active rather than reactive. You can become transpersonal, a state of consciousness beyond the limits of personal identity, rather than personality-based. From this basis, you can create an alternative, consensus-based reality that extends beyond your current limitations. A new reality based on peace, joy, and love. However, to truly embody and maintain this alternative identity, you will have to give up something. You will need to disconnect from others who have a vested interest in keeping you locked into their old, fear-based consensus reality. When you fail to protect yourself, your new energy field may have a tendency to drop back into the old patterns that have been programmed into your consciousness for many lifetimes, remember they could resurface.

If you become caught up in any of these manipulative programs, be fully conscious within. Also be conscious about what others are saying, thinking, and feeling. Then sense how these programs affect you. If it feels uncomfortable or smacks of judgment or criticism, then back off and reject or disconnect from their behavior. It's only their personal *stuff* that has become stuck to them. Just look at that *stuff*, love it, and let it go. You don't need others' personal stuff within your new state of consciousness. There is no judgment of anyone while working through this procedure.

Realize that everyone has personal *stuff* that they are working with as a part of their Earthly lessons. Therefore, it's just fine for them to experience those *stuff*-based feelings and expressions of separation. To protect yourself, be very cautious and avoid making psychic connections. One option you have for protection is to send your love, patience, and kindness to those around you. As they capture some of this love, the stuck *stuff* tends to decrease in intensity.

As you align your unified chakra and create an alternative reality realm based on love, you have proceeded to stabilize your Ascension potential. You have entered a new reality realm where you can raise the frequency of the cells in your body. Request your God/Goddess within to resonate with your body cells at the appropriate state of dimensional consciousness. See your cells resonating at the fifth dimension or above. Then request that your God/Goddess within make an attunement of your multidimensional capabilities within the fourth, fifth, sixth, or seventh dimensions.

As you increase your consciousness, at some point, those humans still in third-dimensional consciousness will be unable to see you; because you will be vibrating at higher frequencies. These higher frequencies are beyond the sense perceptions of a third-dimension human. Your higher frequencies will not register within the retinas of their physical, third-dimension eyes. You will also be unable to communicate audibly because of an inability to make sounds. Your fifth-dimensional vocal cords will be too delicate to move dense third-dimensional air across the vocal cords to create sound. You will be able to project your "Light Body" anywhere on the physical plane just by thought. No longer will you need a car or airplane to travel somewhere. With your Mer-Ka-Ba "Light Body," you can travel anywhere in the Universe, guided by your thought. However, before you begin such trips, confer with the Ascended Masters and others who can advise you on the best techniques for safe intergalactic travel.

* * * * * *

14

Some Theoretical Characteristics of the Future New Reality Realms

Approximately 30 percent of the Earth's current human population has come back from the future to experience "The Shift." Many are aware and remember some of their experiences in the future. The objective of researching what the future of the Earth is like is to assist you and let you know there are many brighter life experiences ahead. Several years ago on the radio show *Coast to Coast AM with Art Bell*, Bell requested that all calls to the show originate from individuals who had come back from the future. A screening of the calls selected those who had truly returned from beyond 2020. The information provided gave the listening audience a glimpse of the New Earth.

What we are considering is the future of humanity. However, keep in mind that time is an illusion and that all reality in the future is "Now." For more information, there are many Web sites with similar information and many books that describe potential futures for the New Earth, this Solar System, and Galaxy.

All past "Now's," present "Now's" and future "Now's" are all really one current "Now." As a result, you can structurally change any conscious creation or event during the current "Now." You can change any past event in your current "Now." Likewise, you can also change your future by currently changing the "Now" which is to become your future. You wonder if you can make these changes during any "Now" event. Yes, you can accomplish this important space-time activity by focusing your consciousness on a visualized experience called a "parallel event frame." Once you visualize the "parallel event frame" (a past or future event) in as many details as possible, you can move along your time track (backward or forward), relive the event, and change it. If you were injured by some accident in the past, go back and relive the event so that the injury did not take place. As a result, you will heal that nonexistent, illusory event rapidly as you send healing energy in to repair the past manifested injury.

What you are experiencing is a form of time travel. To grasp the concept, I suggest you become attentive and open your inner gifts to assist you in visualizing the potential events called "parallel event frames." Some helpful procedures are: open your heart, love unconditionally, seek spiritual guidance in your choices, and know you are practicing for the bright future that awaits you.

The new reality realms will be dramatically different than what you have come to accept as the normal way of life. Remember to keep your expectations to a minimum so you can be open to many possibilities. On the New Earth, you will create as you go because you will not have any reference point on which to plan for the future. Each choice and action will be based on the one choice just made in the "Now" sequence before. You will create your reality base by using your inner guidance and curiosity to lead you.

You will also have help from your Spiritual Assistants. They will give you the feeling that this is the right choice to make. This way of living will be your spiritual pattern of choice. As you evolve spiritually, you drop all of your perceived ideas of what is supposed to be and turn your life choices over to your soul and guidance from God/Goddess within. You are awaking to realize there is no reason for trying to figure out what is or what will take place around the next turn of the road. When each future event arrives, you will know and understand that was your best choice, and you will be there. That's all there is to know. The secret is to *go with the flow* and experience the excitement of the unexpected. These processes will occur much more automatically once you have shed your conditioned responses of the lower-frequency patterns of life. There will be no need to make any future plans. You will become what your soul wants you to be during all sequential "Now" events flowing along your time line.

On the New Earth, you will notice that there are very few words are spoken. This is the sign of an advanced civilization. Communications are carried out telepathically. Spoken and written words are very ancient, inefficient methods to communicate person-to-person. Not only is there wasted energy when communicating with words, but the associated feelings, sensations, and images are frequently missing. With telepathic communications, these components are included.

This is certainly different from the current philosophy that the use of a spoken or written word is a sign of an advanced civilization. Speaking and writing are the signs of a less-developed civilization. When humans adapted the practice of speaking and writing, it dramatically slowed evolutionary progress. Right "Now," within the existing world-wide society, some young children, dogs, cats, other animals, dolphins, and whales, and some native tribes like the Aborigines in Australia, all communicate telepathically. Since this process is not encouraged in children (by adults), their ability to telepathically communicate is rapidly lost after their first few years on Earth.

Telepathy and telempathy are the primary means by which evolved societies communicate. Just think of the gigantic communication system (cell phones, television, radio, newspapers, magazines, and books) currently used by underdeveloped humans for communicating on Earth. Telepathy is a more accurate and efficient communication system. With telepathy feelings, thoughts, and imagery are present to create greater understanding. Telepathy is the primary means of communication throughout the Universe. Imagery, feeling, and sensation provide more accurate messages. The current languages used on Earth do a very poor job in accurately expressing any real meaning. This could be part of the reason humans on Earth, with their many different languages, have so many conflicts; they have difficulty understanding each other.

To understand your future, you must give up the concepts of past lives and karma. These concepts are illusions and only exist in the third-dimension world of duality, of illusory time and space. We chose to incarnate on a third-dimensional planet Earth that was designed for very slow evolutionary progress. Lifetime after lifetime, with repeated mistakes, many challenges, and a hoard of false beliefs, we have in several ways essentially stagnated spiritually. Spiritual growth on Earth has been relatively slow for thousands of lifetimes.

The many false beliefs we have carried for centuries are being replaced with more accurate beliefs and concepts. With these changes, we "Now" realize more than ever that we all create our reality. We attract it to us by what we think and give our attention to. As we increase our level of consciousness and focus our attention, we can move into a fully conscious state and become a conscious, alert being. When fully conscious, there will be no need for sleep or dreaming.

Everyone has had lucid dreams where everything appears real; more real, in fact, than in the so-called waking state. Many times we wake in the morning more tired than when we went to bed because of our many nighttime activities. A question is sometimes asked, "Which is more real, day dreams or night dreams?" Could it be that both are equally real; that is, all of these dreams are illusory movies, and we're the actors? Our daytime and nighttime dream states of consciousness are changing to where those activities will pass away.

Dolphins, the most spiritually advanced beings on Earth, do not sleep, nor do they dream. They are fully conscious. As we physical humans progress spiritually on Earth, we will learn a lot from the dolphins. There will be no third-dimension dolphins on the New Earth; their souls will have incarnated in fifth-dimensional human bodies on the New Earth. This will not be a new experience for the dolphins. Many of the dolphin souls currently on Earth originated from human bodies that died during the explosion of the planet Maldek ("Now" an asteroid belt in this Solar System). You may recall that during one or more of your parallel lives, you incarnated in a dolphin body. Likewise, as mentioned above dolphins have incarnated in human bodies before.

As we shift our consciousness to higher frequencies, it will become easy for the dolphins to incarnate into a high-frequency humanoid body. Science is discovering that dolphin consciousness is higher than that of humans, and they have capabilities beyond those of humans. The brains of dolphins are more evolved than the human brain. This more advanced brain will become a channel through which Higher Creative Powers can flow through these dolphins—our brothers and sisters who are interested in helping humanity. Their connection with Source Energy will allow them to assist humans on the New Earth.

These advanced spiritual beings will teach human souls inhabiting a fifth-dimension body how to live with joy. The dolphins currently experience more joy and fun than any other creature on Earth. For additional understandings about dolphins, trace their history back before they incarnated on Earth. Then strive to understand their evolutionary status and spirituality. Your understanding of dolphins could pay great dividends as a pathway for your spiritual evolution in the future.

In the near future, the government's records of Extraterrestrial activity on Earth will be open to the public. The public is demanding the records be opened. Many humans who realize that Extraterrestrials have been interacting with humans for thousands of years would like to understand their activities. As the programmed fear of alien races is abandoned, we will have opportunities to visit telepathically with humanoids and other physical creations living on many different worlds. On the New Earth, you will welcome the many different Extraterrestrial groups sent to help you adjust to a whole new way of existence. Your acceptance of the Extraterrestrials and their technological assistance will greatly influence the future well-being of the New Earth's inhabitants.

With this off-planet help, all the nations on Earth will instill peace and stop wars. All borders between nations will be removed. We will all live within one global community void of segregation and conflict of any type. Humans will join the forces of Light and focus upon peace. We will join the Intergalactic Federation of Planets and experience the excitement of visiting other societies throughout the Universe and beyond. Humanity on the New Earth will seek liberty of the mind, where each individual is free to follow a spiritual path, rather than follow the manipulators' path. Humans have been manipulated and held in slavery for thousands of years. Social justice will prevail soon. This will allow for a leap in consciousness and accelerate spiritual evolution. The power of consciousness currently eludes a majority of Earth's residents. In the future, we will step into the reality realm of infinite capabilities without trepidation.

On the New Earth, there will be no currency, poverty, or lack of food; thus, no starvation or famine. All of humanity will share and create an ecologically stable environment with sufficient material items created by thought. No one lacks or goes without on the New Earth. People will exchange services and barter for their needed supplies, just as in the past.

There will be no central government. The Internet, set up under guidance from Extraterrestrials, was designed for the purpose of improving communication. With an improved and modified Internet based on telepathic communications, the power of the individual will be restored. Society will be redesigned for the benefit of the individual. Big government, hospitals, the medical establishment and drug companies, insurance companies, retirement programs, secret societies, banking systems, taxation, private property, multinational corporations, large businesses, and religion void of spirituality will all become illusory, archaic societal paradigms of the past. False programming carried out by schools, universities, churches, and the communication media will be completely revised to reflect truth and promote love and peace. No more catering to the promoting of lies, judgmental behavior, political maneuvering, or emphasizing the sensational and bizarre weaknesses of some weak individuals. These tools of the dark forces will be removed from society. We will have more fulfilling lifestyles, greater harmony in society, emotional stability, and healthier eating habits, and sickness and disease will be a thing of the past.

Drunvalo Melchizedek in his book, *Serpents of Light*, 2008, makes an interesting statement about the importance of understanding that you are creating your reality by what you think, quote:

> As you move into the fourth Dimensional Consciousness and you have learned to be a positive thinker you have won the game. If you are there and you are not really ready for it and you start thinking negative thoughts and fear comes in, you will create a scenario which will result in your being thrown back into a lower Dimension. In the Bible, Jesus said the meek shall inherit the Earth. The meek have prepared for Ascension by their positive thinking.

Archangel Metatron channeled a lengthy message posted on www.alienshift.com that states:

"Humans, or third Dimension life forms, will graduate to either the fourth Dimension worlds or fifth Dimensional oneness depending on their level of evolution and their intent."

Every soul will be free to evolve along a spiritual path of love and service to all of creation. Ecologically, all inhabitants of the New Earth will respect every part of creation as having value. Humanity and ecology will become one, since all are interconnected and one cannot survive without the other. A global respect for all of nature will predominate among all living things. This spiritually based respect will help maintain a clean, healthy environment on the New Earth. Everyone will learn how to respect all parts of creation.

The gates of Heaven will open, and you will be surrounded by a glorious new world. There will always be Intergalactic friends willing to help solve pressing challenges. As we approach the "New Earth," we are, in effect, reclaiming the state of consciousness we had during the times of Atlantis and Lemuria. On these continents, many of the residents graduated and evolved to the fifth-dimensional state of consciousness. Many who failed to evolve twenty-five thousand years ago "Now" reside on Earth and await the present opportunity to shift to the fifth-dimensional state of consciousness.

You have been in training as a Creator for thousands of lifetimes. "Now" is your opportunity to use your creative skills to help bring into being the New Earth. Live "Now" as if these events and many others have already manifested. Deep within your memory is a vision of the unique experience of Ascending to the New Earth. The collective consciousness of humanity has a responsibility to create a vision for the New Earth and bring that collective vision into manifestation.

Spirit indicates there are an infinite number of time tracks, time paths, and time lines through which the spirit and soul can evolve back to the Creator Source and God/Goddess. Each soul is constantly faced with choices of which time track, time path, or time line is the most appropriate. No one else can choose for you. Your free will is always honored by God/Goddess. This allows you to complete your lessons and meet the requirements for graduation. There are an infinite number of planets through an infinite number of Solar Systems, Galaxies, and Universes where you can choose to incarnate for a specific type of experience. Your Galactic Universal Assistants are aware of many of these potential opportunities and choices. As you time travel into your future, you can observe that it has been very important to have given up attachments to the past and old duality concepts of the third-dimensional state of consciousness. The process of making repeated mistakes lifetime after lifetime is a pattern of the past. To become fully conscious of where you came from, why you are here, and what it means to "Wake Up" to your potential is a worthy goal. By using your Creator skills, you will have opened an unlimited number of future choices and possibilities.

A global community will be created, and the power of the collective mind will accelerate humanity's evolution. Those humans living in the future may look back at their third-dimensional societies and recognize how primitive they really were. We will then realize the value of joining with the forces of Light and embodying the concepts of acceptance and patience. The Internet was created with Extraterrestrial help to eliminate the secret government and other societal groups that have withheld information about spiritual evolution. On the "New Earth," humanity will be freed from this type of manipulation and control by the Illuminati.

The power of the individual will predominate on the "New Earth," where all will pool their thoughts for the good of everyone. The emotional body will have been brought under control, all fear will have been eliminated, and the environment cleaned and maintained in balance. The availability and the consumption of health-giving plant products will help create balance within all human bodies. The population will be maintained at a certain level by control of births. Global respect for nature will have come into prominence, following the realization that ecological concerns and the survival of humanity are identical. Thus there will be no need to reduce the population through any devious techniques.

"The Shift" in consciousness that began before the year 2000 became the foundation for establishing a global respect for nature and thus helps create a healthy environment. On the "New Earth," the human brain will have an expanded capacity. The activation of dormant DNA energy patterns will assist and expand our mental and emotional capabilities. The opening and expansion of these capabilities will allow various energies from Higher Creative Powers to flow in and optimize the creative energies of all humans. Those new creative powers will help bring into existence a world sometimes called Utopia. In reality, humanity will have reclaimed its long-lost lifestyle and the memory of what it is like to live in joy and peace.

The recommendations brought back from the future tell us that we are to live as if these changes and many more have already taken place; in one sense of the "Now," they have. Living your life "Now" as if the changes have already occurred will help you in making the transition a pleasant experience. You can gain much satisfaction by practicing living on the "New Earth" every day during the years of 2009, 2010, 2011, and 2012. By practicing "Now," you will have helped create the new reality realm—the "New Earth" you have dreamed of.

* * * * * *

15

Some Challenges from El Morya, Guardian of the Ascension Portals

If you plan to Ascend during these exciting times, then it is important to know what the qualifications are and how to prepare your energy bodies. Volumes have been written about Ascension throughout history, but few individuals have set aside or taken time to read this information and then apply what they learn. Many humans are caught up in the mad race associated with their self-centered lives. They are too busy to care about spiritual matters. Many others are just trying to survive; they say they don't have time for spiritual matters.

Consequently, many are unaware of the importance of setting aside time for spiritual matters. When we speak of spiritual matters, I hope you understand that religious matters are not spiritual matters. Time spent in religious activities is most often a diversion from spiritual matters. Jesus Christ never came to Earth to establish a religion and do your spiritual assignments. He came to show all humans how to live a spiritual life and has provided guidance for what is spiritually important. Jesus Christ continues to guide humanity "Now." The book, *Love Without End 1999,* by Glenda Green is one of Jesus's most recent messages to humanity. He continually sets examples in his ongoing messages for all of humanity to follow. In his teachings, Jesus established a pattern that can help anyone interested in preparing for graduation and Ascension.

El Morya, who was embodied as the disciple Peter in the time of Jesus, has recently channeled a very important message. El Morya has been appointed by God/Goddess as the guardian (Chohan) of the portals that open to the fifth-dimension New Earth. Thus he is quite up to date on what the requirements for graduation and Ascension are. In order for you to pass through the fifth-dimensional portal, you will have to be approved by El Morya. Thus, it would be wise to listen to his guidance.

te is channeled by Ascended Master El Morya:
ɔm.

, out of our great love for you, we of the
ɪerarchy, wish to remind you once again
a code of entry that is required for entrance
th dimension. There may be a lot of jokes in
y̱   d about Peter standing at the gate of heaven
and deciding who will or will not be allowed entrance
into the Kingdom. Well, my friends, this joke on Earth
is not so much a joke here. There is more truth to this
than any of you may conceive at this time.

The will of God, dear ones, is that you must pass
through the first portal in order to progress in the right
direction on the spiritual path. Unless you are willing
to surrender your human ego and human personalities
to the Will of God, to be refined and transformed
into the Divine, there is "Now" nothing else for you
to go on a true spiritual path. *Divine Will is the first
portal.* There are six others you must also qualify for
before you can reach the door of the fifth dimension
for your planetary Ascension. To make it through this
first portal, it is highly recommended that you take my
classes at night on the Inner Planes (while your body
sleeps) or take classes from my co-workers of the Will
of God/Goddess who have volunteered to assist me at
this time. You have to pass my tests in your waking time
before you can move on to the next portal. Many of you
reading this message have already moved through this
first portal in this life or in the past, and some of you
have made it through other portals as well. We deplore
the fact that there is still a large percentage of humanity
still living their lives on Automatic Pilot. They have no
idea where they are going, why they are here incarnated
on Earth, nor do they want to find out. They live their
life from day to day, with no conscious direction; their
minds and hearts scattered to the four winds, following
a path of least resistance and spiritual slumber. *Time is*

*getting so short "Now" that if you have not yet made it to
the portal of the Will of God we want to let you know it
is still possible for you to catch up and make it through all
the other portals on time if you choose to do so "NOW."*

There is no more time for procrastination. You
must "Wake Up" "Now" and start very diligently
applying Spiritual Laws in all aspects of your life, living
by the concepts of Love from day-to-day. *Let go of all
your fears and preconceived ideas about God.* Be willing
to embrace Truth that you have been avoiding. Become
the God that you are, right "Now," by becoming Love
in action in all you think, say and do. Love is the only
shortcut you can take in your Ascension process. It is
the greatest key, love of Self, love of God, and love for
all the family of Earth, all kingdoms, including the
animal kingdom. Love and honor all that breathe the
Life of the Creator.

Let go of all judgments and embrace the way of
harmlessness. With enough Love in your heart, you
can make it through all the portals to the Ascension
door on time. Be assured it will not happen for those
who continue to live their lives on automatic pilot.
At this very unique time of Earth history, there is an
unprecedented dispensation by which each soul, with
serious and diligent applications, can make it in a few
years. I, El Morya, shall be there, as the Peter that you
are familiar with, along with the rest of the Spiritual
Hierarchy of this planet and your loved ones to welcome
every one of you Back Home.

In a recent channeling from Adama (at Telos in Mt Shasta) he states
that he has been working closely with El Morya on the Inner Planes
and teaching classes at night to those interested in understanding the
Will of God. Quoting Adama's message posted on https://mslpublish-
ing.com:

I and several other Masters have offered to assist our dear
friend El Morya in this tutoring. Because El Morya's

classes are getting so big. It is my pleasure to invite you personally to come to our classes at night while your body sleeps. If you are willing and ready, you may take our especially designed crash course called; "Ascension by 2012." There are many of us here who are available and willing to give you all the assistance you need. ... There is no fee for our services. All you have to do is make the prayer to your guardian angel at night before falling asleep, and state your intent.

* * * * * *

16

The Lemurian Perspective within the Fourth and Fifth Dimensions

Within Mount Shasta, a majestic, 14,162-foot volcano located in the Cascade Range of Northern California is a city called Telos with over 1.5 million residents. Construction on this complex, multilevel community was begun approximately twenty-five thousand years ago by the survivors of the continent of Lemuria. Work began just previous to the submergence of that continent into the Pacific Ocean and continued for many years thereafter.

Before the Lemurians could build the city of Telos, they had to petition the Intergalactic Federation of Planets and the Agartha Network (an inter-Earth council that represents most subterranean cities) to gain approval to divert the magma flow channels within the volcano away from their potential building sites. Following that approval, they have created a magnificent fifth-dimensional, underground spiritually focused society located at several levels within the mountain. This complex facility and supporting environmental features is described in detail in the *Telos* books (volumes 1–3). Visit the Web site www.lemurianconnection.com for more detailed information about Telos.

The remains of Lemuria are located around the Pacific Rim (New Zealand, Australia, the Pacific Islands, the coasts of North and South America, and the tops of volcanoes that make up the Hawaiian Islands). Many inhabitants of these areas have Lemurian ancestors.

The inhabitants of Telos have maintained their spiritual status for the past twenty-five thousand years, following the most recent shift. They are vegetarians who live long, healthy, and productive lives in ageless bodies that remain approximately thirty to forty years old. Consequently, they are capable of using their physical bodies as soul vehicles for thousands of years when they so desire. When they decide to move on to a higher spiritual realm, they take their bodies with them. They can teleport their bodies to various locations and are invisible to third-dimension humans. Since they exist in the fifth dimension, there is no time. They can change their physical appearance at will. They create their fifth-dimensional homes by thought, and can change them rapidly at will when they desire. If you, as a third-dimensional being, were to be allowed entrance into the city of Telos inside Mount Shasta, you would be unable to see the inhabitants or their fifth-dimensional homes, because they vibrate at too high a frequency for your sensing system.

The Agartha Network of inner Earth cities has an electromagnetic, subway-like system within the Earth (between Agartha Network cities) utilizing trams that travel at very high speeds. These trams travel through a very elaborate network of tunnels. Their advancements in science involve crystal technology that is controlled by their minds, similar to the way many Extraterrestrial races control their spacecraft with their minds. Those living within Telos have a whole fleet of fifth-dimensional spacecraft that operate out of the multidimensional inter-galactic multi-dimensional portal within Mount Shasta, so they can visit other planets. This is also an intergalactic port for spaceships of Extraterrestrials arriving from other planets throughout the Universe.

Mount Shasta is a very special place, much more than a mountain. It is the most sacred location within North America. Large numbers of people throughout the world visit the Mount Shasta area every year because they realize it is one of the most sacred places on Earth. The mountain and associated facilities are a power source for Earth. In addition to being a location where 1.5 million Lemurians reside, it is also a focus for angels, spirit guides, and Ascended Masters of the Light realm.

One amazing feature of the Mount Shasta area is the huge, etheric city of Light located above the dormant volcano. Those of you reading this book that have developed your clairvoyant abilities will be able to see a gigantic, etheric, purple pyramid whose capstone reaches quite some distance into space. The etheric pyramid connects the Earth with the Intergalactic Federation of Planets for this sector of the Milky Way Galaxy.

Some who read about the Lemurians living in Telos may doubt the reality of their existence. That is your individual choice. My intuition, spiritual guides, and *accurate* pendulum dowsing (tuned into Universal Consciousness) all indicate that the city of Telos is 100 percent real. A study of the characteristics of this advanced spiritual group and their current willingness to understand their options during these end times will assist any individual interested in graduation and Ascension. Within your meditations you can know in your heart that many Lemurians still live on Earth's surface and that many spiritually advanced humans reside inside Mt. Shasta. Maybe you sense that you once lived on Lemuria and long for those beautiful times to return. That longing is soon to be fulfilled. Many Light Workers throughout the United States and the world that are helping with the transition and Ascension activities are former Lemurians living within third-dimensional bodies.

The fifth-dimensional Lemurians in Telos have various techniques for monitoring the activities on the lower frequency of Earth's surface. Their measurements indicate that the environment on the Earth's surface has been severely damaged. However, they also detect that many inhabitants living on the surface of the Earth have shifted their consciousness to a higher frequency. Consequently, they believe that as the surface inhabitants evolve by raising their dimensional consciousness, they will be able to interact with the inner-Earth inhabitants.

These Lemurians have available many concepts and scientific understandings to help create the "New Earth" and help set up a spiritually based education system. They also have technology to assist the surface inhabitants to set up a pollution-free transportation system. They have thousands of years of experience in knowing how to grow healthy, nutritious fruits and vegetables. Within Mount Shasta there is an area set aside for growing crops to feed 1.5 million people. We should all look forward to and be thankful for their willingness to help us struggling surface dwellers to create a healthy, beautiful lifestyle on the "New Earth." I recommend reading the three *Telos* books and spending time studying their society as described on the Web site www. lemurianconnection.com.

* * * * * *

17

Take Your Power Back to Optimize Your Creative Potential

Importance of Taking Back Control of Your Life

Many people are desperately looking for someone to tell them what to believe and what to do, someone they can trust. Is that true for you? Why would anyone wish to give his God/Goddess powers to any outside force or group? Many humans on Earth have allowed others to take their power away. Have you allowed others to take your power away? What does it mean to give your power away? What makes you believe you need to allow others to control you? In reality, you don't have to do anything that is not in your best interest and related to the reason you came to Earth in the first place. Examine all of your beliefs and ideas and determine where they came from. Yes, they may currently belong to you, but why did you accept them? Were you forced to believe what your teachers in the educational system told you, what scientists believe is reality, or what your parents, the clergy, or politicians think? Ask yourself if you believe everything you hear, read, or see. If that is true you may have given your power over to others.

A large percentage of the information programmed into your consciousness is illusory. It's based on false beliefs created as a means of maintaining control of the masses. Those who designed and created these illusions had one primary goal in mind. The goal of these controllers was and is to limit your spiritual growth by diverting you from your Spiritual Source (God/Goddess) within.

The solution is to take your power back. First, look within yourself to understand what happened. Ask yourself: Why have I allowed others do my thinking for me? Why do I tend to accept others' opinions without question? Have I lost my connection with God/Goddess within as my true source of understanding? The process of taking your power back involves going within, listening to God/Goddess, and then, with spiritual help, removing all false beliefs.

There is nothing you cannot do yourself. There is no need to call upon someone *out there* in the world to solve your challenges. After all, you came to Earth to take on challenges, come up with solutions, and grow spiritually as a result. When you search out others to come up with solutions to your challenges and problems, you may discover that you have given your power away and, as a result, failed to learn the lessons you signed up for.

There may be sources (counselors, health specialists skilled in preventive medicine, classes, workshops, books, movies, and Web sites) located outside of yourself that can assist you in discovering your truth within. As you seek help, ask the following questions: (1) How does that help feel? Do you sense a warm, fuzzy feeling? Is there light? Is it comfortable and inspiring? (2) Is the help coming from duality concepts promoted by someone dedicated to Service To Self (STS) or is it coming from someone who is promoting the Unity concepts with Service To Others (STO). (3) Does the information provided seem spiritually derived from the higher realms? (4) Is there any fear component associated with the information you discovered? If so, avoid such sources. (5) Is the individual trying to sell something or convince you they have the answers?

Your goal should be to seek help from someone who can help you return to a place of personal power. You want to find someone who can help you discover and understand how powerful you really are. No one outside of you has more understanding about what is happening within your energy system than the God/Goddess within you.

One important tool is to use discernment as you work outside self and inside yourself to find your individual truths. With gaining an understanding of the procedure called discernment comes one of our greatest challenges: an understanding that will enable you to control the ego and overcome fear, especially the fear of fear. Once this task is complete, you are more likely to eliminate hopelessness, find hope, and take back your power.

You and I have a responsibility to try to understand what happened within our society to cause so many individuals to give their power away or allow others to take that power. You may agree that part of the problem is that many have lost the ability to do their own thinking. Also, very few individuals have taken control of their egos and worked on overcoming their fears.

The controllers have known that if you are in a constant state of fear, you are easy to control. You will actually give your power away, thinking that others out there will protect you from an imaginary devil, terrorists, robbers, or other illusory threats. Humans have become lost in a maze of false belief systems, hopelessness, and the pleasant-sounding programs of special interest groups.

Many are realizing that the beliefs of special interest groups and their false propaganda are designed for manipulation and control. Those special interests obviously have a strong tendency towards STS, so they are not to be trusted. Obviously, many old conservative belief systems and special interests are trying to maintain the status quo and stop spiritual growth at all costs. These special interests belong to the lower-frequency duality concepts of the third dimension and are quite frequently judgmental and fear-based. The political system in 2008 displayed some of the judgmental, lying, and self-centered jargon characteristic of low-frequency behavior patterns designed to control others. Exercise caution any time you vote or consider seeking outside help. Your goal is to take your power back and seek guidance from within.

Simply let go and let the God/Goddess within supply the power needed to fill your needs. Then seek out the most appropriate belief system that is compatible with your chosen path and time line on Earth. Get out of the worrying mind trap. Stop giving your old false beliefs emotional energy. Let them run out of steam. Your thoughts and emotions can create and add energy to your false beliefs and illusions.

Always keep in mind that any creation of man is an illusion. To be real and permanent, a creation must have been created by your God/Goddess within. The spiritual part of any creation is a part of God/Goddess, the eternal and permanent unit of each creation. This is why cloned humans who lack a spirit are short-lived. When the clone dies, there is nothing remaining. The spirit of the tree, cow, rock, or human all survive eternally in some energetic form and incarnate somewhere else in form. Within you there is that God/Goddess intelligence waiting to supply you with every good thing. Look closely at your life and notice any imperfections. When you discover them, simply know that somewhere, *elementary errors in thought* created those imperfections.

As you discover errors, just say no. Withdraw the holding energy that maintains those illusory errors.

Use the affirmation given by the angel Asum in the book *Ancient Wisdom Revealed* by Craig Russel, 2005.

"Take this out of me. This experience has served me in my evolutionary growth as a survivor, but I am choosing to be in that place, which is full of grace, where karma is laid to rest. Therefore, those lessons that are steeped in survival consciousness I "Now" set aside that I may evolve through fulfillment."

Those imperfections in our lives, elementary errors in thought brought about by unwise choices, have created many of our painful lessons. They were tools from which to learn; they helped provide us with challenges so that we could understand ourselves. There is no need to continue holding on to these elementary errors of thought unless you have failed to complete the associated lessons. You are at a stage in your evolution where "Now" the goal is to raise your mental, emotional, and physical bodies to higher states of dimensional consciousness. This can be accomplished by setting aside all false beliefs and clearing the genetically engineered and programmed aging processes we have carried during so many lifetimes. We "Now" have a choice to remove the genetically triggered death syndrome. The Creators have opened up a new choice for humanity on Earth. You can choose to take your power back and use your creative talents to create a new reality that will allow you to graduate and Ascend.

Exercising Your Creative Abilities to Create Your Desires

The creative abilities you learned here on Earth are really a complicated function of several energetic interactions on the meta-atomic level, within the etheric realm. The etheric level is unseen by scientists, since it is outside the frequency of the five physical senses in another illusory reality. We all simultaneously exist in several parallel realities. As you exist on Earth in your physical body, you also exist at many other energy levels at the same time. You exist in many frequency bands, and each has its own Laws that govern your parallel activities.

Most individuals reading these words are shifting towards frequency bands within the fourth to fifth dimensions. At the same time, you will continue to exist in many other frequency bands. Throughout your participation within all of these frequencies bands, you have a choice as to where you will put your attention. As you evolve, you will become aware of your other parallel realities and individual soul components of your Oversoul. However, the reality you perceive to be the most important and your primary focus is the "Now" right here on Earth. The rest of your realities are a constant backdrop of all your experiences. For those on the Ascension pathway, these other realities will be joining you in the near future.

Your Oversoul was designed to encompass all of your soul expressions in these different parallel realities. In a sense, the Oversoul could be thought of as your all-inclusive holographic model; your essence, or basic foundation. That is, all of your multiple Oversoul parts (individual souls), incarnated at many locations within the Universe, are contained within your hologram and are a part of your essence. Here on Earth, you are expressing *one* of those potentials within your overall essence. Your essence is your primary quality. It is the energy pattern that is the true you, independent of your expression within any incarnated expression. In full consciousness, you will experience your complete essence, the presence of all your potentials at the same time. Not only will you know your own essence, but you will also be able to recognize the essences of others once you become fully conscious. Even though you are expressing *one* soul experience on Earth at this time, the choice still exists to experience another one of your souls in another "Now" event.

To maximize your creative potential as expressed on the old Earth or New Earth, you must somehow understand that your spirit and soul bodies are part of God/Goddess within. The creative process is a sequential event where all energy bodies become a part of the process. The template for the physical body is the etheric body, located just outside the physical body. The physical body is downloaded or uploaded from the etheric body. The etheric body could be considered a template or blueprint of the observed physical manifestation. Through the processes of thought, you can begin to create by first imagining an etheric template within your holographic design. Once the imaginary thought form is created within the etheric realm; that thought form can then become a physical illusion. These beginning steps of the creative process will function more efficiently and rapidly at fifth-dimensional states of consciousness. "Now" is the time to use your past knowledge, gained in Earth's Creator school, to practice perfecting your creative talents. As you read on, you may think this procedure is all new to you. Everything you are reading, you knew in your previous incarnations. You forgot when the veil of forgetfulness was pulled down over your consciousness. It is "Now" time to ask that the veil be removed so you can remember the creative process. Read slowly and ask your God/Goddess within to clarify the procedure for you.

The first thing to do is visualize some part of your body that needs repair. From this imaginary body part, request that spirit create a basic etheric thought form with two polarities. Then have these two polarities positioned correctly to form a triadic (three-dimensional) template. The triadic etheric template structure should be likened to a proven or established morphogenetic energy field. That is, you need to create a triadic etheric template, based on a proven, functionally efficient energy mold similar to a morphogenetic field (a known energy pattern manifested in the physical world). The template can be based on intuition, or it can be one you have previously observed or studied. For example, you could imagine in your mind a new, healthy liver as the morphogenetic-field-energy triadic template.

Then, within this triadic etheric template, you insert plasmic light energy into the morphogenetic field. Next insert an encodement (DNA- like) language to guide the creative process. This encodement language should first affect the etheric template. This language then proceeds to instruct the etheric template to download or upload the appropriate energy required to create the physical vibrational pattern. Note that at this point, the plasmic light language follows the instructions of the encoding language to make the necessary physical matter arrangements. These arrangements are based in part upon the originally visualized template or morphogenetic energy field.

By closely observing the ongoing process, one can alter the plasmic light to create the most desirable physical structure. Note: When working with the etheric template to densify the energy field, there is an upload or download period called the "time lag." When sufficient light-plasmic energy is provided to the template that energy can become compressed and create the desired physical structure within the physical realm. As this etheric mold downloads or uploads into the physical world, changes in the functional efficiency of the malfunctioning body part slowly takes place. As with any creative activity, practice can help improve the efficiency.

Remember, whatever you think, you create. The time it takes to create from the point of the original thought form to the physical manifestation will gradually become shorter and shorter as you practice and shift to the higher states of dimensional consciousness. In order to insure the most desired creation, several Research Associates have discovered that you will need to go through these creative steps several times to complete the physical manifestation. The steps for the creative process just discussed are not new. Everyone has used this process throughout their lives without defining each step.

The challenge is that you have had difficulties in understanding the creative process; there is also the possibility that you have forgotten how powerful you are. You have pulled back from using your creative skills. Therefore, as you reactivate these skills, exercise caution when setting out to create something. Avoid creating malfunctional objects that could bring into your world new challenges. Make sure your creations are functionally desirable.

One should also consider that the quality of your creation can be improved upon by genetic manipulation through the alteration of neurotransmitters, light and sound frequencies, and adjustments in the basic physical or chemical makeup of the creation. However, realize and always keep in mind that the etheric template creations were based on your thought forms.

We are divine beings; our spirits were created in the image of God/Goddess's unconditional love, centered in the heart. Thus we are a part of God/Goddess, daughters and sons of God/Goddess. Consequently, everyone has the power to come into agreement with the energy of the heart of the Creator, and thus to create. In the past, we gave our creative powers away to the controllers. We allowed others to program us to think and believe we were incomplete in order to limit and restrict our creative capabilities. Why? So that we would bow down to the controllers and seek their help. Our greatest opportunity now is to un-create those controlling programs, restructure those previous lost talents and, as a result, take our power back. This involves the dissolving of negatively charged fields of energy that hold the undesirable illusions in place.

To carry out your responsibility, you must use all the tools you have available. It is the power of attention and intention that contributes to the creative process. With practice, you can manifest many new, illusory thought forms. Once manifested, those creations will need to be held in place with faith, belief, intention, attention, and persistence. Realize that the chair you sit in would disappear if everyone who believed that chairs exist would stop believing that chairs physically exist. The many thought forms of believing that chairs exist is the illusory creation that holds the parts of the physical chair together. Why is the chair an illusory creation? Because a chair lacks permanency, it can be uncreated just as easy as it was created. Everything in the physical world is an illusion, and there is no permanency with anything that is an illusion.

There is a "Cosmic Law that states: *an illusion cannot continue to exist without consciousness energy supporting it.* Remember, everything within the physical world is an illusion. Why? This is because there is no permanent consciousness energy to hold these man-made creations on Earth in a solid, recognizable, physical state. In contrast your spirit and soul are real. They can't be uncreated … ever. They were created by God/Goddess.

> **Remembering cosmic law: a physical illusion cannot continue to exist without consciousness energy supporting it.**

The moment you can change the appearance of something into another something, you have utilized your creative skills to change an illusion. You can change lack into abundance, sickness into health, and hate into love. What was the lack, sickness, or hate? Just one of the many illusions humans create. The vital force that supported and maintained the illusion was your conscious attention, which kept holding on to lack, sickness, or hate. Let go of your false beliefs, withdraw your fear from the illusion, and you have removed the energy that held it in place. The moment that you no longer agree with a less-than-desirable creation and cease giving it your attention, it cannot maintain itself, so it fades away. Creations must have consciousness to support their existence.

Yes, it takes practice to create a new illusion that more efficiently supports your desires. There is an urgent need on Earth for you to help create a new momentum to change the world of appearances. If you are willing to put some effort into working with and practicing the creative and un-creative processes, you can help create this new momentum and accomplish anything.

You have been hypnotized into believing you are powerless. We all have the power to change anything once we awaken and realize we can break free from the hypnotized, programmed conditioning that binds us. We each need to fully understand our ability to take charge of our lives. Preparing for graduation and Ascension is one of those opportunities to create your new reality.

As you work through the Ascension process, you will realize that there will be nothing you need to take with you physically. All of those physical items you consider to be real, and which give you some sense of being, are illusions of the third dimension. Be aware that these illusions will disappear. Let them go with minimal fear. Let go of all those old pictures and keepsakes. There is no way to take them with you. Start clearing house, and get rid of all that junk you thought had keepsake value. As you prepare for Ascension, you will at some point be required to give up your credit cards, car, and cell phone; your home, retirement fund, fame, and status—everything. All these third-dimensional, Earthly things will become meaningless on the New Earth. Remember, no physical things can be taken through the Star Gates.

As you contemplate the future, you intuitively know that these disappearing acts are most likely coming sooner than you think. Yes, some will doubt the reality of these events until they see items beside them disappear. Even then, some humans will reject such events as impossible. It's all about choice and belief in what has happened, what can happen, and what will happen in the very near future. We have had several items disappear in our house. We stopped giving them conscious energy to hold them in the physical world of illusions.

Everyone has a choice to accept or ignore what's happening. Souls who plan to graduate will leave behind all those old, useless emotions and mental thought forms. There will be nothing to hold on to mentally that fails to serve your spiritual path and time line. You may have to give up your ties to family and friends and everything you thought important. Therefore, start clearing out all those false beliefs, negative thought forms, and group activities that have nothing to do with graduation and Ascension. You will need to release anything that could have a tendency to hold you in the lower states of consciousness. The binding power of many thoughts could be destructive to your soul's growth. The process of graduation and Ascension involves letting go of the old and accepting the new.

You may have some important memories you would like to take with you. Your major carryover into the new Earth will be your soul's memories. These are stored electromagnetically within your consciousness. However, if you have failed to keep you Mer-Ka-Ba aligned and spinning appropriately, you could lose your memory when the magnetic field of the Earth drops to zero. Your personal Mer-Ka-Ba magnetic field can help preserve your memories. Also, as you look backwards out of your bus and notice what has happened behind you, you will realize that the only thing that ever mattered was how much love you were willing to share with others.

* * * * *

18

Shifts in Consciousness Related to Graduation and Ascension

The following questions and answers about consciousness have been provided by Adam, the High Priest of Telos. He suggests that you consider your answers to the following questions before proceeding on your Ascension preparation. You may find it helpful to write out your answers.

1. What does it mean to raise one's consciousness?
2. Why would anyone want to raise their consciousness?
3. What happens when one raises their consciousness?
4. Will raising my consciousness influence my daily activities?
5. How will raising my consciousness affect my cosmic evolution?
6. What value is there in making a choice to raise my consciousness?

Once you have carefully contemplated the answers to these questions, you are ready to read on and consider how Adam, from the fifth-dimensional Lemurian society, answers them.

What Does Consciousness Mean?

It means to start becoming continually aware of all your conscious and subconscious activities on Earth. Use all your sensing systems to become more conscious of all aspects of life. Notice how they unfold around you during every "Now" moment. With a higher level of consciousness, it becomes possible to be aware of every event your senses perceive and record in your conscious and subconscious minds. Raising one's consciousness means changing your behavior patterns. No more living on automatic pilot, stuck mentally and emotionally in a repetitive pattern of activities that block out the world around you. It means clearing out activities that have limited spiritual value. It means stopping the madness around you from entering your thoughts and bodies. Avoid mentally and emotionally tuning in to and concentrating on the many negative distractions around you. These distractions have been purposely created to divert your attention and cause confusion in your life. Once humans become confused, they are much easier to manipulate and control. These confusing distractions also limit your ability to raise your consciousness, advance spiritually, and graduate.

Gain control of your chattering mind and focus its activities on worthwhile thoughts. Spend time exploring activities other than those that have entrapped you in a repetitive routine. Seek the real self, the God/Goddess within. Go within and focus your being on your heart. Transfer your focus from the mind to the heart, and its potential guidance for your life. Study how to live from the heart as opposed to living from the mind. Listen to the still, small voice within as your main guidance system. This is an internal knowing, free from the clutter of false beliefs and the many limiting illusions humans have created.

Then use your sensing system to explore everything around you in nature, all the guests Mother Earth has been open to receive. By communicating with and honoring the presence of trees, birds, insects, and animals, you can open up and expand your consciousness. Realize you have become arrogant to think you are superior to others who inhabit the planet with you. No one has a spiritual right to manipulate other creations. Visually sense the features of the landscape around you: the rocks, plants, flowers, and grass. Feel and smell the soil as your source of energy for maintaining the physical body. Examine the characteristics of the air, wind, clouds, sun, moon, and stars, and contemplate how they influence your life on Earth. Give thanks for how they support your life. Realize the love and patience shown by the being you call Mother Earth. She provides life-giving oxygen, water, minerals, and food for your survival as a soul traveling in a physical body. As you thank and honor Earth Mother and all of her guests, she will be ready and willing to assist you in raising your consciousness and vibrational frequency. Just ask members of the Spiritual Hierarchy God/Goddess to raise your consciousness to the most appropriate frequency.

As an unlimited, divine being having a temporary human experience, you can maximize the joy of experiencing the many challenges here on Earth. Concentrate on the wondrous opportunities you have here. Be thankful about your many choices to incarnate back to Earth and complete your third-dimension lessons. Share your insights with others of like mind and find ways to be of service to all of creation. As a result of your journey of self-discovery and understanding of your interconnectedness with creation, you will be assisted in raising your consciousness.

Why Raise My Consciousness?

You should raise your consciousness because the extremely low consciousness of humanity has lost its spiritual connection with reality and is in the process of destroying the planet Earth. For thousands of years after The Fall, the intensity of the duality lessons have become packed full of difficult challenges. Nearing the end of the dark portion of this twenty-five-thousand-year cycle, surface dwellers on Earth have fallen to one of the lowest levels of dimensional consciousness in the Universe. *For the third time in the history of the Earth, humans have Ascended to the heights of glory during the Light phase of a twenty-five-thousand-year cycle. But during and following the dark phase, they have fallen to a very low conscious level.* At this low level of consciousness, a majority of humans have lost contact with their God/Goddess

One sign of this fall in consciousness is evidenced by the current confusion and chaos. Negativity has become so intense that many humans have lost contact with reality. They seek escape through physical sensations or worldly goods in an attempt to satisfy their longings for happiness and joy. Real happiness and joy come from that consciousness connected to the God/Goddess. Many have become so confused about reality they have begun to worship some false, man-made God/Goddess outside themselves, some unknown, ill-defined entity *out there*. They tend to worship an unknown, mystical God/Goddess in an illusory Heaven they created. The real God/Goddess, the -I-Am-That-I-Am, the All-That-Is, or Universal consciousness resides *within* every human, animal, plant, and every other aspect of creation.

What Happens When My Consciousness Rises?

Before examining the many benefits of raising your consciousness, it will be very helpful for you to spend time becoming aware of your feelings about life. Examine the joy of living on Earth, your freedoms, and your capabilities to sense the world around you. Then examine your health, and who or what is in control of your life. Think about how mentally, emotionally, and financially secure you are. Next, spend time contemplating the true meaning of freedom and what freedom means to you personally. Can you locate some factors that limit your freedom or your health? What is the possibility that these factors can be removed? How would you like to see your life unfold? Then decide what you want for your future life on planet Earth.

As you know, everyone creates their reality by their thoughts. You have created every disease you ever experienced. Obviously, you created them for a purpose. The secret is to focus on the thoughts that you want to create, those things you would like to experience in the future "Now." Ask what you can dream about for a better future. Are there activities or events you would like to experience? Do you realize that when you raise your consciousness above your current, limited perceptions, you can have anything you desire? Within the higher consciousness levels, when you ask, you receive. Thus, be careful what you ask for. Your thoughts will be manifesting much more rapidly as you shift your consciousness. As your consciousness moves to a higher level, you have opened your heart and made a more efficient connection with your God/Goddess. As a result, your mind can perceive that perfection and those limitless possibilities are available just for the asking.

During the positive half of each twenty-five-thousand-year cycle, called the Golden Ages, humans have expanded their consciousness and experienced unlimited possibilities. The fall of mankind sometimes referred to in the Bible as related to Eve eating an apple was about partaking of the tree of good and evil. Thus the Fall was about a compromise in values associated with the higher levels of consciousness that had been previously obtained. The Fall was created by humanity's desire to experience polarity (duality) at the lower dimensions. Humans chose to separate from God/Goddess. This Fall in consciousness created a rift in the perfection that had existed in previous lives. As the Fall proceeded, during the dark cycles, humanity gradually descended into the rift of duality that we "Now" experience on Earth. Consciously, you are unaware of the thousands of years you have been on Earth in many different bodies. This means that the real you, not the one residing here on Earth at this time, still possesses the knowledge of all those past lives. We all have the potential to resurrect that knowledge into our current awareness. As you let go of the erroneous and distorted false beliefs and illusions that have limited you for thousands of years, you can begin to remember the great and marvelous being that you are. As you remember those portions of incarnations experienced during the higher states of dimensional consciousness, you can manifest them and bring them back into your physical life on the New Earth.

Will Raising My Consciousness Influence My Daily Activities?

The changes in your life as a result of raising your consciousness are unlimited. Yes, raising your consciousness will gradually influence your daily activities. Raising one's consciousness is a natural process designed by the Creators of all Universes. As your consciousness rises, you become closer to the Creators and God/Goddess. You gradually recognize your real identity as an eternal and immortal part of God/Goddess, a child of love created by the Creators of Love. You will know that you not only came from love, but that by raising your consciousness, your love will ever expand. You can become more aware that you are a child of an omnipotent and glorious God/Goddess, created with all the same attributes. You are a duplicate, if you will, of God/Goddess. As your consciousness is raised to higher frequencies, your lost memories will be restored. Greater understanding will allow you to know where you came from, and what you are doing here. It will also provide guidance for your future paths (time lines) throughout eternity.

Within the higher states of dimensional consciousness, you can move out of the small box in which you have been living for thousands of years and explore what else is available outside your box. You will be able to explore the Earth, this Solar System, other galaxies, and different Universes. You will gradually realize that the little box you have been confined to was an illusion. There is no need to stay confined to your box and all of the other illusions. You can become free and discover you are not alone; you are a part of All-That-Is.

Ask yourself if you are an isolated human living on the only inhabited planet within the Universe. What is your first answer? Are you an interconnected part of everyone and everything? Have you considered that there are millions upon millions of other planets on which inhabitants live and breathe, all connected to the same Creators?

Some scientists now believe that all planets and moons may have inhabitable interior portions. Spirit indicates that on some planets, life on the surface is very difficult to impossible, so the inhabitants must live inside the planet to survive. When we consider that all of creation came about as a result of several Creators all involved in creating many different Universes, then anything is possible. There is no way you as an individual could understand all of creation. It is very logical that biological creation could inhabit both the exterior and interior of billions of planets. And all of these inhabitants are all our brothers and sisters. Can you fathom the concept that you are part of a vast and infinite creation of an unimaginable degree of variation in shape and form? Failing to clear out the false beliefs that place limitations on your spiritual evolution is tragic beyond description. Opening your mind to unlimited possibilities will help you understand you are not alone; the real creation extends beyond your wildest imagination. Why limit your God/Goddess-given capabilities by clinging onto outdated beliefs and illusions? By rising your consciousness to a level that is connected to the God/Goddess self within; it becomes possible to restore all your divine gifts, freedoms, and capabilities. You can receive the gift of spiritual sight and visualize the physically unseen world. You can time travel, bilocate, remote view, and thus experience the joy of exploring past and future events. Your daily life will flow with ease as you focus your thoughts on the beauty of the moment and all it has to offer. You become capable of clearing out all self-punishment, old routines, false beliefs, and illusions that have held you captive for many lifetimes. As an aid to your expanded energy system, you can request that all needed energy-flow patterns without and within your bodies be opened and fine-tuned to optimize your well-being. Grace and magic become available to help you restore your health and stop aging. Within the higher states of consciousness, you have lifted yourself above the pain and suffering of the present physical, mental, and emotional limitations of the third-dimensional state of consciousness.

Will My Shift in Consciousness Influence My Spiritual Evolution?

Assuming you plan to follow the outline of evolution designed by the Creator, God/Goddess then the process of raising one's dimensional consciousness will continue from a glory to greater and greater glories on into eternity. The Lemurians living within Mount Shasta in Telos have sensed that the majority of humans residing on Earth are dreaming of going to a New Earth when they leave. Could it be that the "New Earth" they are dreaming of is right here? "Now" at the end of the twenty-five-thousand-year cycle and the beginning of a new cycle unfolding on this planet, you will no longer have to die to go to an illusory heaven with streets of gold. The real Heaven on Earth will manifest right here as a parallel "New Earth" for all of those who choose to ride the wave of graduation and Ascension. For those who reject this opportunity, there are other options available. Therefore, you have a choice of whether or not to answer the following yes-or-no questions about your reason for coming to Earth. Many have already answered these questions.

1. Did you incarnate on Earth to *remain* in the little box of duality consciousness and continue living on some third-dimensional planet like Earth?

2. Do you still require lessons and challenges to complete a part of your contract within the little box of duality before you graduate?

3. Did you come to Earth to complete your third- and fourth-dimensional lessons in this incarnation before moving out of the little box and into Unity/Christ Consciousness?

4. Did you come to Earth to shift your consciousness to the fifth-dimensional frequencies and thereby graduate and take your renewed physical body to the "New Earth"?

Do you understand the significance of your answers to these questions? You may have already decided or are close to making your decision about graduation and Ascension. Everyone has a choice to make. There is no judgment as to what your answers are. Your choices and decisions about these four questions will significantly influence your current "Now" status and the status of your cosmic evolution for thousands of future experiences.

Keep in mind that within the spiritual realms there is no time or space. Thus you have an eternity to chart your path. However, there may be an advantage of speeding up your evolution by answering *no* to the first two questions and *yes* to the second two. By choosing to answer *yes* to the second two questions, you will be moving out of duality, away from the lessons and challenges that pain and suffering have provided you. The decision to shift into a higher, fifth-dimension frequency is a choice to embrace Unity/Christ consciousness by passing through the Star Gates to the "New Earth." With this decision, a whole new reality realm opens up to a cosmic path for your spiritual evolution. Opportunities within the higher levels of consciousness have unlimited potentials.

Discussion about Choosing to Raise Your Consciousness

One method for raising your consciousness is to focus your conscious intent on sensing the characteristics of all aspects of God/Goddess creations. Tune into nature and all the characteristics of that creation. Open your heart and mind to all human, animal, plant, and mineral kingdoms, and to spirit beings residing on and around Earth. Seek to know and understand the many different people, animals, and plants, and their behavior patterns. Try to understand the purpose of each one. They each have a specific purpose and a support role to play in your life on Earth. Study the names of the many different animals and plants. Thank the angels, divas, and fairies for their service to each human and plant. Thank all of the spiritual entities for all their loving care. These higher-dimensional spirit entities have a consciousness and a sensing ability in order to understand your thoughts.

There is value in working with the soil and growing plants. Placing your hands in the soil and watching a plant grow have been scientifically proven to bring in healing energies. Open your heart to all of that which is above and below in the visible and invisible world. Strive to communicate with the invisible world that exists within the higher frequencies. Start to open your spiritual sensing system to become aware of those realities beyond your five physical senses. Develop your sixth sense to communicate with the angels, divas, and fairies, those higher-frequency creations. Believe that anything is possible. Remember, your beliefs create the foundation for the thoughts that create your reality. Open yourself to sense the unconditional love present within all of the wonders of creation. You will be raising your consciousness to all of the new energies that are flooding the Solar System and planet Earth.

By shifting your consciousness to the higher frequencies at this time in history, you will be closing out the thousands of lifetimes you spent on the low-frequency planets. Your labors and many challenges throughout the centuries will be crowned during graduation and Ascension. Never in the history of the Earth has the Ascension process been made as easy as it is currently. The Creators have given permission for Mother Earth to Ascend, and she has chosen to do so. Mother Earth welcomes all who would like to join her and Ascend.

The goal of mass graduation has eluded humanity for thousands of years, primarily because that opportunity only occurs every twenty-five thousand years. You can now realize that your goal in continuing to incarnate on Earth was to raise your consciousness so you could eventually Ascend with your physical body to the "New Earth." The Creators and God/Goddess have chosen to offer this opportunity to you. There is still time to "Wake Up" and decide to graduate. However, if you prefer to wait for the end of another twenty-five thousand years to graduate, that is, at the end of the next cycle, that is an acceptable option. For those who were unaware that graduation time is near, this is your "Wake Up" call. For those of you making preparations to graduate, continue your efforts.

Some have asked if humanity "Now" has an opportunity to graduate from third-dimension Earth, why haven't we haven't heard of this opportunity in the communication media. The major communication media—radio, television, and the newspapers—are controlled by the Illuminati and specific Extraterrestrial groups. They would rather keep you on an Earth-like planet as slaves in the third dimension for another twenty-five thousand years than let you know of this opportunity.

The subject of Ascension has been discussed in hundreds of books throughout history, and there are now close to one thousand Internet Web sites that discuss and outline helpful suggestions for your graduation and Ascension. Obviously, there are many false beliefs about how you achieve Ascension. Go within during meditation, use discernment, and you will know the most appropriate path. It is up to each individual to be willing to work at finding and following their own spiritual path. No one else is responsible for you. Over two thousand years ago, Yeshua (Sananda or Jesus Christ) came to Earth to show humanity the way to live in order to graduate and Ascend. His basic instructions were simple: start by loving yourself, and then love your neighbor as yourself.

In summary, the best advice for you in the days to come is to start each day with a total commitment to embrace and align your spirit and soul with the God/Goddess within. Then request that your heart and God/Goddess within take charge of your activities during the coming days so that everything unfolds efficiently and gracefully.

The following quote comes from the Web site www.ascendedearth. ishcom.net:

> "My Beloved God/Goddess Within, I AM in you and you are in me. Hold me this day in the tenderness of your care. Send to me all the protection, guidance, and understanding I need to make progress in becoming the Christ I AM. Let me be a Living demonstration of your Love, Kindness, and Beauty this day."

* * * * * *

19

Initiations and Disciplines Taught Within the Ascension Temples

Souls planning to Ascend to become an Ascended Master are required to have completed spiritual initiations as taught within the Seven Temples of Ascension. Duplicates of each accession temple are available for your use and are located in Luxor, Egypt, Telos in Mount Shasta, higher-dimensional Shambhala in Tibet, and at Mato Grosso in Brazil. Many humans on Earth have completed some of the initiations in one or more of these Ascension Temples or in other disciplines. Each one of these temples is positioned within the fifth-dimensional state of reality consciousness. Thus if you reside within the third-dimensional state of consciousness, your physical sensing system lacks the ability to see these temples. However, as a higher part of your multidimensional reality, you can travel out of your body at night and visit these temples.

It is my understanding that passage through all seven of these temples is not a requirement for passing through "The Shift" and Ascending to the "New Earth." However, attendance in these temples and completion of many of the lessons and disciplines are recommended. This is especially true of the first four temples. To become an Ascended Master you will be required to complete all the lessons, disciplines, and initiations as you pass through all seven temples in sequence. Before you are allowed to enter any temple, you must have completed all the lessons and disciplines in the temples preceding it.

The initiations within these seven temples are briefly discussed below. As an advanced soul, all of these Ascension requirements are stored within your super-consciousness. The objective of working through each of the Seven Temples of Ascension is to bring these disciplinary patterns back into remembrance. Then, once these principles are integrated within your heart, you can utilize them for your daily activities on the third-dimensional Earth and the new fifth-dimensional Earth.

These requirements can be brought into remembrance by actually attending the sessions held in each of the Ascension Temples. Many North Americans have attended one or more of the seven temples in Luxor, Egypt, or a duplicate set located at Telos in Mount Shasta. Your

194

other options are to ask to attend similar temples located in Tibet or Brazil. Each night as you fall asleep, make your applications on the inner spiritual planes to go to the temple of your choice.

Call upon the Office of the Christ, under the direction of Lord Maitreya and Lord Sananda (previously known as Jesus) and assisted by the Great White Brotherhood. Then members of your High Self Spiritual Council and/or Divine presence within will go with you and assist in any way needed.

The disciplines outlined within each individual temple must be completed before moving on to the next temple. Approval to move on to the following temple will be based on how you consciously live the disciplines taught in the preceding temple. You must pass the disciplines of temple one before moving on to temple two, temple two before moving on to temple three, and so forth. Following your attendance and activities within each temple, members of the Great White Brotherhood will observe your Earthly activities to determine if you mastered the lessons and "Now" qualify to move on. Everyone on Earth is being monitored to determine their spiritual status.

With the new dispensations put in place by the Creators, God/Goddess this initiation sequence can be completed much faster than at any previous time in the history of the Earth. Many reading these words have already completed the required remembrances within the first three to four temples. Over three hundred and forty thousand souls on Earth have recently completed the disciplines of all initiations outlined in these seven temples.

Working with the disciplinary challenges outlined within each of the seven temples will be very helpful for anyone interested in passing through "The Shift," graduating from third-dimension Earth, and Ascending. These internal, conscious disciplines will prepare your new physical bodies to qualify to physically pass through the portals (Star Gates) leading to the New Earth. According to spiritual sources, over 2.5 billion souls out of the seven billion plus present on Earth have considered Ascending at the end of the end of this twenty-five-thousand-year cycle. A large number of these 2.5 billion souls, all over planet Earth, are now attempting to discover how to prepare them-selves to accept the upgraded features of their new bodies and the coming Earth changes. Once they discover how to prepare and have prepared, they have an opportunity to become actively involved in helping create the newly developing society on the New Earth. You may want to carefully consider the opportunities associated with Ascending and/or in becoming an Ascended Master.

You can start "Now" by requesting entrance to temple one. Or you can ask members of the Great White Brotherhood to reveal to you what temple you are "Now" ready to enter.

Temple One: The Temple of God/Goddess's Will

The mastery of the first temple involves the candidate's ability to transform all thoughts and feelings by bringing them into alignment with their divine self. The candidate is given guidance in learning how to commune with his own God/Goddess presence within and to develop true humility in the presence of the divine self. Guidance for these classes is provided by Master El Morya and his assistants. The candidate will learn how to dissolve all rebellion against God/Goddess's will in all components of his Oversoul (individual souls) located anywhere within the various Universes.

Emphasis will then be directed towards removing any rebellion against self-discipline and self-correction and other serious barriers to real spiritual progress. Any thoughts and feelings that in any way damage the physical, mental, and emotional bodies are counterproductive and destined to destroy that which is sacred. Any activity or destructive behavior that would be termed self-punishment or self-persecution for the sake of escape from reality or trying to satisfy cravings of the senses needs to be brought under control.

The implications are that the candidate interested in completing the requirements in the Temple of God's Will must take care of his physical, mental and emotional bodily temple, where God resides. This means taking diligent care of your body by obtaining adequate rest (generally eight hours of sleep with one hundred minutes of deep delta sleep) and adequate nutrition (including minerals, iodine, water, and oxygen). You should exercise, abstain from drugs and the poisons found in tobacco, liquor, coffee, processed foods, soft drinks, and prescription and recreational drugs. Also avoid X-rays and all nerve or metabolic poisons and toxins (e.g., MSG and NutraSweet) and toxic heavy metals. Avoid micro-waved foods, foods containing radioactivity, foods altered by genetic engineering, foods containing excess sugar and salt, toxic food preservatives used to store food-like products over long periods, poisonous colored dyes, artificial flavoring agents, and a host of other adverse energies. Many of these chemicals have purposely been placed in drinks and foods to destroy your life forces and weaken the body. Those individuals who do not wish to accept these self-disciplines and self-corrections may not have developed an interest in becoming their best. A highly desirable spiritual goal is to become the highest and greatest expression of a God/Goddess incarnate that you can be. The items listed above are just a few examples of the lessons and disciplines that you will need to consider as you participate in completing the requirements outlined for temple one.

Note 1: Within the higher states of fifth-dimensional consciousness, there are no secrets. Every thought and every action taken by anyone is known by all. Therefore, it is very easy for those within the higher-dimensional spiritual realm to accurately sense and record all your thoughts, activities, and behavior patterns. Nothing is hidden. The Ascension Great White Brotherhood will have examined your recorded activities and notify you when you have completed the qualifications for each preceding temple before you can move on.

Note 2: The transformation that you are about to experience is very unique to planet Earth. As one of the Earth's residents, you have become one of the brave ones, living upon the showcase of this Universe. There are millions upon millions of higher-dimensional entities in Extraterrestrial spaceships with large crews and visitors watching you daily. They are rooting for you to embrace self-discipline and sending their love and support as you prepare for Ascension.

Temple Two: The Temple of Learning

Within the second temple there are a host of Ascended Masters and members of the Ascension Brotherhood who provide instructions about Universal Laws and the Law of Cause and Effect. To help you to have a better grasp of the classes within this Temple, spirit has requested that you carefully study Section V of this book, where several Universal Laws are discussed. For example, the Law of Cause and Effect, with which almost everyone is familiar, needs to be understood. For example, for every action taken in thought or deed, there will be an effect that must be balanced.

There are other Universal Laws that many humans are unaware of and thus lack an understanding of their importance. Very few humans on Earth have been exposed to, or have spent time studying and applying, the multitude of Universal Laws. As a result, many are unaware of how important Universal Laws are. The Law of Karma relates to the Law of Cause and Effect and other Universal Laws. Many of these Laws will be taught in the "Temple of Learning. Through an understanding of these Universal Laws, individuals will be able to fine-tune their skills to develop harmony and synchronization with the all-knowing God/Goddess within. Time spent in Temple Two is a happy time of learning how to bring into perfection your talents for STO. In Temple Two, people of every profession (artists, musicians, mechanics, and teachers) gain an understanding of how to improve their talents. Here, one learns how to find a place of service where one can apply their God/Goddess-given talents in STO. These understandings will serve many useful purposes as you prepare for future service within the higher states of dimensional consciousness. Following graduation from third-dimension Earth, you will reside within a society free from drudgery, confusion, and other features of the world of duality. The Temple of Learning provides a foundation on which to further build your talents as a member of that reality realm called Unity/Christ consciousness. In Temple Two, you are preparing to be ready to use your individual talents to serve the whole of society as a means of creating Heaven on Earth. Once you have learned how to apply Universal Laws to your life, proceed to Temple Three.

Temple Three: The Temple of Love

Instructions within the "Temple of Love are under the direction of the "Beloved Paul the Venetian." Here, emphasis is directed towards learning the discipline of unconditional love and harmony as a means of balancing your own life stream and your ability to convey unconditional love to all of creation. As a learning tool, the candidate is placed in living quarters with those who have within themselves tendencies which are particularly aggravating to others. Within the Temple of Love the candidate is faced with a challenge to live peacefully with his fellow man. The challenge can become somewhat dramatic. Imagine yourself held in living quarters with others who have a tendency to transfer their lack of love for self into behavior that is not only aggravating but downright disgusting. Consequently, those new to the concept of unconditional love, the neophytes who have a dislike for anything new, jump up and run to the door.

With great relief, those who remain are then able to get down to business and receive guidance on the importance of love for self and others. To live peacefully with one's fellow men is one of the greatest tests of the un-ascended state of consciousness. The beauty, kindness, and graciousness of the great master, Beloved Paul the Venetian, are so astonishing it can melt a heart of stone. Through his example, he requires that you learn tolerance, compassion, and understanding of all components of creation. Also within the instructions and subsequent practical applications, everyday challenges are recalled and played out in class. Some individuals may be severely challenged when making these practical applications, drop out of class, and go on their way.

Love is the foundation on which all Universes and their components were created and continue to be created. The Creator of Love is the foundational energy for creating each spirit and soul from *light*. Love operates from the heart, not from the ego-based, self-centered mind. Thus, concentrate on living all your activities of tolerance, compassion, and understanding from the heart. Heart-centered guidance is more closely connected to God/Goddess. The God/Goddess source working through you can assist you in mastering the applications of unconditional love in your life. Just ask for assistance and be open to receive.

During the months of March and April of 2008 an increased concentration of Light and Love energies arrived on Earth. These incoming energies continue to flow to Earth and can help you center your being in Light and Love. Visualize this Light and Love flowing from the cosmos, through you, and out to the Earth's soil, rocks, plants, birds, animals, insects, microbial life, and all other components of creation incarnated on Earth. Then direct it to your family and friends.

Once the Ascension Brotherhood grants permission, ask to enter Temple Four.

Temple Four: The Temple of Ascension

Ascended Master Serapis Bay, the Chohan of the Fourth Ray, will assist you in your instructions within the Temple of Ascension. Serapis Bay has had over 11,500 years of experience since he brought the Ascension Flame from Atlantis and helped construct the Temple of Luxor in Egypt. The Ascension Flame is still maintained by the Ascension Brotherhood in Egypt. Reminder: Serapis Bay is a stern disciplinarian and in charge of the Ascension portals (Star Gates) to the "New Earth." There's no messing with him.

In Temple Four, the candidate must draw enough purity from within his consciousness to observe his "I-Am" presence of God/Goddess within and his Holy Christ self" face-to-face. The candidate will be faced with tricks of the ego self, and subtle appearances must be dealt with and brought under control. Remember, the ego self wants to be in charge regardless of the damage caused to any of your energy bodies. In fact, the ego self can be so controlling that it can cause all kinds of pain and suffering in order to maintain control. During the instructions, Serapis Bay himself will stand within the aura of the candidate and observe any remaining energy imbalances of a discordant nature. As a result, the candidate frequently hears many strange voices coming from within that have been lodged inside the inner and outer bodies. These imbalances need to be drawn out so that the candidate may discern the "Voice of the Silence," the God/Goddess within. As the candidate becomes aware of all of his past negative creations and transgressions, these must be transformed into Pure-White Light.

Serapis Bay has been feared for centuries because of his strict discipline. The following quote is his message for you.

> I am dedicated to seeing that you pass through the fires
> of purification, and that you, who desire the opportunity
> to gain your Ascension might persevere until that day of

victory. Angels of the Ascension Temple gather all praise, adoration, songs, devotion and blessings sent upward by individuals and congregational for individual worship. These energies are created by devotional practices that are carefully woven into the ever-widening spiritual streams of energy. Each soul who attains Ascension Status makes it easier for the next life stream to avail itself of the fully gathered cosmic momentum of those who have gone before.

Once approved, you proceed to Temple Five.

Temple Five: The Temple of Consecration

The disciplines of the fifth Temple involve taking seriously the cer-emonial placement of the garment of consecration on you by Master Hilarion or Beloved Raphael. All body systems are consecrated for pu-rity in order to prepare for Ascension. Golden sandals are placed on the candidate's feet, and a silken robe is donned. Then individual parts of the body are consecrated. The consecrations of the hands and feet are infused with the Flame of Healing. These infusions assist the body's movements. Next, a consecration of the lips takes place to invoke that Sacred Words be uttered as a means of manifestation of healing powers from the spoken word. Then the eyes are consecrated to guide the eyes to see and call forth the perfection of spiritual sight and understanding. These procedures are a few examples of the many activities that take place within the fifth Temple.

Temple Six: The Temple of Service

The sixth Temple is sponsored by Lord Sananda and his beloved twin flame, Nada (they were previously known as Jesus Christ and Mary Magdalene). Lessons within this temple are designed to guide the candidate in Service to Others. Those entering the sixth Temple are expected to temporarily put aside their worldly pursuits in order to be of service, first to self, family, neighbors, friends, and others who reside within their immediate locality. Then that service is to expand to include all of those in need. Here the candidate is required to find what the needs of others are and how best to be of service. The candidate is expected to volunteer some of his time in planetary service, utilizing heart-felt energy to help lift others back on their chosen paths. Through this planetary service, the candidate is becoming aware that by meeting the needs of the few, the needs of many are reached by influence and example. Guidance is continually given by Sananda and Nada as the candidate goes out from the Temple of Service to become a ministering servant. The services provided by the candidate should extend beyond the physical needs to the mental, emotional, and spiritual needs of humanity. As a ministering servant, the candidate utilizes teaching talents in response to those who call for help. The candidate calls upon others in the community and world to assist him in serving others.

The lessons and guidance provided within the Temple of Service must be put into practice through becoming humble and disciplined. This means providing selfless service to other humans on planet Earth. Before one can Ascend and become a Master one must learn the lessons of service to move on to Temple Seven. This means becoming sensitive to the guidance of the Ascension Brotherhood and becoming obedient to implement the concept of true brotherhood for all. This responsibility means being dedicated to enhancing the consciousness of all of humanity. As an individual candidate who has completed the requirements provided in the Temple of Service you will be recognized for and by your dedication to serving and assisting organizations that provide for those in need. Many who have completed the Temple of Service requirements actually spend a large portion of their lives with an inward drive, goal, and dedication to be of Service To Others (STO) as their chosen professions.

Many have completed the requirements for the first five temples in previous lifetimes. This is true of some of you reading this report. Many have tried to meet the requirements of the sixth Temple, but have failed, and were unable to move on to the seventh Temple.

The following comment from the Ascension Brotherhood illustrates the challenge: "In the past, too often, Serapis Bay saw many of you leave Luxor, ready to set the world on fire, only to recede back as you went down the steps of the great temple. This is where a great number of you lost your opportunity for Ascension in many previous incarnations."

From this statement, we come to realize that each of our spirits and souls have been aware of the requirements for Ascension for many, many lifetimes. In fact, we have apparently gone to the Temple in Luxor to proceed through the Ascension process several times before. During this incarnation, we again have the opportunity to return to Temple in Luxor or Temple Six in Telos to complete the requirements for graduation and Ascension in this current lifetime. This time, may you make every effort possible to succeed.

Once approved by the Ascension Brotherhood, you proceed to Temple Seven.

Temple Seven: The Temple of the Violet Flame

To enter the Seventh Temple you must have accomplished the challenges outlined within the "Temple of Service. Activities within the seventh Temple are like putting the final touches on all of your individual energy systems. These attunements prepare the candidate for receiving and sending out spiritual, life-giving energies from God/Goddess within that are absolutely pure. Activities within the seventh Temple in Luxor, Egypt, and at Telos in Mount Shasta are under the direction of Master Saint Germain, Lord of the Seventh Ray. Saint Germain brought the Violet Flame from Atlantis to Egypt over 11,500 years ago. He has worked with these energies ever since.

Because of the developing critical situation associated with the end of the age on Earth, Saint Germain petitioned the Ascension Masters in approximately 1987 to release the use of the Violet Flame to anyone interested in evolving spiritually and in helping themselves and humanity. As you read on, I believe you will understand why this petition was requested and subsequently granted. Humanity "Now" has available one of the most powerful spiritual tools known; "The Violet Flame."

> **A very important message:**
> **Use of the violet consuming flame is the most powerful spiritual tool known.**

Saint Germain states: "The use of the Violet Consuming Flame is more valuable to you and all of mankind than all of the wealth, gold, and jewels of this planet."

Then in 1998, the Silver Ray of Grace and Harmony, under the guardianship of Archangel Zadkiel, was merged with the Violet Flame of transmutation to create the Silver Violet Flame of transmutation and mercy. This combination has significantly amplified the spiritual energies available for humanity's use in the purification of all human energy bodies.

The Violet Flame is associated with the color violet and has long been associated with spirituality. It has the highest frequency within the visible spectrum. However, the Violet Flame also includes a combination of colors from lavender through lilac to deep violet. Behind this physical spectrum of the Violet Flame, mystics have glimpsed a spiritual spectrum of light energy emanating from a brilliant inner, divine light. These spiritual light energies are more radiant and pure than any found within the physical realm. This unique Violet Flame has the capabilities to accelerate spiritual development and preparation for Ascension. You can add love and gratitude to the Violet Flame, and/or the Silver Violet Flame and consider either "thought form" a dear friend to provide you with mercy, forgiveness, and freedom. In addition, these "thought forms" can provide cleansing, purifying, transmuting, and transforming for any creation.

Many spiritual teachers indicate that the Violet Flame is a divine, living, intelligent spiritual being. When called upon appropriately by a candidate on the Ascension Path, the Violet Flame has the capability to consume all obstacles not in divine order. The Violet Flame can function to completely purify every energy system within the human physical body (atoms, electrons, molecules, cells and tissues.) Also, the Violet Flame can purify and cleanse the mental, emotional, and spiritual bodies. Thus, everyone can and should purge their energy systems of all past and present life attachments, pain, anger, disease, guilt, weaknesses, blame, and all mental, emotional, and spiritual thought forms that hinder spiritual growth. Call on the Violet Flame to transmute all energies that do not serve a divine purpose.

Invoking the Violet Flame of Saint Germain for Clearing:

You need to call on Saint Master St. Germain to invoke the Violet and Silver Flame of transmutation, compassion, and forgiveness to cleanse and purify all of your energy bodies. These flames are a combination of blue rays for power and pink rays for love (divine masculine and feminine, respectively). The main role of these flames is to create positive change. Visualize the violet flame pouring love, forgiveness, and compassion across and through your bodies. Then anticipate and know that all undesirable energies are being transmuted.

In the past, thousands of souls have Ascended after using the Violet Flames to prepare themselves By daily calling forth the Violet Flame, souls have gradually changed all the dark, negative energies from many "Now" lives (past, present, and future) into pure, positive, healing, golden liquid light. Many souls who have used the Violet Flames to assist their Ascension process "Now" reside within the fifth-dimensional state of consciousness or higher, enjoying all the new realities available.

Saint Master St. Germain suggests you start your day by calling forth the Violet Flames. Ask the Violet Flames to sustain you for the rest of the day, throughout all of your activities. Stay detached from the outcome of each activity. If you begin with a specific desired outcome, you will likely miss the boat. One needs to allow space for the most appropriate outcome to manifest.

Your Higher Self knows what is best, and the God/Goddess within can help with creating the most desirable outcome. The God/Goddess within can guide you along your path. You will learn that the Violet Flames' energies will be one of the most spiritual tools you have available. The most important thing at this juncture is to be able to let go of your own personal agenda so you become receptive to guidance from God/Goddess within.

Within Unity/Christ consciousness your agenda should be in tune with those around you. Otherwise, you have maintained your separation within a world of duality consciousness. Many people are afraid to let go of their personal agendas and allow the wisdom of their Higher Selves and God/Goddess within to take charge. They have become so identified with their *misaligned human egos* they have lost sight of their heart-guided, spiritual connections. You may consider using the following channeling from Saint Master St. Germain for invoking the Violet Flames.

> In the name of the I AM of my being, in the name of God/Goddess, I "Now" call forth the action of the Violet Flames of transmutation, of compassion, and forgiveness in my auric field, for the cleansing and purifying of every thought and feeling in my solar plexus and in all of my chakras. I ask the action of the Violet Fire to permeate every cell, atom and electron of my four body systems at this moment and at all times each day of my life, 24 hours a day, 7 days a week for the healing of all distortions in my energy field from past and present misunderstandings. I ask the energies of the Violet Fire to start healing all distortions in my physical, emotional, and mental bodies. With much gratitude, I "Now" ask for the action of the Violet Fire to manifest in my energy fields in full power. And it is so.

Note 1: Everyone can work with the Violet Flames to help themselves, their families, and their friends, regardless of whether they have completed the lessons outlined within each of the seven temples. However, the ability to which anyone can efficiently work with the Violet Flames appears to be correlated with the degree to which an individual has progressed through and applied the lessons outlined in all seven temples of Ascension. The degree to which your request will be met relates to your level of spiritual development. Obviously, it is still very important to complete the lessons of Temple One the Temple of God/Goddess's Will, as soon as possible. In addition, those individuals who have set as one of their goals to complete the instructions outlined in all seven temples of   Ascension will greatly benefit through those efforts. The fact that you have dedicated time and effort to working on your spiritual development allows you to use the Violet Flames of Ascension.

Note 2: When you, the candidate, have completed the lessons of Temples one through six and worked to use the Violet Flame of Ascension (outlined in Temple Seven), your activities will be appraised by the Ascension Masters. They will be looking for your degree of dedication to the assigned guidelines and your proficiency in applying those guidelines.

When they give their approval, you will be granted the opportunity to experience a graduation ceremony, the Ceremony of Ascension. Once the ceremony is experienced, the candidate will have completed the requirements to become an "Ascended Master.

* * * * *

20

Qualifications and Requirements for Graduation and Ascension

Note: The objective for listing these qualifications is to help you qualify for graduation. It is in no way designed to make you feel that these goals are unattainable and thus inspire hopelessness. Your Spiritual Assistants know you can attain an appropriate level of consciousness for graduation. That is, when you decide to dedicate time and effort to working through these requirements. Many different Spiritual Assistants when asked will help you meet the qualifications in a reasonable amount of time. Thousands all over planet Earth have recently awakened to the need to make these changes in their lives on Earth. Consequently, many souls are meeting these Ascension qualifications daily. With dedication and perseverance, you can also meet the qualifications for graduation. The dividends for giving this opportunity your best shot will be so magnificent there are no words to describe them.

There is nothing you have to do outside of self to meet these qualifications and requirements. All qualifications and requirements already exist within each individual's consciousness. Thus, the objective is to remember and make the necessary adjustments within self to fully embrace the divinity within. Each individual is to tap into the wisdom of the heart and, as a being of love, bring out the God/Goddess within to assist you.

To complete these qualifications, spirit recommends working in a group to encourage each other. This creates a tremendous advantage because fifth-dimension consciousness is a consciousness of Oneness. Each individual adds a synergistic energy to the group to create a much more powerful connection to All-That-Is. All members of the group can contribute their energies and learn to relate to others within a consciousness of Oneness. As each individual contributes, he or/she becomes a part of the created group Oneness.

Listed below are third-dimensional tools for helping meet graduation requirements.

Knowing Who You Are and Belief in Creator Source

Your first and most important conscious activity is: *knowing who you are and believing in God/Goddess within.* You are an eternal creation of spirit and soul created in the image of the Creator Source (God/Goddess, ALL-THAT-IS.) Thus, the one primary requirement for Ascension is to know who you are. You are a spirit with a soul that is evolving through a series of incarnations throughout the Universe. Your magnificence is beyond imagination and has no limitations.

The degree to which you know who you are significantly determines your spiritual status. Also the degree to which you connect with your God/Goddess within also influences your future

> **Your most important spiritual understanding is to know who you are. Then become One with your God/Goddess.**

capabilities. We all have a responsibility to strengthen our beliefs and connections to Source. Once this connection is strengthened, from that point forward you can be open to receive rewards wherever you are in the Universe. Multitudes of opportunities beyond anything you could imagine will become available if you are willing to invest time in becoming "One" with your God/Goddess within. As you listen to guidance from within, your capabilities for soul development will accelerate geometrically. Reality is a spiritual concept that comes from being committed to allowing the Light to flow through your energy system to the Earth and other parts of creation. The books *The Power of "Now"* and *A New Earth: Awakening to Your Life's Purpose* by Eckhart Tolle should be required readings for your Ascension preparation. These spiritual guidelines will provide you with an understanding that can help keep you on track for your future experiences, regardless of where you are in your consciousness evolution. For example, in *A New Earth*, by Eckhart Tolle, there is a section entitled "The Peace That Passeth All Understanding."

Paraphrasing, the question is: What gives you your sense of identification and worth? Since the ego identifies with form, what would happen if you lost your identification with form? Who are you then?

Hopefully you realize you are not a form or profession; you are consciousness. That realization is called the peace of God. The ultimate truth of who you are is not I am this or I am that. That is, you are not a plumber or housewife; you are not a male or female; nor are you a physical person. You are Spirit consciousness, a component of The I-Am-That–I-Am, a spiritual part of God, an eternal creation with unlimited possibilities.

Preparing All of Your Bodies for Ascension

Ascension to a higher dimensional state of consciousness will require creating a new, healthy body. Within our research to understand "Subtle Energy" we have been working to develop procedures for manipulating "Subtle Energy." Listed below are a few major, important procedures (out of thousands) that need to be monitored in order to insure that your bodies are in the most desirable condition for achieving Ascension. You do not need to understand each procedure to ask for help; just ask. Spirit recommends you use accurate pendulum dowsing in communication with Universal Consciousness to monitor each of these procedures before and after you ask for help. Readings can be taken on a scale of minus ten to plus ten, where plus ten is the ideal. The object is to monitor the requested changes until they read within the range of plus five to plus ten.

(1) All holographic patterns (templates) should be completed and periodically updated by your spirit helpers. (2) All morphogenetic field patterns need to be cleared and balanced. (3) All 617 soul facets should be located, cleaned up, and properly installed in relation to all others. Then check to make sure all soul facets are harmonized with each other for maximum functional efficiency. (4) All twenty-two (plus) human energy bodies should be harmonized, synchronized, and integrated with your Holy Spirit Body. (5) External grid patterns around the body should be in place, balanced, and connected appropriately to the external and internal chakras and to all meridians and collaterals. (6) All three Mer-Ka-Ba tetrahedrons should be positioned appropriately: one stationary, one spinning clockwise, and the third spinning counter

clockwise, centered on the prana tube and balanced for optimum efficiency. This part of your "Light Body" is extremely important. (7) Until the physical body reaches "Light Body" status, each individual should supply the physical body with adequate minerals and vitamins and a balance of foods. Once "Light Body" status is accomplished, your body will require only a limited intake of external nutrients, because it will utilize available prana and photons. (8) All body cells should be constantly hydrated with clean, structured (meaning the molecular clusters are polarized and spinning counterclockwise) water that contains the love energy. (9) The pH and pOH of all body cells should be brought into balance so that the hydrogen (H^+) ions and the hydroxyl (OH^-) ions maintain a pH in the range of 6.5 to 7.0. (10) All adverse past life imbalances (discordant programs, karma, parallel event frames, and various vows, contracts, agreements, etc.) need to be uncreated and/or cleared from all energy bodies. (11) The emotional body's functional efficiency should be maintained with an ability to deal with all upcoming and potentially upsetting emotional situations. When the emotional body has been severely damaged and its efficiency is questionable, obtain a new one. (12) Each individual is responsible for clearing out all false beliefs, eliminating all forms of fear, and un-creating all third-dimensional illusions that have no purpose within the fourth and fifth states of dimensional consciousness. (13) Work needs to be underway to move from duality consciousness into Unity/Christ consciousness and to establish "Light Body" status. (14) The ego of the mind must be brought into balance and made respectful of the sensing systems of the heart and body. (15) All of the body's internal energy-flow systems need to be cleared and optimized so that all organs and glands receive proper energy. This involves centering the prana tube and clearing and balancing all of the outer and inner chakras (major, intermediate, and minor), brain strings, slip strings, axiatonal lines, meridians, collaterals, and core star. There are many other desirable energy-flow patterns. (16) Everyone should constantly monitor the availability of minerals, vitamins, iodine, electrolytes, and basic nutrients for optimum health. (17) Archangel Metatron, master of light, indicates that the energies of platinum and palladium are energies of Ascension. These rays are the most pristine vibratory rays in the Solar System. They can also assist in the recreation of all your new body parts. These platinum and palladium energies are available upon submitting a request to your Spiritual Assistants and should be drawn into your heart as you prepare for Ascension.

Within a channeling by Archangel Metatron, www.crystalinks.com, Metatron emphasizes the importance of the platinum ray energies.

> The energy of the platinum ray is a multidimensional frequency that has a unique utility that is manifested and drawn into the Ascension phase of planetary systems and humankind. In truth, dear ones, it has been used by many of you in other dimensions and planetary systems, and many of you chose to be here at this time to re-experience what you already know and to help others in their experience of Ascension. The platinum ray is the ray of crystalline light. Draw it into your hearts as you face the quickening of this marvelous event. You are entering the threshold of a cosmic leap, an enormous graduation, and it involves many aspects. It encompasses many tools, many components, and copious events that may or may not resonate with your sense of the Ascension.

Archangel Metatron goes on to discuss many copious events that must take place. For example, hurricanes, tornadoes, solar storms, earthquakes, and volcanic activity. Many of these events and others will be localized as opposed to global. In contrast, there are also global events such as global warming, changes in the weight distribution of water and land masses on Earth, the Earth's axis tilt, and reversal of the Earth's magnetic fields. The timing and details of these copious events are unknown. It is impossible to predict time line events because everything on Earth is in a state of flux and in reality clock (calendar) time is an illusion. That many of these events will occur is certain. They are part of the cleansing and preparation for Ascension. It would be helpful for you to prepare a chart of the above seventeen procedures to record their changes during specific time periods using accurate pendulum dowsing.

Clearing Limiting Duality Beliefs

Once you understand you can change anything, you will begin to understand there is neither good nor bad within the world. Who instilled within your energy system the idea that anything is good or bad, better or the best? Why did you accept these false, limiting, illusory beliefs? And why did you buy into all of the other duality beliefs as having reality? Spirit indicates that each illusion had a purpose in helping you suffer while here on Earth. Your challenge was to overcome that suffering.

However, for those interested in moving to Heaven on Earth within a new reality realm, a belief in good and evil is unnecessary and will no longer have any constructive value spiritually. All of creation *just is*. Enjoy the variety available without placing judgments on any one thing or any person as being better than another. Stop giving things labels, and stop putting things into preconceived boxes that hold like illusions. Erase your slate, empty those boxes, clean house, and let all that accumulated *stuff* go. Exercise patience, kindness, understanding, and acceptance, and believe that everything is in divine order. Then, as you avoid

> False, illusory beliefs created in the duality experiment need to be cleared. They cannot be carried into the fifth dimension.

passing judgment on anything, you can enjoy the wonderful variety of all your experiences. You can stop judging differences, live with less stress, and bring joy and balance into your life.

Requesting That Your "Light Quotient" Be Optimized

Live in the Light; Light made of photons is the primary building energy for all components of creation. In order to graduate and Ascend, one's flow of photon energy (Light Quotient) ratio should be at least 80 percent of its desired energy intensity on a scale of 0 to 100 percent. Use *accurate* pendulum dowsing to measure your "Light Quotient" percentage. The amount of light photon energy flowing through an individual is termed a "Light Quotient" and is related to your frequency acceleration. The "Light Quotient" can also be measured in Hawkins energy units, with a minimum of one thousand required for Ascension. You can also use accurate pendulum dowsing to measure Hawkins energy units. Living in the Light will help activate your DNA coding and open the necessary portals involved in increasing your dimensional consciousness. Many factors influence the rate of your frequency acceleration. People can request help from their Spiritual Assistants to bring the flow rate up to its appropriate level. The "Light- Quotient energy-flow rate should be gradually increased within safe limits in relation to any resistance. Continue to ask your Spiritual Assistants to remove any resistance and bring the flow rate up and maintain it above 80 percent, or close to one thousand Hawkins units.

What I Perceive Outside Me Is Really Within Me

The experience of reality is always a subjective experience because it is only through perception that you can know anything. Any experience of sight, sound, touch, taste, smell, feelings, thoughts, or subtle energy is completely dependent upon you being there to perceive it. There has been much said about the illusory nature of the world. The truth is that the world exists, but it does not exist outside of you as it seems. Your perceptions bring you the facts of anything outside, thus the world that appears outside is really in you. When you perceive anything at all, it belongs to you. *To perceive it is to own it.* The world belongs to you because it is you and only you who can perceive it. If there is someone or something in your life, it is because you can perceive it.

You have been taught that you are a part of the world. However, spirit says this is not a good understanding. You are much larger and grander than you have been taught. As you awaken to your true identity, you will recover your greatness, freedom, power, and strength of purpose that was lost when you fell asleep long ago. You will know the truth when you "Wake Up." You and only you can choose what

> What everyone "thinks they know" has always eventually been proven to be untrue.
> Knowing is relative to truth.

you will perceive. This is the most important gift you have—the free will to make choices. Therefore, the meanings or interpretations that you give your perceptions are highly important. What everyone "thinks they know" has always eventually been proven to be untrue, even though it seemed certain until it was questioned and disproved. Everything is relative, and there is much more than meets the eye. Here is where God/Goddess consciousness comes in. Once you understand that everything is inside you, the choice to experience Unity/Christ consciousness opens up a whole new world. You then better understand the phrases, "As above, so below" and "as within, so without," and that everything is energy. Nothing can exist without its antithesis (opposite) to balance it. Truth is Universal and Eternal. It needs no explanation and cannot be captured by words.

The spiritual lessons posted on the Web site www.God/Goddess channel.com are highly recommended. The world is a part of you; you are not a part of the world. What you bring inside you, via your perceptions, are illusory creations. What you experience *out there* is consciousness manifested and held in place by belief. It will be very important to find time to continue your studies about truth and reality, because that understanding will help acccelerate your spiritual progress.

Striving toward and Implementing Unity/Christ Consciousness

Uniting your consciousness reality with the Unity/Christ consciousness reality is required as a means of moving out of duality consciousness. Some boundary requirements and specific criteria have been put in place to help guide individuals towards Unity/Christ consciousness. Raising one's consciousness to the level of Unity/Christ consciousness is one of the primary requirements for graduation and Ascension. All individuals who are unable to embrace their Christhood will have to exit planet Earth because their frequency will be too low to physically survive on or within a fifth-dimensional planet. Many concepts within this book are briefly discussed to help you start implementing Unity/Christ consciousness.

There are many other third-dimension duality planets available within this Universe and other Universes that one can transfer to as a means of completing your specific duality lessons. If you prefer to remain upon a third-dimension planet, just make your request known to your High Self Spiritual Council and obtain a list of options. There are no judgments about your decision to remain upon a low-frequency planet. All is within divine order and related to your soul's spiritual evolution. Many Extraterrestrial groups are standing by to help you work through the various options and to help transport you to your planet of choice.

Applying the Twelve Golden Principles for Ascension

Lady Guinevere and Ascended Master Kuthumi have outlined twelve golden principles they consider the beginnings of Ascension. These principles are designed to help you fully know yourself. The objective for using these thought forms is also to help you to know *full Ascension*. Remember, the objective is to move your consciousness from a lower to a higher state. Because of the rapid changes on Earth, life is gradually becoming more frantic. One helpful tool for dealing with these frantic feelings is to shift your consciousness to become more balanced between masculine and feminine. It will also help to ask that your body move from *a low-frequency, carbon-based metabolism to a high-frequency, silicon-based metabolism.* To help facilitate this change, one good source of silica is the horsetail plant; other sources include fibrous plant tissues.

Recall that all plant cells contain silica as a means of creating structural rigidity. Plants must contain silica for strength in order to stand upright. The cell walls of plant stems have a high concentration of silica, the most abundant element on Earth. All rocks, sand, and soil contain high concentrations of silica. The human body is unable to metabolize silica in sand and soil. In order to metabolize silica select a carbon-bound source of silica in plant stems to bring your silica up to the appropriate level.

On the New Earth, we will become vegetarian. However, your major source of energy will be from light (photons) and prana, since we will inhabit lighter bodies.

Ascended Master Kuthumi on www.kuthumischool.com introduced a channeling discussion by stating:

"Now" let us briefly give to you the twelve golden principles that every single person on this planet will have to work through. This is true for everyone, regardless of their plans.

1. Truth: Truth is about being true to you. Acknowledge truth. Speak your truth and live your truth. Your truth should be in alignment with the truth of your God/Goddess within. Go within to listen for the truth (the still, small voice) and use that voice as your guide.

2. Love: Love is about practicing unconditional love and loving self. It is breaking out of conditional-love consciousness. Placing conditions on love is less than pure love. We are to love ourselves, others, and all of creation without questioning or judging.

3. Communication: As a member of the human race, we have a responsibility to communicate with our brothers and sisters and within all parts of nature and God/Goddess's creation. To communicate means to make meaningful contact with each other: humans, animals and plants.

4. Non-judgment: We must realize that to make valid judgments of others, we must have walked in their shoes. That is, we must have lived their lives. Any judgments you make will reflect back on you as one of your weaknesses. In many cases, judgments are actually reflecting what is lacking or in severe pain in the life of the person doing the judging.

5. Creativity: Creativity acts as a means of unconsciously processing that which is deeply wounded within a person. It allows a person to process what is being suppressed, repressed, or depressed. Creative process therapy is very important.

6. Consciousness: Living one's life unconsciously is living one's life irresponsibly. Living consciously means

always being aware of what is happening in your "Now" experiences. Be alert and attentive to everything happening around you. Living in a fog, separated from events around you, is dangerous and could cause serious injury.

7. Responsibility: Responsibility is simply the ability to respond to life. That means to take direct responsibility in your ability to lovingly respond to whatever life presents to you. Become responsible to deal with anything that comes your way.

8. Respect: It is very important to respect all of God/Goddess's creations, from the tiniest ant to the giant whale. All life forms have a purpose, and all deserve respect. It will be very difficult to respect yourself when you fail to show respect for anything else.

9. Loyalty: Be loyal to those who have trusted you and those who may come to cry on your shoulder. The dog is an example of loyalty. To develop your loyalties, listen to nature and notice how spirit communicates through music, art, and the channeled word.

10. Passion: Having passion for life brings forth creativity so one can fully experience life. Creativity is the life-giving force which guides the life you live today. Passion allows you to express your divinity and God/Goddess-given talents to assist others.

11. Justice: Justice brings balance. Be fair in your relationships and with yourself. This covers forgiveness of self and others; one of the most important healing processes known is forgiveness. Justice is for healing wounds. Every wound within self or afflicted on others must be healed before Ascension. Be prepared to face your past for healing; otherwise you will find yourself running in circles, like a dog chasing its own tail.

12. Faith: Faith allows one to keep one's eye on the Light of God/Goddess, even during the darkest of times. Faith will open a pathway out of stressful situations. Faith allows you to move mountains. Faith is your tool that becomes the key to your success in life.

These principles should be a part of everyone's life on Earth. Some individuals have been severely abused by others on Earth. Some have been known to manipulate these principles for their own selfish purposes. As a result they are trapped in their own pain and suffering. Everyone should be given a chance to find their own inner truth and the courage and strength to face their pain and suffering and move forward consciously. Some of these experiences have resulted in a buildup of guilt. Guilt-ridden people frequently take on poverty consciousness and have difficulty expressing love for themselves and others. Thus the importance of removing guilt consciousness. Everyone is required to live these principles as a part of their preparing for Ascension.

Become Emotionally Stable by Controlling Fear-based Feelings

The mental and emotional bodies should be cleared of all the low-frequency negativity stored during all past lives and in the present life. This means clearing out all discordant programs, all implants, attaching cords, imprints, karmic records, pain memories, anger, grief, sorrow, sickness, addictions, low self-esteem, miasmas, stress, tension, depression, and all destructive thought forms lodged in any energy body or body part. These energies need to be released from the subconscious mind, solar plexus, mental, and emotional bodies. One clearing procedure is to increase the high-frequency Love intensity until it cancels out the lower, negative frequencies. If you become highly emotionally charged about something, that state of being could lead to confusion and chaos. If the emotional experience spirals out of control, you can enter into an arena where you become unsure about whom and where you are. As a result, you could lose your sense of direction and stray from your spiritual path. Thus, avoid becoming emotionally charged over any event.

To become emotionally stable means to become centered emotionally. You have the appropriate amount of emotion to sufficiently sense your reality. If you lack emotional control, the chances are that you have some suppressed energy overlaid with an intense emotion. When this occurs, release the intense emotion. When you realize you are becoming excessively emotional about anything, you have strayed from your goals and ideals. These occurrences of excess emotion require considerable energy and help precondition the body for many imbalances that can lead to disease, sickness, and death. To become highly emotional about anything brings on extreme energetic imbalances that divert you from that position in your life called the "Centerline of Love. This process of living on the Centerline of Love can awaken the realization that you are the Creator of your every dream. The energy saved by avoiding becoming excessively emotional about anything can be used to create your dreams. The energy required to become emotional about something is quite intense. Frequently, those out-of-control emotions cause more harm than good. The warrior personality is more inclined towards Service to Self (STS) and uses emotional outbursts as a weapon.

When you spend energy on activities other than those on your chosen path, then that energy could have been used for more beneficial purposes. All available energy can move your life along your time line or path towards health, well-being, and the fulfillment of your reason for coming to Earth. You start with Service To Others (STO) rather than STS. This Center of Love pathway is a place of calmness that can lead to emotional healing when you focus your intent towards that goal. Emotional healing takes place when you can experience the completeness of all possibilities without any extremes, living calmly in the "Now."

To proceed on a path of enlightenment and Ascension requires that you bring into balance your world of emotions and feelings. If you are emotionally imbalanced, the process of shifting consciousness will stop short of your desired goal. Balancing your emotions means accessing the status of your feelings, gaining control, and creating a healthy, stable emotional body. I repeat: negative emotions create all kinds of stress which may become stored in a body part, and cause disharmony and thus damage your energy bodies. Many stresses can be correlated with an imbalance within your emotional bodies.

When you lose control of your emotions, closely examine your energy bodies. You will discover that negative thought forms can become lodged within that body part which is weak. I repeat: a majority

> **If you are emotionally imbalanced, the process of shifting consciousness will stop short of your desired goal.**

of all diseases have an associated emotional imbalance. These imbalances trigger changes within the chemical and electrical nature of your energy patterns.

One major reason you came to Earth was to gain control of your emotional bodies. You have five bodies that influence the functional efficiency of your third body, called the emotional body. Constantly monitor the functional efficiency of your Emotional Body using accurate pendulum dowsing. When your Emotional Body's energy becomes excessively low, determine the cause and seek help to heal your emotional body. You also have the option to request and receive a new Emotional Body if your old one is severely damaged. *When appropriate*, request your God/Goddess within and/or your High Self Spiritual Council for permission to obtain a new emotional body. If you obtain an affirmative to your request, ask your Spiritual Assistants to locate and install that new Emotional Body.

To avoid damaging your emotional body, when some hurt feeling comes up within the physical body, focus your consciousness on that part of the body. If the feeling is unpleasant, focus an energy ball where the feeling is most intense and just let it sit there briefly. Next, let go of all concern or any judgment associated with the feeling. Then move that ball of energy into your heart. Hold the ball of energy in the heart until it has shifted into a ball of Love. The old ball of damaging emotional energies is being replaced with a new, healing ball of Love energy. "Now" *believe* that the Love energy can heal all disturbances, and you can return to your "Centerline of Love.

The most efficient means of bringing fear under control is to become Love. Fear is the primary force that *stops* a person from growing into the Light and taking on "Light Body" status. Most fear represents a past life wound that we came to Earth to heal. The solution is to return to the Light and replace it with unconditional Love. Love energy is the force that propels one towards Ascension. The challenge comes when we endeavor to maintain that love as we shift to a higher state of dimensional consciousness. During the process of shifting, less-than-desirable stored emotions and fears frequently come up to be released. As these less-than-desirable thought forms come up, they must be cleared as soon as possible. To hold on to them is a significant error. Unless they are cleared, these adverse thoughts could rapidly manifest into your energy system, become amplified with thought and cause damage to many of your bodies. The Spiritual Hierarchy will work with you to identify and help clear your adverse thoughts.

It is a fact of nature that when any form of fear arises, humans have a tendency to play out their own fears. Once these fears have manifested in our daily lives, we have reduced or even destroyed our ability to balance our emotions and feelings. We have forced ourselves to deviate from the spiritual path and reduced our ability to shift to higher states of dimensional consciousness.

The Egyptians realized how important it was to control their emotions. They built temples for the specific purpose of gaining emotional control. *Caution! Be Alert!* When you have evolved to a higher dimensional state of consciousness and allowed fears to manifest in your consciousness, that behavior pattern can drop you back into the lower dimensions. Those attempts to move out of duality consciousness may have taken lifetimes. All that effort can be negated by one misguided, ill-created fear. An inability to control fear indicates you have failed to complete your third-dimension lessons. Thus back you go, right into the third-dimensional world of duality. You cannot take fears, associated negative emotions, or any mental or emotional instability into the fourth or the fifth dimensional state of consciousness. All such emotional imbalances would be very damaging to your high-frequency bodies and cause you to return to the third dimension. To remain within the higher-frequency states of dimensional con-

> **Avoid bringing any low-frequency thought form with you into the fifth dimension. It could propel you back to a lower dimension.**

sciousness requires that you overcome the duality consciousness fears and adverse thoughts of the third dimension. This will help you to shift towards Unity/Christ consciousness of the fifth dimension.

As you study the characteristics of those who have evolved to the higher dimensional states of consciousness, you will observe that they seldom exhibit any adverse emotional behavior. When you observe most Extraterrestrials, Ascended Master, and the Spiritual Hierarchy, you will notice emotional calmness as they interact with others. Also note the degree to which the soul called Barack Obama has control over his emotions.

Were you to carry any low-frequency thought forms (anything less than divine love) into the fifth dimension, these thoughts could be amplified over a thousand times in your mind and feelings. This would be so traumatic, it would be impossible to stay in the higher vibrations for any length of time. Prepare your Emotional Body for Ascension by filling it with love to help clear all low-frequency thoughts. That love will then radiate out to others as a healing energy. Radiating love energy is a high priority for maintaining a fifth-dimensional state of consciousness.

Being Receptive, Open-minded, and Discerning

To advance spiritually is very difficult for those who are closed-minded and have already figured everything out. A closed-minded, highly conservative person who is afraid to change and venture out into the unknown is a person who is in deep trouble and needs help. Fear of changing the old, familiar patterns could cause a challenge for those with closed minds. Spirit indicates that fear of change is unjustified. It indicates a lack of faith in God/God-

> **Humans who are closed-minded and think they have everything figured out will need to become receptive and open to new thoughts.**

dess to provide guidance in all you do. Much spiritual help is available upon request for those who need assistance. However, you must ask to receive it.

The spiritually minded soul is receptive and open-minded to the opportunities available. Obviously, one must use discernment to know the most appropriate pathway (time line) that leads your soul and spirit back to God. *Using discernment means to judge well with spiritual insight.* Take time to listen to the still, small voice within from God/Goddess and write down those thought forms, messages, on paper. Use those thoughts to develop a constructive plan to focus on. Start concentrating on those items in your "Now" life you would like to change. Once a plan is formulated, stick to the plan unless directed by God/Goddess to make changes. *For those on a Spiritual path, failure to develop a plan for your life and missed opportunities to focus on needed changes will no longer be acceptable. Nor will failure to discipline your-self be acceptable. These activities are a part of your preparation for Ascension.*

There is no place for complacency within the higher states of dimensional consciousness. The need to make changes is obvious to those who have realized that there will be many opportunities available at the higher dimensions. The secret is to dedicate your-self to the task of making the appropriate changes "Now." As each human works to make love-centered changes in his life, group consciousness will assist in bringing about the reality realm of the New Earth.

Understand Time and How to Control Time

Ascending humans are to become the masters of time. We all realize that our human spirits chose to go through "The Fall" and live within the world of illusory time and space on the third-dimension Earth. However, we are not bound by the illusion of time and space from a spiritual perspective. We are advised by the Spiritual Hierarchy to be in control of time and space, rather than having time and space control us. Spiritual evolution, Unity Consciousness, "Light Body" status, Graduation, and Ascension are all beyond the limitations of time and space. Ascension combines the spiritual world of non-time and the physical world of time. Love is the key to helping make this combination work in harmony, since love is truly in the "Now" moment and beyond time. Love always occurs within the "Now" moment, separate from time. When you live in the space of love, you are beyond time; there is no time but the present moment.

Many of you have had the feeling that time stood still when experiencing love—for example, when you were truly in love with someone else. All other time stood still and was perceptual only within perceived references related to past and future beliefs. When you under-

> **When you understand spiritual time, you will come to know it is a gift you can control to meet your needs.**

stand the perceptual nature of spiritual time, you can function consciously beyond time and change time to meet your needs. Time can be under your control. You can alter time for an intended purpose. You can shorten time or lengthen time, depending on your perception about the time required to meet your needs. You can be in control of time from your perception. Time is a gift, an energy force available to facilitate your creations. Following Ascension, you will be able to manipulate time to assist you in manifesting your thoughts. Start practicing "Now" to manipulate time.

In the book *Teachings from the Sacred Triangle*, the Arcturians, channeling through David Miller, discuss several key points concerning time. As you evolve spiritually, your concept of time will take on a totally new meaning. To understand what is happening, it is important for your conception of self to be integrated with time. This process relates to being in the "Now" where the past, present, and future all consciously exist simultaneously. You have then shifted your different selves within multiple time frames into "Now."

The Arcturians state:

> If you lose your multi-time reference, then you could make yourself vulnerable, especially when traveling inter-dimensionally to a planet in a lower dimension than the one you reside within. You could expose yourself to time warps when you are in a time shifting consciousness. Exposing yourself to the time shift without proper protection and training, could result in you're becoming caught in a time warp and be thrown back into the third dimension. This has happened to some of you before.
>
> One secret of all great healers on Earth lies in their ability to time shift. Time shifting helps you to Ascend and transform yourself. The secret of interplanetary travel is also linked to time shifting. Time shifting is the basis of entering the Jupiter corridor in your Solar System. When one goes through a time shift corridor, then one can travel great distances without losing biological time.

The Arcturians go on to explain how power spots on Earth can assist you with your ability to time shift. Also, using tones as part of your meditation can be a valuable tool for time shifting. Spirit suggests you become aware of the importance of working with time. As you proceed down your spiritual path, seek spiritual help for comprehending the process of time shifting. Seek additional helpful guidelines in books, on the Internet, and in workshops that will assist you in understanding time shifting.

Take On Perseverance, Faith, and Trust

Ask for strength to persevere and the faith and trust to complete the task that you volunteered to carry out when you came to Earth. Have faith and trust that you will be able to make the necessary adjustments to create a new you—to create a new body. Trust those who walk with you to find their own truths without bugging them about the truths you have discovered. Your opinions may be welcomed … when requested, and when you can express them diplomatically. Be accepting of others and yourself. Guide your Ascension and transition onto the New Earth with an open mind, grace, ease, laughter, and joy. Be ready to change your beliefs in order to accept new realities when they become self-evident and available. Remember, you are not your beliefs; you are spirit consciousness. Perseverance based on stubbornness and holding on to old illusions and false beliefs is unfounded and can sabotage your spiritual efforts.

> **ALERT!**
> **Holding on to old illusions and false beliefs can sabotage your spiritual efforts.**

By taking on perseverance, faith, and trust, you have opened a flow of energy to help manifest your desires. The opposite of these procedures blocks energy flow. Become fearless in searching for truth, knowing that there are multitudes of guides and Spiritual Assistants available to assist you at a moment's notice.

Know That What You Think, Pray for, and Verbalize, You Create

The danger of looking for a health problem or thinking about any health imbalance has been demonstrated to have a very undesirable *down side.* Practice avoiding thinking about a health-related imbalance within your body or another's body. Those thoughts could increase the severity of an imbalance or could actually create an imbalance. When visiting health care practitioners, exercise extreme caution in accepting their opinions. If you must give your power to a health care practitioner, consult more than one and ask God/Goddess about their accuracy. What you believe and fear is what you draw to you and create.

For example, recently an article was published about a woman dying of cancer. She was grief-stricken and did not understand why she had gotten cancer. She stated that she had *prayed all of her life not to get cancer.* The writer went on to explain that what you think about, you create. Her lifelong focus on cancer helped create the cancer. Other published information indicates that people who contribute to the American Cancer Society's drive for funds are more likely to get cancer compared to those who avoid contributing. Again, by thinking about cancer, individuals have increased the chances of creating that which they fear.

The medical profession and drug companies are very aware of the connection between what you think and what you create. A good example relates to the advertisements about potential diseases in relation to the promotion of drugs. The pharmaceutical industry advertises on television with the following suggestion. *You should ask your doctor if this drug is right for you.* By suggesting a potential problem, they create new customers. Other advertisements indicate a person should periodically get a medical checkup to see if anything is wrong within their body. As many observe, this is a great way to have the doctor or whomever look for something and bill the insurance company and make some steady money.

The material world exists because of the expectancy of the observer and his thoughts. In the movie *The Secret,* the producers do a good job emphasizing how powerful your thoughts are. However, if you believe in and want to use the services of health care practitioners, exercise extreme care in what you think about and avoid accepting any single opinion. Until you learn to heal yourself you should be grateful for the services of health care practitioners. However, to depend on someone or some drug to maintain your health means giving your power away to an outside force. Your body was designed to heal itself. By going within, you can ask God/Goddess and many other Spiritual Assistants to respond to your request for assistance.

Remember, many things we are told or have heard are opinions based on false beliefs and a limited understanding of Spiritual Law and how to manipulate Subtle Energy. If you are excessively open-minded to accepting others' opinions without question, then you may want to exercise caution when listening to and accepting negative thoughts broadcast on television or from any other source. By planting negative thoughts within an individual's consciousness, these manipulators create another client and thereby take that client's power and money away.

Being Aware of Your Every Thought

Be self-aware and prepared to monitor your thoughts every moment of the day. Realize that every thought is composed of Subtle Energy and can become a creation when focused upon. Focus on love, and you create love. Focus on fear, and you create fear. Those thoughts not only create your reality but also impact on the energy patterns (reality) of others. One good example is the power that a large group can have when its members focus their unified energy towards a specific opportunity to bring about change. When enough people think there is a need for rain, then rain comes. Years ago on *Coast to Coast AM with Art Bell*, Bell asked his millions of listeners to visualize rain in two areas of great need: a drought

> **Thoughts create your reality. Be very careful what you think. At the higher frequencies, thoughts manifest very rapidly.**

in Texas and a forest fire in Canada. In both cases, rain fell within hours. Many scientifically designed experiments have proven how the power of mass consciousness can influence a multitude of events on Earth, for example, weather modification and the alleviation of stress along fault lines in Earthquake-prone areas. One key to the successful manipulation of matter when using Subtle Energy is to generate positive thoughts based on divine will and the concepts of love. Keep in mind, the opposite of love is hate. Love is the most powerful force in the Universe, and you can utilize that force to help create a New Earth.

As your consciousness increases to the higher frequencies, be very careful what you think. Thought forms manifest much more rapidly at these higher frequencies. When you verbalize a thought, you add additional Subtle Energy to that thought. So be aware of what you say out loud. Sometime it is better to say nothing when additional energy could divert the thoughts of others towards expressing their warrior tendencies

Within the fifth-dimensional state of consciousness, it is possible to create anything you desire, even a new house. Once you raise your consciousness and Ascend, you can create your dreams. You can create new bodily features when you so desire. Recall that during the process of creation you visualize, create an etheric mold, add a control program, focus your intent, and fill the pattern with creative Subtle Energies (energies like love, light, and joy). In the fifth-dimensional world, the whole process of creating is very simple and quick. "Now" is the time to become aware of your every thought and gain control of those thoughts for your benefit and the benefit of others.

Finding Your Own Truth and Acting upon It

When a request is made for an expression of what is truth for you, it's very important to act upon your truth. It would be unwise to accept and express the truths of other well-meaning clergy, counselors, advisors, or friends. Also never falsify or exaggerate your truth for the supposed purpose of appearing superior (a know it all) and/or as a means of manipulating others. Anyone who lies about anything will pay a severe personal penalty, as the event is recorded in the nucleic acids of the DNA (your body cells) and your Akashic Records (your eternal records). All karmic wrongs have to be balanced to create an energy pattern that stands the test of time. Many patterns of imbalance can be traced to a failure to act on truth, even many lifetimes ago. Everything is happening "Now," and everything had and still has its purpose as a part of your lessons.

It may help to realize that your truth may not be anyone else's truth. Therefore, cease believing you know anything about what is true for anyone but yourself. There is never a need to try to convince someone else of your truths. When asked for your opinion, just say, "This is my truth, and it may have nothing to do with your truth." There is no such thing as "my truth is correct and your truth is wrong." Judgments of others are unacceptable in any form. Judgments are based on false belief systems, the ego's loss of control, and limiting illusions, all of which inhibit spiritual development and Ascension. Cease all judgments to avoid paying a stiff penalty in the future.

Importance of Honesty and Honoring Your Commitments

Regardless of how commitments are made, they should always be honored. All commitments should be honored regardless of the original intent or of ever-changing circumstances. When you commit within yourself or to commit to another, your intention is to carry out a task. Failing to follow through on that task indicates a lack of understanding of Spiritual Laws and the importance of being honest. Honesty with self is one of the high priorities for individuals interested in maintaining their health and well-being. Dishonesty sets up an energy pattern within the body that changes the DNA and destroys healthy metabolism, creating serious biochemical imbalances.

> **Dishonesty sets up an energy pattern within the body that changes the DNA and damages healthy metabolism.**

A truthful person will *walk his talk*. Any time you commit to anything, it is highly important to follow through. If the commitment was a mistake, then that should be immediately addressed and the commitment revised with all parties involved, thereby avoiding various repercussions, emotional pain, and many possible embarrassments. It would be better for you to limit all commitments until you understand

230

Universal Law and how to follow through with honesty. Honesty is the best policy.

Prana Life Force and Pranic Breathing—Body's Future Energy

One important procedure that will help bring all energetic changes into perspective is to practice Prana Breathing. Prana Breathing will pull in needed life-force energy from the Earth and Source that can help stabilize all your energy bodies.

Prana is a Sanskrit word that refers to a vital, life-sustaining force responsible for maintaining all living systems. Thus, prana is called the vital energy or life force principle of all natural processes of the Universe. The root word prana means "to fill with," in this situation, to fill with the life principle in action. The presence of prana within the human body is what distinguishes a living physical body from a dead one. As a living physical body dies, the prana, or life force, leaves the body through one of several orifices. Prana is in the food we eat, in the water we drink, in the Earth, the sunlight, and in the air we breathe. Prana is a subtle form of energy, a life force that apparently originates from the Great Central Sun, Alcyone, in the Milky Way Galaxy. Astronomical evidence has revealed that many solar and star systems revolve around this Great Central Sun. The Great Central Sun, Alcyone, is located in the center of the Pleiades star system, and is a major source of prana energy for our solar system.

> **Prana is a subtle form of energy responsible for maintaining all living systems.**

Prana is the energy behind all motion in the Universe. Prana provides the energy for the flow of rivers, the flow of thought, and the energetic force that activates your "Light Body." Through an understanding of prana and pranic breathing, you can cleanse and rejuvenate, and thus create your new bodies. As a result, you can dramatically increase your life span to the number of years you desire. Prana Breathing in combination with the intake of photons will become the energy sources for your fourth and fifth dimensional energy bodies on the New Earth.

In the future on the New Earth, obtaining oxygen for the physical boy will be for very specific purposes. The intake of Prana and photons will be your primary source of energy for most purposes. Thus, the requirement for edible food on the New Earth will be dramatically reduced.

During incarnations upon the continent of Lemuria and during other Golden Ages in the Universe, we naturally breathed prana. This is why the soft spot is present on the heads of babies. This is the area of the body where humans should naturally take in prana. But pranic breathing is not currently a natural practice with many humans on Earth. Currently, most humans obtain their prana in their food and through normal respiratory breathing. As humans eat less natural food, breathe polluted air, and drink poisonous water, they ingest less prana life-force energy. The lack of prana is evidenced by the physical, mental, emotional, psychological, and spiritual imbalances (diseases) rampant on planet Earth. On the New Earth you will need to breathe prana and take in photons. Spirit suggests that it is "Now" time to start practicing prana breathing and take in more light photons. Spend time in the sun every day to obtain adequate photons.

Traditionally, the yogic school of thought indicates you should bring in prana by doing pranic breathing through the lungs. In fact, if you cruise the Internet you will discover many Web sites on the science of Prana yam. Spiritual sources indicate that most yogis do not realize that proper *pranic breathing is not accomplished through the use of the lungs. Prana breathing is done by taking in prana through your pranic tube.* Your pranic tube is roughly the size of a fluorescent light tube, and it extends vertically directly through the center of your body. It passes through the pineal and thymus glands and your perineum. It does not bend with your spine. The upper portion is connected to the crown chakra site and extends out into space to tap into a prana source. The lower portion extends down through the base chakra site and is connected to a prana source within the Earth.

Pranic breathing will be especially useful when the Earth's magnetic shift is taking place. Your body is essentially a bipolar magnet. Around your body is a tube torus, doughnut-shaped magnetic field. Down the center of this doughnut shaped field is your prana tube. Recall that scientific research indicates the magnetic field of the Earth is dropping towards zero. In order to maintain a healthy body and retain your memory and reasoning capabilities, you should consider the following: Keep your prana tube centered through the middle of your body and keep your Mer-Ka-Ba "Light Body" centered and spinning appropriately. Make sure that your external grid energy patterns are balanced, your external and internal chakras are functional, and all energy cords are connected to the meridians and collaterals. These flow patterns are all required to deliver energy to all functional bodies and body parts. In order to deliver that energy efficiently, all of these energy-flow patterns should be appropriately balanced and harmonized every few days. There is also is a need to balance all polarity points in the body and insure that the electrical system is working appropriately. There are many Spiritual Assistants to call upon to help maintain these energy-flow patterns.

I repeat: currently your memory and awareness are tied to and held in place by the magnetic fields of the Earth. If you fail to maintain your Mer-Ka-Ba appropriately during "The Shift" when the magnetic field of the Earth drops to zero, you will lose your memory and reasoning ability. When this has happened in the past, the soul essentially reverted back to caveman consciousness. When the memory is lost one major choice would be to incarnate on another third-dimensional planet and start over again with a new contract and a revised spiritual path.

In addition to maintaining your Mer-Ka-Ba in good working order, you must also concentrate on learning to do pranic breathing. It is very important to bring this prana life force down from the cosmos and up from the Earth into your heart chakra. The prana flow should be continuous. As you train your body to use pranic breathing, a procedure it has forgotten how to perform, you will need to practice training your body to establish a pranic breathing pattern. The objective is for your pranic breathing process to become automatic all of the time. As the prana flows into the heart it should create a prana sphere. Then as you draw in more prana visualize this prana sphere expanding to encompass your entire body. When this happens, the continuous prana energy flow will enliven your body and also help activate and maintain your Mer-Ka-Ba. When your Mer-Ka-Ba is maintained, it creates its own magnetic field to replace the lost magnetic field of the Earth. By maintaining a functionally efficient Mer-Ka-Ba, you will have helped protect your memory, awareness, and reasoning ability.

These are choices and personal responsibilities you have to make in order to graduate and Ascend to the New Earth. No one else can make these choices for you, or muster the discipline required to maintain your Mer-Ka-Ba and other energy systems. You have many choices to make. You can ask for help from your Spiritual Assistants in making these choices, attempt to do everything on your own, or ignore the whole complicated process.

The creation of your pranic tube, the process of prana breathing, the maintenance of your Mer-Ka-Ba, and maintenance of the energy-flow circuits within the body are all designed to help you create and maintain a healthy new body. That healthy new body will assist you in shifting your consciousness from the third dimension to the fourth and fifth dimensional states of consciousness. The creation of the pranic energy body is critical to raising your frequency to the higher states of consciousness. In other words, to raise your consciousness and maintain that state will require prana energy.

There are many factors that can deplete your prana energy. Everything you do on Earth requires energy. All conscious and physical activity requires prana energy. To understand how these factors build or diminish your prana is beyond human comprehension. However, it is well established that the amount of prana within the body determines the quality of physical, mental, and emotional health. Maintaining a high level of prana is currently very important. It will become more important during the upcoming turbulent times. The presence of a strong prana body and a highly functional and balanced Mer-Ka-Ba "Light Body" will help protect you from the undesirable, dense, and destructive energies emitted by all conscious beings on Earth, including the Earth itself. Some protection is available by calling upon the Creator of Shields. Request that they adjust your Mer-Ka-Ba "Light Body" appropriately, and have them install a pyramid shield and a cocoon shield around your body, house, car, and property. Also request they add various surface features to the shields: mirrors, gold, white light, and gels that restrict the flow of adverse energies into your body.

Pranic Breathing Procedure

Begin training your body how to prana breathe by initially standing in your bare feet on a soil surface or on the grass, when available. Otherwise you can sit comfortably on the floor or a chair and visualize your Earth connection. The objective is to start by visualizing a connection to the Earth. Now visualize your prana tube extending through the center of your body, out the top of your head to as far away as possible, and down into the Earth for an appropriate distance.

Step 1: Begin with a physical, inhaling breath to bring prana up from the Earth, into your base chakra, and through the prana tube into the heart chakra. Continue the visualization of a continuous one-way flow of prana from the Earth into the heart. Note that the flow does not go in and out; it just flows up from the Earth. You should sense a feeling of life-force energy flowing up from Earth.

Step 2: Now breathe in prana from the cosmic realm from far above your head, down through the crown chakra, through the pineal and thymus glands, and down into the heart chakra.

Step 3: Next, visualize both of these flow patterns occurring simultaneously. Draw in prana from the Earth and from the Cosmos in a continuous flow pattern.

Step 4: As the simultaneous prana breathing continues from below and above, you should create a prana sphere in the heart center. Then request that this sphere increase in size to fill your entire body. Keep practicing these simple steps until you know the process has become automatic. Once you have developed a strong visualization of these steps, you can relax and allow your head to rest on something.

Step 5: Then, without thinking about the procedure, realize that prana is flowing throughout your body. If your mind won't shut up, just sit and watch it think until it becomes bored and stops. Then you can allow all thoughts to briefly come and go. Let everything go as you relax, allow all body parts to receive prana, and thus recharge all conceivable parts of your various energy bodies.

Bringing Balance between the Heart, Body, and Mind

Balancing of the heart, body, and mind will be required to create balance within your body's mental communication system. Everyone on Earth has been experiencing a war between the heart, body, and mind for many lifetimes. The heart, body, and mind each need to be allowed to optimize their individual and unique communication capabilities. The heart has intelligence and actually communicates with other hearts on planet Earth energetically. Your heart is literally talking to other hearts throughout the Earth. Every single beat of the heart sends out an electromagnetic pulse that extends out thousands of miles. Your heart has a sensing system that receives vibratory information by knowing and feeling. The body also has its own sensing system and picks up vibrations of light by sight, odors by smell, and hearing, touching, and tasting through other senses. The mind, working from the brain, gets its information by thinking and processing various vibrations stored within the body.

The balancing of the heart, body, and mind is a matter of letting each do its job and not more than its job. The mind's task is to take the heart's sense of knowingness and feeling and applying them in ways that allow thoughts to be in harmony with the body's sensing system. The mind's attempt and constant demand to take on the job of the heart's knowingness and feeling is a grievous error. This is the out-of-control ego mind trying to dictate to the heart. Likewise, the heart should never attempt

> **Balancing of the heart, body, and mind is a matter of letting each do its job. What is the job of each?**

to take on the tasks of the mind and attempt to apply its knowingness and feelings. The mind is the energy system that makes the applications. The body's sensing system should never reason that it is capable of knowing and feeling, nor attempt to apply the knowledge and feelings of the heart.

Remember, the heart, body, and mind each have their own way of receiving and/or working with vibratory information. Slow down or even stop that blasted, chattering mind. Many times, it thinks it knows and feels everything. That is a false belief; the mind lacks the ability to know and feel anything. The mind, controlled by the ego, has become overly cluttered with false beliefs, fears, judgments, and erroneous concepts. When all of these thought forms are put together, they could literally ruin your life and have for some humans. A majority of humans on Earth have abandoned their heart energies long ago to give priority to the mind. The mind does not have the wisdom of the heart and is unable to offer you the wisdom of the consciousness of God/Goddess.

The mind is limited by the information stored within the consciousness, much of which is total illusion and false beliefs. Real knowing comes from God/Goddess, that still, small voice within, which connects to All-That-Is, and to all other hearts throughout the Universe. The mind should be limited to its purpose: the processing of information from the heart and body. If you really want to improve your well-being and joy, stop listening to the ego-centered mind and start listening to the heart. There is intelligence and memory energy within the heart that is brought in from All-That-Is. The heart has the ability to choose the right action and guide your mind to be selective. The heart does not analyze; that is the mind's job. It's your responsibility to make sure the mind is doing *only its* job. The importance of these guidelines is beyond measure. Your state of well-being and graduation depends on your ability to balance the functions of the heart, mind, and body.

By learning how to listen to the heart, you will be provided with intelligent information to alleviate any imbalance within the body. By learning to live from the heart, you can limit any disease. Your heart's functional efficiency will improve as you speak from the heart and avoid speaking from the mind. Read these paragraphs several times. Implant these thoughts into your consciousness, and then make appropriate applications to your everyday activities.

Understand that the ego-centered mind attempts to satisfy itself through material means. The mental and emotional drive instilled by the ego towards gratification only increases man's misery. Spiritual discoveries have revealed that the ego-driven mind has no qualms about killing the body. We are all aware of how the mind can create addictions and self-punishment through such avenues as the use of alcohol and drugs. Such addictions also include a craving for processed, adulterated drinks and foods. Avoid paying attention to your mind's advice about how important the taste of any food or drink is. Very seldom does the taste of a drink or processed food, by itself, determine the quality of the item being tasted. Taste is for the joy of experiencing differences. Drink water and consume fresh, natural, unprocessed foods to obtain greater nutritional value and enjoy how each natural product tastes. Obviously, if something tastes moldy or poisonous, don't eat it.

Realize that the soul's hunger for spiritual food can never be satisfied by the body's drive to indulge the senses as a measure of value. This includes indulging in the body's cravings through excessive sex, tastes, and smells, hearing discordant sounds, and other short-lived feelings of ecstasy. These urges come from the mind; they do not originate from the heart. Follow the messages of the heart. Trust your heart; ask your mind to analyze what the senses detect in order to keep your body safe from all of the garbage marketed to you in this game of life on Earth.

Slow down. Go into your quiet place and listen to the heart. Develop a continuous state of peaceful meditation. The heart will inform you, as you listen, that you are made in the image of God/Goddess, whole and complete without the man-made illusions of drugs and many false beliefs about how the body's sensing and metabolic systems work.

> **Your Truth comes from the heart, not from the ego-centered mind. The ego-centered mind can ruin your life, even get you killed.**

These are illusions of the mind and the building blocks of the ego. The ego-driven mind wants you to think it knows what truth is. Your truth comes from the heart, not from the ego-centered mind.

As you bring into balance the heart, body, and mind, you can more accurately embrace the way of harmlessness in all areas of your life. The heart will guide you to respect and honor all of God/Goddess's creations. These abilities require the activation and use of the "Love Body." You will then be in a position to be of Service to Others a love-centered performer.

Every human on Earth is being monitored by advanced technology on board the Extraterrestrial vehicles of the Intergalactic Fleet from the "Confederation of Planets and Ashtar Command. Computers on board these spacecraft detect and record the extent to which your twelve strands of DNA have been activated, the functional efficiency of your internally designed Mer-Ka-Ba, the extent to which the Love

Body is aligned to activate your "Light Body," and the degree to which the heart, body, and mind have been balanced.

A certain percentage of the human population on Earth are bringing into balance their hearts, bodies, and minds. Also as they embrace love and compassion toward all life forms and all physical kingdoms (e.g., minerals and water) they are preparing for Ascension. These shifts within the consciousness of Ascending humans must take place before the Extraterrestrials and inner-Earth inhabitants will physically come to assist and educate humanity about how to live on the New Earth.

Here is a quote from Ahnahmar located in Telos, Mount Shasta, CA: *Telos Volume I,* by Aurelia Jones, 2004.

> But I say to you that the heart is always the Creator. In the pool of wisdom that the heart is, resides the true inspiration for all that surrounds you. The heart's language is subtle; however, it is often timid, for you have not given much support to the heart's frequency in your Dimension. In truth, the high incidence of heart disease on your plane is a direct symptom of this, as is most other disease.
>
> In your world, the leadership of the mind over the heart has led to strife, both internal and external; for the leadership of the mind tends to separate instead of unify. Yet the mind is a necessary tool in the process of creation, so then how do you reconcile this? To return to full consciousness, as divine being, it is imperative that you begin to turn the leadership over to the heart, and allow the heart to rule rather than the mind.

For a greater understanding about many aspects of Ascension, refer to the books by Aurelia Louise Jones, Telos Volumes I, II and III. Visit the Web site www.lemurianconnection.com to learn about a fifth-dimensional Society living in California.

Clearing Your Soul and All Bodies of Imbalances

Your Ascending body should be free from self-punishment, sickness, pain, and suffering so that when you shift to a higher frequency you are prepared to work on the new lessons outlined for your future on the New Earth's spiritual path. There is no value in taking an unhealthy body, one that is suffering pain and a host of mental and emotional imbalances, into the higher dimensional states of consciousness. Can you imagine what it would be like to arrive at Heaven on Earth within decrepit physical, mental, and emotional bodies and with a spiritually weak, inefficient spirit and soul? Such a body would have difficulty functioning within third-dimension consciousness; it would be almost nonfunctional within a fifth dimensional state of consciousness. One good place to start preparing your bodies for Ascension is to make sure all 617 soul facets are present, properly installed, and harmonized.

Also, search out procedures for working with your soul and its facets. After all, one of the reasons you came to Earth was your soul's evolutionary progression towards perfection. A fractured and damaged soul presents a serious challenge to its owner and calls for immediate action. Study and take workshops about how to maintain your soul. If you are unfamiliar with the structure of your soul, this should be a very high priority. The degree to which you keep your soul facets present and functional is very important. Seek help from your Spiritual Assistants when soul damage is detected.

There are literally hundreds of methods for clearing your energy bodies of imbalances. In fact, there are many books and Web sites about various clearing procedures. It is your responsibility to search out clearing procedures appropriate for you. Spirit indicates there is no value in holding on to all of the various imbalances that interfere with your health and well-being. Failure to work diligently to clear all of the harmful imbalances could have ramifications that slow your spiritual progress for centuries.

Letting Go of Your Third- Dimension Connections

Letting those third dimensional aspects of ourselves die and be transformed is an ongoing process that is required to Ascend, become a cosmic human master, and eventually become an Ascended Master. Your individual spirit and soul must let go of everything that could in any way bind it to the old, third dimension paradigms and duality illusions. This process has become a very difficult task for many humans on Earth. Regardless of the consequences, many have a tendency to hold on to old, outdated lifestyle patterns because of habit and fear of change, regardless of the consequences. This means that if you are serious about evolving spiritually, you need to let go of everything that gives you an Earthly identity and illusory self worth. Yes, that means letting go of family, friends, relationships, jobs, material possessions, plans, home, race, gender, sexual preference, and anything else that gives you some form of temporary happiness or fleeting satisfaction. One must also let go of all concepts and duality beliefs that bind you to the Earth plane. Let go of all the illusions and false beliefs you have learned from your parents, religious programming, and propaganda from self-centered interest

> **Let go of all your connections to the third-dimension. That's a major requirement for Ascension.**

groups disseminated through educational classes, workshops, and the media. *Let go of everything in your life that has no spiritual foundation or real, lasting value.*

All of these illusions, false beliefs, and limiting concepts need to be released to make room for the spiritual understandings needed within the higher dimensions of consciousness. The objective is to release anything that separates you from your belief about the God/Goddess within. Humans are requested and advised to allow everything that serves no useful spiritual purpose within the future higher reality realms to pass away.

This also means surrendering all your pain, wounds, attachments to suffering and victimhood, and any concept of enemy consciousness. There are no enemies except those you have created as illusions. The objective is to realize you are not a profession or a job title; you are nothing other than a great spirit, that essence of God/Goddess that can create all things within the new reality realm. Once you grasp what the fifth dimensional reality realm is like, as discussed in the three *Telos* books: TelosVolume1, TelosVolume2, TelosVolume3, and on the Web Site www.lemurianconnection.com, you can better understand the need to clear all impediments that could interfere with your future creations.

Clearing away and letting go of those aspects of yourself that have held you in bondage can open energetic space for the many new energies arriving on Earth. As you become aligned with the new energies and drive your bus backwards, you can examine your experiences and determine what worked for you in the past and what will not work in the future. In fact, by continuing to hang on to the old patterns, those self-destructive emotions and unhealthy relationships could create serious hostilities, and damage all your bodies. Some hostilities could become so intense that they interfere with your graduation.

The choices you make "Now" should be centered on the joy and happiness you feel and know every day. There is a need to focus on the rightness of any situation in which you are engaged, as guided from the heart. In any future decisions and/or relationships, it will be helpful to determine: (1) how you feel about the circumstances under which the decision and/or relationship was created, and (2) how you feel about the way the decision and/or relationship is maintained. Once these two criteria have been clearly resolved within your heart and mind, all other considerations will fall into place. From that solid foundation, you have established a pattern for developing a clear understanding for all of your future decisions and relationships. Then you will have opened up an opportunity and a pathway (time line) to explore and enjoy life as you never have before. All future activities and plans can originate from thoughts received from your God/Goddess within and guidance from your heart.

Importance of Gaining Control of Your Ego

Gaining control of the ego should be a high priority for those who are aware that they are being controlled by their ego. The original function of the ego has been altered over the centuries, and it can become very destructive when it creates a superiority complex. Start practicing "Now" how to introduce your own thoughts (not the ego's) into your consciousness. This process requires that you know the difference between the ego's unfounded directives and your mind's analysis of the heart's sound guidance from All-That-Is. Alter the activities of the ego so that it becomes your friend. That is, restore the ego to its original purposes: providing self-esteem, personal identity, and worthiness.

If you sense that you are judging or fighting anyone, then you are no different from the warrior; you are asleep and have strayed from your spiritual path. You are caught in the world of ego, where judgment, conflict, and warrior consciousness predominate.

Exercise extreme caution when listening to the mind as opposed to the heart, since the ego, tied to the mind, is quite frequently out to destroy you at all costs. In truth, your ego is what limits your life span here on third dimension Earth. When you admit to yourself that you need to get your ego under control, you can lengthen your life span.

The ego, within a majority of humans, is not a friend. Determine if your ego is your friend. The important task of controlling your ego is serious business. Some individuals' egos w''l seek to destroy any unsuspecting human when it fails to have its way. Many human deaths are triggered by an out-of-control ego. When the ego is out of control, it functions as an imbalanced mental and/or emotional system. Your ego's functional features

> **CAUTION:**
> **The ego, which is tied to the mind, can get out of control and destroy you.**

can be identified by asking your Spiritual Assistants. Your task is to make every effort possible to get to know your ego and thereby take control of it.

There is a great spiritual danger when it comes to the ego. The ego can become so enhanced after an individual obtains spiritual power and understanding that the ego will take that ability and seek personal power and material gain. Or the ego may instill fear and a false belief that faith in God/Goddess and spiritual power is insufficient to survive in this world. Either way, the ego can stop further spiritual growth until it is brought under control. The spiritual journey for many souls has been sidetracked or delayed by the ego. However, since no one is truly lost forever, there's always another chance down the time line, within this life or in a future lifetime, to get back on track. Why wait any longer to take control of your ego, a very important step? Act "Now."

Spirit recommends that you learn to live from the heart. In a majority of situations when the heart takes control of your guidance system, the ego will be restored to its original purpose. Learning to live from the heart will take dedication and practice. In the meantime, until you learn to live from the heart, cease listening to the thousands of thoughts the chattering ego presents to your mind. There will be no death to the altered ego, only transformation when you gain control.

Within the fully awakened human there will be a merging into what is termed a Balanced-Source Ego. Once you have awakened and brought the ego under control, you will have reached a state of Balanced-Source Ego. Then your altered ego can become your friend. Rather than listen to its insane voice flooding you with endless thoughts, choose to stay in your heart and use your mind constructively by inducing your own thoughts. Keep out of any battling mode with the ego.

When you struggle with a thing by giving it excessive attention, it can become more intensified. Avoid focusing attention on the ego. Doing battle with the ego can cause unwanted consequences and will deplete your energy. Simply inform your ego that all of the thoughts within your mind are to agree with the heart-felt consciousness within. *Then understand the power of directing your attention towards listening to the heart.*

Here are some meditative thoughts for assistance in helping stabilize your mental and emotional bodies: "I will withdraw the power I have given anything that could limit me. I suspend all judgments. I suspend all of my false beliefs. Furthermore, I "Now" understand and accept the reality that this world is one of illusions. This world does not have Laws that maintain or sustain those illusions; therefore, I can change my illusory creations and experience joy in everything. I "Now" choose to live by Universal Laws."

Love Body Attunement: Preparing for "Light Body" Activation

The foundation of all your creation needs to be guided from your God/Goddess within, in cooperation with The Council of Creators, including the Creator of Love, to bring everything you desire into existence. Creative thought forms all emanate from the void and from the concept of "Let There Be Light," the building block of all of creation. Thus these thought forms can all be equated to the heart of God/Goddess within or, as some believe, equated with the source of All-That-Is.

An important part of the current divine plan for spiritual evolution is to heal and activate the Love-Body, (the fifteenth body). For those who are receptive to following the divine plan, it is very important to activate and balance the Love Body. Originally, the Creator of Love willed that the divine masculine and divine feminine attributes would come into existence through the power and energy of Divine Love. These two attributes were originally in total balance and were housed within our fifteenth energy body, called the Love Body. When our souls chose to experience a state of separation during "The Fall," the masculine and feminine qualities split into two separate energy currents. That separation process damaged the Love Body. As a result, the energy of Divine Love became distorted, and the energy that passes through the "Love Body" to the Light Body also became distorted.

The state of duality separation, characteristic of the third dimensional state of consciousness, is a distortion of the energy state of Oneness. Hence, this state of separation brings about a distortion of the Divine Love energies in your Love Body. These distortions have allowed the entrance of adverse energies, those that are the opposite of love, called hate energies. For example, negative thought forms and false beliefs (hate-and fear-based energies) have become lodged within the Love Body. These distortions are anchored within Love Crystals that make up the Love Body and they are called discordant soul memories. These discordant soul memories also create energy blockages within all of the "Light Body" parts, including the Love Crystals, outer and inner chakras, water pathways, and the Diamond Plates. As result, your soul cannot anchor the quotient of Divine Love or Divine Light when these blockages are present. Healing the Love Body is therefore an essential prerequisite to taking on "Light Body" status. Also healing the Love Crystals, Diamond Plates, and the Love-Lines are essential for healing the Love Body and optimizing your well-being for spiritual evolution.

The Divine Mother's message on the Internet Web site www.star-knowledge.net discusses how important it is to heal the Love Crystals. In fact, the Divine Mother indicates that the healing of the Love Crystals is so important it could make a difference in the survival of the human species. You have an obligation to yourself and to your family, friends, and fellow man to gain an understanding of why the survival of the human is at stake because of damage to the Love Crystals. First of all, realize that to Ascend you will be required to obtain "Light Body" status. One place to start is on the Web site www.light-elixirs.com of the Ascend Foundation, distributed by Dr. Lillian Corredor. Accurate pendulum dowsing, tuned into Universal Consciousness indicates the information on these Web sites is quite accurate.

The Divine Love energies and Vital Life Force that emanate from "Spiritual Sources (for example, The Great Central Sun) are transferred across the Cosmos through *water*—that is, through Etheric Water within the Etheric realm, and through physical water in the physical realm. Therefore, the divine plan to heal the Love Body involves the healing of the waters of the Earth. This spiritual project was started by the Spiritual Hierarchy in the year 2000 AD and was to have been completed in 2007 AD. Light workers and many Spiritual Assistants from around the Earth's surface and within the Middle Earth and other internal Earth reality realms have been working during this period to heal the oceans, lakes, rivers, and underground waters. The healing process involves working with and opening the Love Portals of the Earth and healing the Love Portals of each human's Love Body to be receptive to the incoming Divine Love energies.

Everyone should check the functional efficiency of their Love-Body using accurate pendulum dowsing to make sure it has been cleared, repaired, and is capable of transferring Divine Love energies and Vital Life Forces into your "Light Body." Your responsibilities are to accurately pendulum dowse and ask for assistance from your Spiritual Assistants when dowsing indicates there is a need.

These activities are so important, spirit would like to repeat. Go within and request help from your God/Goddess to locate spiritual help to clear out all discordant soul memories. Then request that Spiritual Assistants repair all energy-flow pathways, including external and internal chakras, water pathways, and the Love Body, Love Crystals, and Love-Lines, and Diamond Plates. Also, request that all flow channels for divine energies be repaired to allow for optimum flow of Divine Love into and through the Love Body in order to activate the "Light Body."

"Light Body" Activation

One of the most exciting and important aspects of Ascension is the activation of your "Light Body." One of the most effective and efficient methods of activating your "Light Body" is working together within a spiritual group. The group should be specifically organized for the spiritual purposes of growth, STO, love of all creations, and "Light Body" activation. The process involves raising the frequency of your physical body (shifting to a higher dimensional consciousness) and lowering the frequency of your spirit body so they can merge together completely. These processes will need to be timed and synchronized with the amount of "Light Quotient" you are holding within your cells. The higher the Light Quotient is the less dense the physical body. The objective of the "Light Body" activation is to merge your physical body and your Higher Self into one energy system just preceding "The Shift," so it will be functional during Ascension.

> An exciting aspect of preparing for Ascension is the activation of your "Light Body."

There are twelve steps for "Light Body" activation that you will need to request help for implementation of the activation. Seek help from your Spiritual Assistants, God/Goddess within, various Creators and/or Archangels, and any other Spiritual helper you work with. Ask them to help you carry out the following steps to completion.

*Steps one through six: M*any individuals reading this material have successfully completed these initial steps (one through six) many years ago. In fact, most of your Spiritual Assistants completed these steps long ago. If you are initiating your spiritual program, ask your Spiritual Assistants to help carry out these first six steps.

Steps seven through ten are focused on one individual specialized area needing attention. In 1988, the Earth completed step three in its task of taking on "Light Body" Activation. The following approximate dates indicate when Earth herself completed the other steps: step four in 1989; step five in 1990; step six in 1991; step seven in 1992; step eight in 1994; step nine in 1997; step ten in 2001; and step eleven in 2005. Earth is "Now" completing step twelve. Thus Earth has completed most of these steps. Humans are "Now" in the process of catching up with Earth's "Light Body" Activation.

Earth's accomplishment of completing steps four through eleven has created a problem for those humans who are working on steps seven through eleven. Those individuals who are working on the steps below nine quite frequently experience some physical pain because they lack harmony with the higher spiritual frequencies of Earth. They may have more headaches, earaches, and muscle and joint pains. They also may have acquired increased nerve sensitivity that register as pain throughout their bodies.

Note: Several individuals are working on more than one step simultaneously. That is quite appropriate because of the collapse in available clock time and an unknown Ascension date.

Step Seven-Spiritual Changes: Step seven involves going through your first descent in the frequency of your spirit body and a noticeable spiritual awakening. At the same time, it will be very helpful to request that your physical body's dimensional state of consciousness be increased to approach the frequency of your spirit body (which is descending in frequency). The objective of these changes is to facilitate a merging of your physical body and spirit bodies within the same frequency range.

Step Eight-Physical Body Changes: Changes associated with step eight are more involved and require many months to complete. To accomplish these changes, an audible light code is being beamed towards your body. It is sensed as a hum that you can hear. The objective of the audible light code is to activate the physical body in order to get your attention. Your Spirit Guides will increase the intensity of the audible light code to a level that is safe but also loud enough that you can hear it. They would like for you to let them know if you hear or have heard the hum. If the hum becomes too loud, ask your Spiritual Assistants to turn the intensity down.

Those who have gone through step eight frequently experience extreme bodily changes, such as reduced physical body density. For example, with the density drop of the physical body, there may be an increase in body size and an increase in weight. The objective is to provide more space to contain the incoming spiritual energies. This weight gain may be reduced by frequent physical exercise such as swimming, bicycling, running, or weight training. You can help this process along by using any exercise that helps build muscle mass; in fact, this is the preferred approach. The increased muscle mass will help protect the nervous system and adipose tissue from the increased energies.

Note: Adipose tissue is used to store fat, and it will not protect the nervous system from the new spiritual energies like muscle mass will. In fact, the adipose tissues could fry when the incoming energies become too intense, causing damage to the insulin receptor cells. If at any time you sense excessive energy flow, ask your Spiritual Assistants to slow the flow rate.

Step-Nine Integrating Spiritual and Physical Changes: Step nine is designed to integrate the spiritual changes in step seven with the physical changes completed in step eight. These integrative processes have been designed to improve various aspects of your everyday life. During integration within step nine, the primary focus is on improving relationships. Step nine frequently begins and ends with fairly significant conflicts with those around you. As a result, you may be forced to seek out new relationships as guided by your still, small voice within. What happens is that any previous or current relationship that is based on control or manipulation, by you or someone else *becomes intolerable.* When this occurs and these relationships end, *it's a good thing.* As a result of the changes in your relationships, you may find yourself essentially alone. That experience is really OK; after all, the most important relationship you have is with yourself. When the time is right, new relationships can and may develop.

Step Ten-Energy clearing to manifest spiritual gifts: Step ten is very important because of its ability to help you become energetically clear. As you become energetically clear, your ability to use your spiritual talents and gifts will begin to manifest. Then you are better able to chart your own desired reality. One major objective of step ten is to change the way that available energy is stored within your bodies. At the lower states of dimensional consciousness, available energy is stored in the emotional and mental bodies. At higher states of dimensional consciousness, your primary energy-storage site needs to be changed to the spiritual body. Once this change has been accomplished, you can then transfer some of that energy stored in the spiritual body to any appropriate place for later use. That spiritually stored energy will become available upon demand.

To move your available energy to the spiritual body, ask for help and guidance from God/Goddess within to locate the most appropriate Spiritual Assistants to complete this task. As you proceed through step ten, it may feel as if you have been newly born and are very tender. You also begin to take on the talents of a *Spiritual Master* so that the newly developed spiritual gifts can be used in your everyday physical pursuits. As a result, you will want and need to live by your spiritual gifts. For example, if you are clairvoyant, that talent will literally overtake your sensing system

You may also begin to have many unique experiences. One day as you walk along a street, you will clearly see that the sidewalks have three curbs. This may initially be confusing. You will be seeing the physical curb, the etheric curb, and the fourth-dimensional curb. If you rely upon your clairvoyant sense, not your physical sense, you will know where to step. If you use your physical sense of sight, you will miss the curb and trip a few times. During these activities, you are releasing thought forms you will no longer need. These old thought forms are characteristic of the lower dimensions and have been stored within the mental and emotional bodies. Your current goal will be to practice relocating your spiritual body energy to the higher dimensions. Once accomplished, that energy will be readily available any time you need energy.

Appropriately using the energy stored within the spiritual body can create what many call miracles. The ordinary, low-frequency humans have their available energy locked up and stored within the memories, false beliefs, and emotions of the emotional and mental bodies.

The *Spiritual Master* has cleared his emotional and mental bodies and all other available energy and stored it within his/her spiritual body. The spiritually stored energy can then flow into the emotional and mental bodies to activate or energize their intended purpose. After the emotion or thought is completed, any excess energy automatically flows back to the spiritual body.

There is another significant advantage in making these changes in your energy-storage pattern. When you store your energy within the spiritual body, it remains in place until called upon for use. As a result, this stored energy has not been consumed by a chattering mind and by various types of emotional instability that can consume large quantities of energy. Completing step ten will make available more energy and allow you to perform miracles by manifesting your thoughts. You will be able to manifest your thoughts very rapidly, so exercise caution in what you think about.

Step Eleven-Involves continuing to manifest your spiritual abilities: Step eleven is a natural progression from step ten; many times the transition is very easy and hardly noticed. One's spiritual abilities continue to develop, and the physical body begins to change in appearance. During step eleven, your physical body may gradually become luminous. It may actually glow and appear more beautiful. Your friends and family may comment on how young you look. They may ask what is happening or what you did to bring about these changes. You may find yourself bringing up some of your deepest fears so that they can be cleared. When these thought forms come up, they should be released rapidly; otherwise, they could manifest within your daily life. You have nothing to fear but fear, when working through and experiencing the completion of step eleven.

Step Twelve-Completion of "Light Body" Activation: Step twelve is where "Light Body" Activation is being completed. Once you have completed it, you will have a new Ascension vehicle. This experience is characterized by the movement of your Mer-Ka-Ba into the heart center of your body. This Mer-Ka-Ba, sometimes referred to as a golden ball of light, is your vehicle of Ascension. This experience is the beginning of your physical body's Ascension into the fifth dimensional state of consciousness. There is no specific illusory time during which this event of the movement of the Mer-Ka-Ba into the heart center, takes place.

These Ascension events are personal events and can take place when you are alone, within a group, or as part of a collective experience of many souls. You will Ascend when you are ready. Ascensions are currently occurring all over the Earth and will continue to occur daily. Because you will have disappeared to the eyesight of third-dimensional entities, you could become a missing person. Very few humans on Earth are qualified to understand such an occurrence that you are missing because you Ascended.

Ascension is really a very simple thing. It is an event that has taken many years of preparation but occurs in an instant. But remember, you are still exactly where you were before you Ascended. The sun will still shine and the stars will twinkle, just as they always have. You have changed frequency and will experience other almost miraculous changes in your new reality. They are too numerous to mention. The whole process is a bit like when someone dies and moves to the fourth dimension in spirit form. Sometimes these spirit forms (disincarnates) become Earth bound and are unaware they are dead. As a result of thinking they are still alive in a physical body, they continue their daily activities.

Many light workers constantly encounter disincarnates needing help in returning to their chosen time lines. Helping them find the light, move through the tunnel, and progress to meet their Spiritual Assistants can be of tremendous help to these disincarnates unable to figure out various aspects of the spiritual realm.

One of the easiest ways to know you have Ascended and are still within a physical body is to notice the joy you have within. It is that state of consciousness that brings about a feeling of oneness with God/Goddess. It is a feeling that spiritual energies can and are flowing from All-That-Is through you. Another sign that occurs shortly after Ascension is the rapid manifestation in response to the fantasies that come up in your activities. These so called fantasies actually manifest very quickly as a discernable event or physical creation.

When the majority of those humans who plan to Ascend give up the game of polarity and move by choice into *joy* and *oneness*, then mass Ascension will occur. Until that time, "Light Body" Activations will continue. Mass Ascension ("The Shift") will occur when Spirit and the collective group of Spiritual Assistants decide the timing of the great event has arrived. When mass Ascension begins, everyone on Earth will sense something dramatic is happening. When "The Shift" is actually in full swing, it will be an event that has been anticipated for centuries.

As you work with your consciousness, implementing the qualifications listed above, you can create and become masterpieces of *joy*. Evaluate your life and clear everything that does not bring joy. By focusing on joy, you will establish a foundation on which to become the Spiritual Master you have always desired to be. By your very presence, others will experience joy. In fact, your spiritual energies will radiate out to everything in your area of influence. This path of joy, and the realization that one person can make a difference, makes the Ascension process not only very simple but brings much pleasure to everyone. There is no ego or sense of superiority with this feeling of joy, just a feeling of Service To Others (STO).

As you activate your "Light Body" you actually impact the planet Earth and its changes. Some of these changes may be somewhat frightening if you are unaware of their potential. Since you are on your spiritual path of Ascension, you have nothing to fear; you will be accepting of whatever happens. You "Now" know a little bit about what will take place during the Ascension process, and are ready for the experience of a lifetime. The joy and excitement have just begun. Have faith, believe, and know you are on your chosen path (time line).

* * * * *

21

Changing the Human Energy System to Create New Bodies

Unleashing Your Genetic Potential: DNA Activation

Within each cell of the human body there is a genetic blueprint for life called the double-stranded DNA helix. When the human soul reincarnates lifetime after lifetime, the DNA patterns present within your bodies are gradually altered to adjust to the new energies they encounter within each new environment. All of these changes on Earth and many more can be correlated with a change in human consciousness. Simultaneously, as the Earth shifts to a higher state of dimensional consciousness, the harmonics of the DNA within our physical cells and other forms of DNA are undergoing changes. The DNA changes that occur in combination with changes in consciousness are a very important part of the graduation and Ascension process.

Scientifically and energetically, it has been established that your DNA codes can and do change frequently. If you believe in a fixed genetic code, the usual scientific approach to understanding, then you must look outside yourself for healing. You may believe that some physical, scientific manipulation can be performed to alter your DNA and bring health. If you believe in a variable DNA code, then you are part of a spiritual and cultural transformation. You can look inside yourself for healing. You have within your consciousness the power to change your DNA and bring about healing without any outside influence or interference.

When a healing crisis develops within society, as is currently the case, humanity begins to look for more effective control alternatives. We can search for a weakness in the body's energy system that could account for the sensed demise. That weakness is quite frequently associated with a damaged DNA coding system. So how do we repair that DNA damage?

The very foundations of those weaknesses are believed to be stored within our DNA. All disturbances that the human physical body experiences while residing at the lower-dimensional vibrational frequencies, are known to alter our DNA. Sometimes that alteration results in metabolic damage to our bodies. The metabolic damage is caused by the action of low-frequency vibrations which alter the helical structure and the arrangement of the molecular components of the DNA. When the DNA becomes damaged, flaws develop within the communications between cells. This in turn alters normal metabolism. Such flaws are known to weaken the immune, lymph, and nervous systems. Each person needs to ask the question: What are those low-frequency vibrations that have the potential to damage my DNA? As you think about the differences between high- and low-frequency (love and hate) vibrations, you should be able to come up with some answers.

Experimental evidence is also available to indicate that DNA responds to thought forms. For example, several laboratories, experiments at the Institute of Heart Math in Boulder Creek, CA. have indicated that DNA can be changed in structure in response to an emotional thought, see www.heartmath.org. Comparisons were made between the emotions of love and fear. To set up one experiment, DNA was extracted from individual donors and placed in test tubes. Then other individuals held the test tubes, generated either love or fear, and directed those thought forms to the test tubes.

The results of the experiment revealed that the extracted DNA in the tubes changed in structure in response to the thought forms held in consciousness. When love energy was directed towards the tubes, the DNA molecules relaxed and unwound. In contrast, when fear was directed toward the tubes, the DNA molecules become tightly wound. Also, the donors of the DNA experienced love or fear feelings similar to that which was directed toward the tubes. That is, the emotions of the donors matched the emotions of those holding the tubes of DNA. By projecting love- and fear-based emotions to the extracted DNA, there was communication between the extracted DNA and the donors.

One system in the human body where changes in DNA take place is within human blood. In ancient times, when humans obtained food primarily by consuming dead animals, there was only one type of blood. Everybody had type O blood. About fifteen thousand years ago, a new blood type was detected. This change in the blood has been correlated with the period in Earth's history shortly after a great comet struck Earth off the coast of Atlantis. After the comet struck, the human population slowed their hunting of animals and started gathering and farming vegetables and grains as a food source. A shift in the diet caused a shift in the DNA. This new blood type, called type A, came about because of changes in the DNA. The new DNA coded for the production of new enzymes required to digest these new foods. Thus, type A blood came into existence as a result of the changed lifestyle.

As time progressed, two more changes in diet occurred with corresponding changes in DNA and the creation of blood types B and AB. Humans "Now" have four major blood types. However, additional changes have been detected by several research laboratories indicating that a potential new blood type is currently beginning to appear.

As consciousness increases, additional changes have been observed in many children. For example, the DNA of the newborns in China started changing in 1974. The Chinese have a large research program dedicated to understanding DNA differences in these new children. A detected DNA change within a Chinese boy was correlated with his ability to see with his ears. He actually had better sight with his ears than normal children have with their eyes.

These genetic changes appear to be related to a shift in consciousness. Children being born all over the world have many new and different characteristics. Some of these children are called Indigo Children and they currently account for 90 percent of the children born. In some parts of the world, these new children have a different liver, one designed to allow the body to consume junk food without adverse side effects. Again we see how food intake triggers a biological mechanism within the body to alter the DNA for survival.

Scientists have attempted to understand these environmentally induced changes by studying insects and animals. For example, it is well known that when cockroaches are fed insecticides in an attempt to eradicate them, many at first get sick and die. However, in a small percentage of the cockroaches, the DNA mutates so it codes for enzymes that metabolize the insecticide.

A somewhat similar pattern has developed in children exposed to HIV and AIDS; these children have undergone genetic changes that appear to have developed spontaneously due to the presence of AIDS. There is a new DNA pattern that creates a resistance to HIV. For example, a child in California at an early age was found to be susceptible to HIV. However, after exposure to HIV, the body responded with a genetic change in the child's DNA. As a result, the virus was eradicated from the child's body.

In more recent studies, scientists have reported that a large number of children are developing resistance to HIV. In addition, other children have developed DNA changes that render their bodies resistant to developing AIDS. Recent research studies statistically suggest that there are now sixty million people on Earth who have changed their DNA and "Now" have immunity to HIV. As the energy patterns around us change, we change genetically.

Drunvalo Melchizedek indicates that all of humanity is changing genetically as we move from the third- to the fourth-dimensional state of consciousness and higher. It is also interesting that scientists have discovered that the brains of Indigo Children's appear to be somehow connected to computer technology. Those who have kept deeply held secrets are concerned about the ability of these children to tap into their secrets. Some have called them hackers because of their capabilities. These children are much more capable of meshing with computer systems and have the mental capability to improve upon the features of computer hardware and software. Computers respond to their thought forms. These Indigo Children have a multitude of new characteristics that their parents lack. It has been proven by the Chinese government and other research groups that these new children can move energy by thought.

For example, one youngster demonstrated before an audience in China how he could move pills through a sealed bottle. As the youngster focused on the bottle of pills, he gave a command to the pills. The pills then passed through the glass bottle (without breakage) on to the table. In a related experiment, a coin was placed on the table outside of a bottle; at the command of a youngster, the coin entered the bottle. These are some simple examples of the fourth-dimensional consciousness capabilities that will be available for those who plan to graduate and Ascend.

The reason for describing these examples is to stress that everyone involved in Ascension will need to have their DNA repaired and changed to adjust to the new states of dimensional consciousness.

Without these changes, it will be impossible to Ascend to the New Earth. So how do we repair and adjust that DNA damage?

It is imperative that you take personal responsibility for requesting that you're DNA codes change for your new shifts in dimensional consciousness. That means the DNA code changes should be recorded in the majority of your energy bodies. For these changes to hold, you will need to transmute the carbon-based molecules within your body's structural features to silica-based crystalline molecules. The silica molecule is one primary feature of computer technology. Obviously, it will be very helpful for you to increase your intake of silica to assist this needed molecular change. The objective is to prepare the body cells and DNA to be able to receive the higher-frequency crystalline matrix of light that passes through the crystalline grid of the Earth and into your cells.

After you have increased the silica available, you will need spiritual help to carry out the required DNA changes. Request that you're God/Goddess within or High Self Spiritual Council call in Spiritual Genetic Engineers (Encodement Technicians) to help tune the emotion energizers, also called "Matrix Crystals" in your body. These crystals are in the cellular matrix within the subcutaneous walls of your physical cells. These "Matrix Crystals" regulate the pulsation of each DNA strand. In turn, each strand directs changes to its equivalent non-Physical or etheric DNA strand in the higher-frequency bodies. With these instructions, various physical and etheric DNA strands are altered structurally and energetically to function at a higher frequency. This is part of the preparation for "The Shift," graduation, and Ascension. Evidence indicates that you can consciously monitor these DNA changes to determine your spiritual status. To be more efficient, it will be very helpful for you to study genetic codes (DNA and RNA)and how they function; also seek guidance from the still small voices within so that you can phrase the most appropriate request. Then request that your God/Goddess within seek the most qualified Spiritual Assistants, Genetic Engineers and Encodement Techniques to make specific changes in your DNA

DNA within the human body has also been demonstrated to code for some chemicals introduced into the body. For example, in the 1960's I attended a medical workshop on LSD where it was reported that LSD flashbacks occurred several months after LSD exposure. The research team discovered that the flashbacks were caused by the body's production of LSD. The DNA within the body sensed the LSD (lysergic acid diethylamide) molecule and created an Artificial Encodement for its production. Similarly, my DNA has encoded for the production of acetylsalicylic acid (aspirin) after taking baby aspirin for three weeks. I am allergic to full strength aspirin that causes a swelling of my legs and feet. After three weeks on baby aspirin the aspirin concentration in the blood increased and my legs began to swell. To reduce the swelling I stopped taking aspirin and requested that my Spiritual Assistants remove the acetylsalicylic acid from my body. As the aspirin concentration came down the swelling started to decrease, but within three days the acetylsalicylic acid increased in the blood and swelling started up again, without taking aspirin. Pendulum dowsing indicates the presence of Artificial DNA Encodements for production of aspirin. To keep the aspirin concentration and swelling down these Artificial DNA Encodements had to be removed. When there is a need to know use accurate pendulum dowsing to monitor your DNA changes. These measurements will insure you that the appropriate changes have in fact taken place.

Many humans are in the process of changing their DNA for "The Shift" into the fourth-dimensional state of consciousness. Many individuals have requested that appropriate DNA changes take place in all their bodies to facilitate their new multidimensional capabilities. These changes will help shift all of your energy systems to the fourth, fifth, sixth, seventh, and eighth states of dimensional consciousness. You can change your life as you change your DNA. For additional helpful guidelines, read and study the book *Change Your DNA, Change Your Life* by Kathy Chapman as channeled from the Goddess, (Amma). Also study the channelings (through Cathy Chapman) from Amma published in the *Sedona Journal of Emergence* each month.

As you make concerted efforts to make the required changes in your DNA, you can become healthier. You may need to continually request that all of your energy systems be elevated to the most appropriate state of dimensional consciousness to help lock in the requested changes. These changes in consciousness can provide the foundation for creating new body parts.

The Ascension process will be much more efficient and less stressful when you have finished creating your new physical, mental, and emotional bodies. Before these new body parts can be created and maintained, the appropriate changes in DNA are required. Once the DNA is upgraded, clear and fine tune all energy flow patterns in order to supply the appropriate energies to maintain the new body parts.

In addition to the physical DNA, there are ten etheric - spiritual strands of DNA that have been dormant since the beginning of recorded history, approximately one hundred thousand years ago. When the Pleiadians came to Earth, they installed spiritual equipment (DNA) within one of the twenty kinds of humanoids present on Earth. This one group of humanoids had evolved to a higher-frequency state whereby they were ready to receive the genetic changes available. As a result, this humanoid group had a more functionally efficient DNA. As recently as twenty-five thousand years ago, human DNA was more adapted to the higher frequencies than it currently is. The Fall in consciousness resulted in damage to the human DNA. Humans "Now" have an opportunity to repair that damage.

Throughout history, many changes in the human DNA have occurred through genetic engineering, emotional imbalances, and changes in the environment. Human DNA is like a computer chip; different sections can be either in the on or off position. A torsion wave pattern from the soul actually programs the DNA, much like the operating system and software tells the chip in your computer to run. As a soul reincarnates lifetime after lifetime, its spiraling, torsion-wave, energetic signature will transfer the DNA inherited from the parents to create similarities in facial appearance, personality, and many other body characteristics. A new understanding indicates that the spiraling torsion wave of DNA radiates an energy field. One example of how this radiated wave influences another person's DNA is well known. When two people live together for many years, their torsion waves radiate out to each other, and these waves influence the other's DNA. Over time, the torsion waves alter both sets of DNA, and these two people begin to look and act alike.

There are many other examples of how the DNA molecule relates to man's evolutionary status. The importance of the features of human DNA is well known throughout the Universe. Extraterrestrials races working to assist Earth in the Ascension process have reported that they have equipment to monitor the human DNA of everyone on Earth. That information about a person's DNA structure is one good measure of an individual's spiritual status.

If you have chosen to Ascend, it is time to start creating your new, ageless body. That new physical body will be needed to pass through the Star Gates. If that is your choice, pay close attention to what is happening within the DNA located within your physical, mental, and emotional bodies.

To better understand the functional features of your bodies, it would be wise to listen to your spirit guides. For example, Joanna Cherry (refer to www.Ascensionmastery.com) tells of an experience during one of her Ascension Mastery workshops. Ramtha, a spiritual guide, had revealed to her that the pituitary gland (the master gland located two inches down from the top of the head) produces a death hormone in response to humanity's belief that the body must age and die. This death hormone causes various abnormalities to help bring on death through a series of metabolic and physical changes.

Learning of this information from Ramtha, Joanna asked her pituitary if this was true. The answer was, *"Yes, that is true."* Realizing that an individual can talk to any body part, Joanna talked to her pituitary as follows: "My beloved pituitary gland! I thank you and acknowledge you for having produced the death hormone in the past. That was exactly what I commanded you to do, and you have served me perfectly! I want you to know that I have remembered who I AM. I AM an unlimited God/Goddess-being who has absolute choice to determine all my life experiences! I have chosen to rejuvenate this beloved body. Therefore, it is time for you to cease producing the death hormone, and begin producing a life hormone. I ask you to do this "NOW."

Joanna then described her experience. "My head felt like it flipped off! Light began pouring in through the crown chakra. Within my pituitary gland I felt ecstasy! Then I heard this message from my pituitary. Thank you! Thank you for freeing me from a job I hated, and letting me do my real work, helping this body to be more alive and strong and beautiful every day!"

Since then, Joanna has requested that her RNA-DNA be shifted from the two helixes per cell to twelve; the number we had when we were vibrating at a higher state of dimensional consciousness. Joanna says it is very important to tune into the body and feel what is going on within each body part. By talking with each body part and knowing their individual conditions, you have a knowing of what to request. To ask and receive means you need to know the question and what spirit team to ask.

Joanna's experiences began in 1982. In 1998 she heard the thought from within: "Your body has now reached a non-dying state." Since then, Joanna has discovered that her ego has been against her rejuvenation efforts. In fact, the ego would come up with punishing experiences if she went against its suggestions. Old "aging" thoughts still resurfaced to hinder her rejuvenation. From Joanna's experience, we can gain some insights of how important it is to clear out all old false belief systems and continue to ask and receive. Anyone can ask that one's state of dimensional consciousness be raised to the most appropriate level and that the twelve strands of DNA be activated. You will then be in position to ask for your new body parts and your new Ascension body. For additional helpful suggestions refer to the book *New Cells, New Bodies, New Life,* by Virginia Essene, http://hilarion.com. Virginia provides a more complete description of how rejuvenation of the pituitary gland and other organs and glands can help rejuvenate your worn-out physical body.

The death hormone is the result of a DNA change and thus another illusion created by humans. The activation of the death hormone and deactivation of the rejuvenation hormone occurred at the end of the last twenty-five-thousand-year cycle during "The Fall of Atlantis. These changes, which resulted in a reduction in the life span of the human body, were created by altering the DNA codes and the light connections to the endocrine glands. These DNA changes increased the production of the death hormone and decreased the production of the rejuvenation hormone. Hormones produced by the endocrine glands are secreted into the body to regulate all kinds of metabolic patterns. Thus it is very important to work with your Spiritual Assistants to bring about repatterning, restructuring, and rejuvenation of all organs and glands to balance your energy patterns.

Scientific research at the National Institutes of Health at George Washington University and other research centers has discovered many factors that relate to aging and the onset of disease. For example, factors such as decreasing consumption of oxygen, low Thymosin, and low concentrations of DHEA (dehdrepiandrosterone) are all associated with aging. Dr. Norman Shealy discusses several (biochemical) factors related to aging in his book, *Life Beyond 100: Secrets of the Fountain of Youth*. In order to prepare your body for Ascension and "Light Body" status, your DNA must be re-patterned to bring all hormones back into balance to stop and/or reverse the aging process. One method of repatterning, called the "Melchizedek Program" is described on several Web sites (www.bethcoleman.net, www.light-elixirs.com, and www.unexplainable.net). Study all the information available on the Internet to help create your new body. One objective should be to align your "Light Body" through the chakra system. Then you can use the power codes and mantras described by Kalina Raphael Rose. These procedures can be used to deactivate the death hormones and reactivate the rejuvenation hormones. Follow these guidelines closely on the Internet, because as your Spiritual Assistants make hormonal changes, various emotions may be released. You need to be aware of this and ready to deal with them. That is, you will need to rapidly clear those undesirable emotions so as to avoid creating additional emotional imbalances.

Another factor related to the shortening of the human life span is damage to the light filaments connecting the DNA strands to the endocrine glands. We need to repair these connecting light filaments. Optimum performance of the endocrine glands is very important in raising the vibratory rate of the body to incorporate Unity/Christ Consciousness. It has been well established in scientific research that after puberty, via a programmed command, the pituitary gland begins to produce a death hormone. Remember that this command and others can be reversed, since the human physical body was originally designed to live for thousands of years. The possibility of living for thousands of years is still present. Your challenge is to learn how to regain your God/Goddess given potential and use that to change your evolutionary pattern.

Repatterning and Restructuring the Physical Body

Following the implementation of the procedures outlined in chapter 20 and here in chapter 21, you will have begun to make preparations to repattern and restructure your physical body for Ascension. We humans on Earth are faced with a significant challenge. If we are to take our bodies with us to the New Earth, we have no choice but to prepare our physical bodies to withstand the upcoming changes associated with "The Shift." The objective is to prepare your body for the conditions under which it must function during "The Shift"(transition) and on the New Earth.

To accomplish this challenge, you will be required to call upon various Spiritual Assistants who have the capabilities and tools to respond to your requests. The first objective is to decide that you want your physical body to be in total balance with your holographic template, which is in balance with your God/Goddess designed pattern stored within. Through desire, intention, meditation, prayer, faith, and belief, you can come to the realization that every part of your current physical body is the product of your holographic template and your thought processes. That is, you have helped create the body your spirit is "Now" riding in. If you have created a body that is imbalanced, then you can restore balance. Each balance and imbalance you created had a purpose. Both of these experiences within the Creator School called Earth, have provided you with an opportunity to understand your creative potential and grow spiritually.

When your body is in total alignment with God/Goddess, it is in perfect balance. In contrast, when there is a lack of balance somewhere within your body, something is out of alignment. To become whole, aligned, and healthy, the part of the body that is out of alignment with the God/Goddess within must be rebalanced.

Spirit indicates that the holographic template of your potentially perfect body is located within the God/Goddess "Master Cell." When we began our physical incarnations upon Earth, we came as a spiritual part of the Creator. The original "God/Goddess, Master Cell" resulted from the uniting of the sperm and egg during conception. That cell represents our beginning as a physical creation on Earth. As the God/Goddess, Master Cell divides and multiplies, the developing fetus takes on some of the characteristics of the parents, in addition to the God/Goddess aspects stored within the original Master Cell. Each cell within the developing body contains a replica of the genetic features that direct cell replication to create a specific body part. These genetic features within the DNA codes that originated from the holographic Master Cell create various electrochemical messages that control all biochemical systems in the physical body. Each human is, in reality, a part of God/Goddess that originally manifested within the holographic God/Goddess, Master Cell.

Once the soul of the incarnate enters the newborn (generally, close to the time of delivery), it provides its own coded information about its historical aspects. That is, it brings in various physical, mental, emotional, and spiritual patterns, those characteristics carried along with the evolving soul through many lifetimes. These energetic patterns are then stored within the God/Goddess, Master Cell. Thus, there is a need to clear some of the past-life programming encodements deposited into the God/Goddess, Master Cell carried over from your ancestors and past lives. Otherwise your past life encodements may become activated and magnified in this life.

To insure that the God/Goddess, Master Cell contains a relatively perfect hologram will require various clearings. To approach this ideal will require that undesirable past-life programs, carried in the incarnating soul, be cleared before you can create your new body parts. Once cleared, all other cells in the body can look to the God/Goddess, Master Cell as the ideal. Then you have the option to request help from your Spiritual Assistants to rejuvenate, repattern, and restructure all of your body parts and, as a result, obtain a new body. The physical body was originally designed to remain in perfect health for thousands of years. Why is this true? It is true because each cell within the physical body contains the ideal holographic template of the God/Goddess, master pattern. Our original cell that divided to create who we physically are was brought into existence from God/Goddess during the conception process.

That part of our humanness on Earth has been called the "perfect light of God/Goddess" that shines out through our God/Goddess, Master Cell. Many believe that this representative part of God/Goddess is a holographic spiritual template that is ever evolving. That template, brought into existence by the Creators of the Universe, and guided by Creator of Light and Creator of Love is a perfect replica of the God/Goddess within. As God/Goddess evolves to become more complete due to the activities of creation, the human God/Goddess, Master Cell has the potential to be constantly upgraded, that is when you request the upgrade.

As a result of The Fall, that perfect replica of the Holographic Template stored with the Master Cell has been altered by incarnating within a low-frequency, third-dimensional Creator school called Earth. With your decision to come to Earth, you took on duality consciousness. Within the duality aspects of creation, love is the highest frequency. Love is that which builds. The lowest frequency of creation is called hate; it is that which destroys. To repeat, love builds, while hate destroys.

To restore the God/Goddess, Master Cell and build balance throughout the body, we need to call upon the Creator of Love to instill within us total Love. With love, we can center all of our activities with positive, loving thoughts. In order for you to create your new, balanced, physical body, you will be required to strive towards becoming Love, expressing only positive thoughts throughout your daily walk on Earth. When you have shifted your consciousness to align with the God/Goddess within, you can pull in prana energy (via prana breathing) from All-That-Is. Channel that prana through your God/Goddess, Master Cell to direct the holographic templates therein to carry that potentially ideal pattern to the potentially ideal etheric mold that already remains within all the cells of your body. Utilizing these procedures as guided by your Spiritual Assistants will help create your new body.

You can then consciously direct prana and positive, loving, healing thoughts to that part of the body that needs balancing. Once the perfect etheric mold is patterned after the upgraded holographic template and it has been superimposed over the imbalanced cells, then the prana energy can download or upload so that the ideal pattern can manifest within the physical realm. As a result of the manifestation, the previously existing imbalance is brought back into balance. To assist all of these requests, additional Creators have expressed their interest in participating. Thus, you can call upon The Creator of Love, The Creator

of Light, The Creator of New Body Parts and The Crea
and their staff to respond to your request. As you prepare y
have a very clear understanding of your desires, and have
phrased question before you call upon these Creators for assi

Mycoplasma as Co-factors in Diseases and Maintaining Health

Those humans on Earth who plan to stay healthy, graduate, and
Ascend to the New Earth need to become aware of the threat Mycoplasma organisms pose to their health and survival. You may ask, what
are Mycoplasmas? Mycoplasmas are the smallest know free-living mi-
croorganism on Earth. They do not have a cell wall surrounding their
protoplasm like bacteria. Rather they have a pliable membrane - like a
tiny jelly fish. Individual cells take on many shapes depending on the
species and where they reside. As they grow in mass they create a fungal strand like structure, hence the name "Myco" designation for their
fungal features. Their mucous like appearance gives them a plasma
feature, thus the name Mycoplasma.

Mycoplasma were first isolated and identified in animals in 1898 at
the Pasteur Institute in France. The first human pathogen Mycoplasma
pneumonia (a pneumonia
incitent) was first identified
in the 1950s. Over one-hun-
dred species of Mycoplasma
have been isolated from
plants, animals and humans.

> **What are Mycoplasmas?**
> **Smallest know free-living organisms**
> **capable of threatening survival of**
> **all living systems.**

There are eight human pathogenic species: Mycoplasma pneumonia,
M. genitalum, M. fermentans, M. hominis, M. incognitos, M. pene-
trans, M. pirum, and Ureaplasma urealyticum. According to accurate
pendulum dowsing 84 percent of the worlds` human population and
97 percent of the U. S. population is infected with Mycoplasma. Because of their potential as significant human pathogens Mycoplasmas
have been genetically engineered as biological warfare agents. They
were used experimentally in the Gulf War and have been a significant
ingredient of aerial sprays categorized as "Chem-trails." Thus they are
easily disseminated in the air.

Mycoplasma can be easily disseminated from person to person by coughing and on the surfaces of objects. Once they enter a host (e.g. human) they become attached to the cells walls. They contain an unique plasma and protein coating that can mimic the cell wall of the host cell. Consequently they are called "Stealth" pathogens since they cannot be differentiated from the body's own cells; as a result they go undetected even with an electron microscope. Mycoplasmas are considered parasites because they rely on the nutrients of host cells for their energy source. Mycoplasma can also parasitize host cells without killing them, thus there is a reduced lack of symptoms to reveal their presence. They enter a cell and take control of the host cells RNA and DNA, inserting artificial encodements. Also once inside a cell they act like a living thorn; a persistent foreign substance that causes the host's immune defense mechanisms to wage war against healthy cells. As the pathogen grows within the cells it produces hydrogen peroxide and superoxide radicals they diffuse out to surrounding tissues to cause stress. This type of stress results in tissue symptoms that appear swollen and heated, and with painful inflammation, typical of many autoimmune disorders. They can invade and parasitize white blood cells and phagocytes (natural killer cells) that weaken the immune system. Once the blood cells become infected the Mycoplasma can spread to every part of the human body via the circulatory system. Once the immune system is compromised the Mycoplasma can damage the heart, liver, thyroid, pancreas, joints, skin, nervous system and any other body part. Once they enter the body cells they become hidden away like a spy who has infiltrated the defending army

Accurate pendulum dowsing has revealed that with some humans a large percentage of all body parts contain some Mycoplasma. These potential pathogens can cause specific diseases but generally they act as co-factors with many other disease inciting agents. Evidence indicates that the Mycoplasma can weaken body tissues rendering them more susceptible to other infectious agents or in other cases they invade tissues in which the immune system has been compromised by a lack of proper nutrition and/or the presence of toxins and heavy toxic metals.

A few examples of human diseases in which Mycoplasma have been incriminated as a major part of the disease complex are: fibromyalgia, chronic fatigue syndrome, cancers, multiple sclerosis, heart diseases and circulatory problems, intestinal diseases, cardititis, urinary tract infections, meningitis, encephalitis, Crohn's disease, ALS, lupus, AIDS, Gulf War Syndrome, rheumatoid arthritis, anemia, diabetes, asthma, leukemia, chromosomal aberrations, malignant transformations, tachycardia, eye and ear disorders, infertility, Scleroderma, endocrine gland disorders, gingivitis, periodontal (tooth) diseases, CNS disorders, Gullian-Barr syndrome, polyradiculitis, and low birth weight in infants.

Treatment options from health care practitioners are very limited. The use of conventional antibiotics indicates that since Mycoplasma lack cell walls they are resistant to many antibiotics. Why? Most antibiotics were designed to attack cell walls of bacteria. However some medical doctors continue to treat patients with several strong antibiotics. Frequently the side effects of the antibiotic treatment are more severe than the disease they are treating. Some health care practitioners are using natural antibiotics in an attempt to reduce Mycoplasma infections. For example: antibiotics from olive (olive leaf extract), and Neem leaf or seed extracts. Regardless of whether chemical or natural antibiotics are used these chemicals do not differentiate and can destroy the beneficial gastrointestinal organisms, helpful for digestion and elimination.

An alternative approach is to reduce the severity of Mycoplasma infection is to secure help from various Spiritual Assistants. There are many Spiritual Assistants who have the capability of transmuting, un-creating, phase shifting, or removing these organisms. Also one should consider asking for the use of the Violet ray or a sequence of colored light scanning's over the body to deactivate these microorganisms. However just removing them from the body does not solve the challenge these organisms pose. Shortly after their removal one can become re-infected unless attempts are made to develop resistance to their invasion. We have made requests for the Creators of New Body Parts, Light, Love, and Health to come up with a new immune system that could be installed within the human body of the third and fourth dimensional consciousness individuals. That request is currently under review and possible implementation. However, spirit indicates the most logical solution to the Mycoplasma challenge is to shift all body parts to a higher dimensional state of consciousness. Current experimental evidence indicates this poses a challenge. A request from our

Spiritual Assistants can result in the consciousness shift of a body part to a higher frequency, say within the fifth to seventh dimensional states of consciousness. The problem is holding that body part at the higher frequency. Over time, unless adjustments are made to clear all past life and ancestral carry over imbalances they pull the body part back into the lower frequency. The challenge is to detect these low frequency holding patterns and have them removed so we can become free of diseases.

Until we are able to clear our bodies of discordant programs and holding patterns our ability to create a new healthy high frequency body is limited. Without that new body the potential for passing through the Starr Gate to the New Earth is questionable. An unhealthy weakened body containing low frequency of second to fourth dimensional disease inciting agents, like the Mycoplasmas, is incompatible with the fifth to seventh dimensional frequencies of the New Earth. Consequently the need humans have to create new body parts and new bodies that meet the qualifications for graduation and Ascension.

* * * * *

Section V: Universal Laws and Shifts in Consciousness

22

Understanding Universal Laws and Shifts in Consciousness

Universal Laws provide the foundation on which the Universe is governed. Everything happens in accordance with Universal Law; whether one recognizes this reality or not makes no difference. For example, Edgar Cayce stated in one of his readings, "Every jot and tittle of the Law will be fulfilled." Only when individuals learn to live with and understand these Universal Laws will they come into harmony and into a state of Love and Well Being.

In order to increase the accuracy of your belief systems, raise your frequency of vibration, shift your consciousness towards oneness, and accelerate your Ascension into the higher dimensions, you will be required to apply Universal Laws to your life. All humans need to understand the importance of applying Universal Laws to their daily activities. Every thought you have will attract similar thoughts. These are stored in your subconscious mind and in your eternal Akashic records. Always remember that every thought is a prayer. To move forward on the Ascension pathway, one must take complete control of the mind by monitoring every thought. The use of positive affirmations, positive thinking, and visualizations of the preferred path (time line) can assist the mind with these tasks. Reject any thought that is not God/Goddess centered and in alignment with unconditional love for self and others. You could greatly benefit concerning an understanding of Universal Laws by studying the book *The Universal Laws of God* by Joshua David Stone and Gloria Excelsias, 2002.

Universal Law of Oneness

Since everything (Galaxy, rock, plant, animal, person, insect, and microbe) is created by God/Goddess, then all is Oneness. We are One with All-That-Is. We are One with God/Goddess: we always have been and always will be. *A Course in Miracles*, a book designed for spiritual enlightenment, says: "the one problem in life is separation from God."

This problem originated from the fact that everything humans sense on Earth is an illusion. Because of the mind, the prevailing belief is that what is sensed and thought about while on Earth is real. Humans have a tendency to live from the mind. The mind fails to understand that what is seen and thought about is a world of separation, a world of illusions. Without mind, all of these illusions would disappear. The illusion is a state of hypnosis; it only exists in our minds because our five senses thought the school play on Earth was real. Based on this sensed illusion, our perception of the world results in a belief system that is less than 10 percent accurate. The real world is not the physical sensing world our minds have created. The real world is a spiritual world vibrating at higher frequencies.

In order to apply the Universal Law of Oneness we must "Wake Up" and end the dream of the physical world. For many lifetimes we have lived this nightmare, this daily illusion that reality exists in the physical dimensions—the second and third dimensions, where we chose to experience duality and separation in order to work our way back and Ascend to the higher dimensions. That is, prepare to return to Source from where we came.

We have a responsibility to live a life of Oneness and realize that every thought we create affects every part of creation. We are One created body, a part of the all God/Goddess. Each of your thoughts affects everyone else in creation. This fact will become very important as you Ascend to the higher states of consciousness, where thoughts manifest rapidly. Below the fifth dimension there is a time gap, a buffer zone, between a thought and the manifestation of that thought into the physical realm. This is not true at the higher dimensions; the buffer zone is very small. As we evolve on the Ascension path, the manifestation time shortens. Therefore, within the higher dimensional states of consciousness, we will be required to apply the Law of Oneness in order to work with formless matter that is in chaos.

We should be learning how to use our creative skills in a manner that takes into consideration responsibility to ourselves and others and thereby reduces chaos and confusion. These efforts will help prepare us to function within the arena of Unity/Christ consciousness, characteristic of the higher dimensional states of consciousness. One of our goals is to become completely humble, gentle, and patient, bearing one another's burdens and living with unconditional love for all parts of creation. Through implementing the concepts of Unity/Christ consciousness, we will be in position to become co-Creators for the betterment of the whole of creation.

Universal Law of Manifestation

The Law of Manifestation involves the evolutionary development of the four major minds: conscious, subconscious, super-conscious, and soul-consciousness along with the cosmic consciousness, so that they can come into perfect balance and alignment with each other. All minds and energy bodies must be aligned for the rapid manifestation of that which you have asked assistance in creating. For this process to occur our minds must be attuned to our soul, High Self Spiritual Council and God/Goddess within. This is the key to working with the Law of Manifestation. As we implement this Law, it is important to realize that the Law of Manifestation operates whether we are consciously aware of it or not. Whatever we tell the subconscious mind, it responds to and acts on those thoughts. When you achieve a specific level of Ascension and become vigilant about every thought, then you can have everything you desire or need. Through the use of meditation and prayer, one can go within and manifest as a soul rather than as an individual personality. If we manifest from the consciousness of the personality, we will see ourselves as separate from our brothers and sisters, and separate from God/Goddess and Creation. This separation will cut us off from the source of spiritual energy flowing through us. By manifesting creations from the Unity/Christ consciousness level, our manifestations will be in alignment with God/Goddess, All-That-Is, functionally efficient, and capable of creating harmony. Subatomic malfunctioning creations are just the opposite; they create disharmony.

A good example of the misuse of your creative potential would be to take on and magnify warrior consciousness. You can frequently observe this destructive pattern by an individual's desire to fight. During the 2008 presidential election, one of the candidates continually used the word "fight" in his talks. That philosophy and behavior pattern is a very good example of low-frequency, third-dimension duality consciousness, as opposed to a more spiritually advanced, high-frequency, fifth-dimensional state of the Unity/Christ consciousness.

Your thoughts should manifest that which is beneficial to all of mankind and other components of creation. Any time you experience anything but perfection in your life, immediately pray and seek help from your God/Goddess within and from your High-Self Spiritual Council to neutralize any subatomic malfunctioning creations. In fact, it is always wise to seek the assistance of your Spiritual Councils in all of your manifestations. With their assistance, the possibility of creating a subatomic malfunctioning creation is reduced.

Before asking for a manifestation, ask permission from Universal Consciousness to make sure the proposed manifestation is in the best interest of all concerned. A positive answer insures that the free will of any or all other individuals in creation is not violated.

Another very important aspect of manifestation is not to become attached to the exact item you are trying to manifest. Attachments will short-circuit the flow of creative energy. Surrender is the key to success. Surrender your request, or, when the pattern for manifestation has been created, surrender it to God/Goddess and/or to your Spiritual Assistants. Throughout the process of manifestation, ask for God/Goddess's will to be done for the highest and best interest of all concerned.

In all prayer and creative manifestations, visualize the positive. Remember every thought is a prayer. To pray with a negative thought is a negative prayer. Visualizing a sickness before praying for healing, and then visualizing perfect health, are two prayers: one negative; the second positive. Visualizing a sickness adds sickness energy to the imbalance, increasing its intensity and severity. Since every thought is a prayer, the secret to the most appropriate thinking patterns is to learn to think and visualize positively, and always pray positively. Always exercise caution when applying the Law of Manifestation. The creative forces are perfectly happy to manifest the negative as well as the positive; they do not differentiate.

The Laws of Manifestation operate from our thoughts whether we are consciously aware of those thoughts or not. Your subconscious mind will follow whatever instructions you give it. The subconscious mind has no reasoning capabilities. If you constantly hold a negative thought for any length of time, it will manifest somewhere. If and when a negative thought enters the mind, immediately ask three times for it to be cancelled. Why three times? Nine is a completion number, and three threes equals nine. It's complete; it's done away with. When you forget to cancel, be prepared for the manifestation of an undesirable thought pattern.

Every moment of your life, day and night, the Laws of Manifestation are operating. A negative thought within your dreams can also manifest. Thus you must learn to control your dreams. It is easier to be very vigilant during our waking hours and to monitor every thought that enters our conscious minds. Remember, a large portion of your night dreams are reviewing various waking activities that can be just as real as day dreams. To help avoid negative creations during the night dream cycle, allow only positive thoughts of perfection, love, patience, tolerance, and health during the day cycle. The alternative is to allow negative thoughts to create scary dreams and nightmares.

In order to maintain continuity with Source energy, continually commune with God/Goddess during the daytime. It will be very helpful to establish a desirable daily pattern. Training the mind to have positive thoughts will assist us in having everything our hearts' desires and more. At this level of consciousness our four minds and cosmic mind are in harmony, balanced and integrated into Oneness. This process requires self-discipline. We must learn to discipline our minds, emotions, bodies, and all levels of our consciousness. These activities will hold the proper vibration for attunement of the soul. The goal will be to experience Oneness for the next phase of our soul growth. By using your God/Goddess-given potential for manifestation, your creativity will be maximized. Always strive to work with your internal guidance system as a means of helping bring Unity/Christ consciousness to Earth.

At all costs, avoid bowing down to the illusion of your ego. The ego can be very destructive when out of control. An individual ego that has established goals for recognition, glamour, money, and control has placed a roadblock in your path to manifest creations for the benefit of

all. The illusion of ego says, "I am better than those others. I am edu-
cated; I know what's best for them." What has happened? Ego has created the illusion of separation. Sometimes the problem is that we have
missed the mark in living the words of Jesus Christ when he said, "Love
thy neighbor as thyself." If you lack self-love, you feel undeserving. If
one is undeserving or lives with the philosophy of separation, one's ego
seeks recognition. To compensate, the ego tends to dominate. It creates
contradictions within the belief system that can enter into the creative
process to block the requested manifestation. When you truly learn to
master the Law of Manifestation, you realize that God/Goddess has
already given you everything that is needed. Failure is not a possibility.
When your request is not for the highest good of all concerned, then
your request may appear to have been denied. In reality, your perceived
denial was within the divine plan.

Manifestations are more likely to accelerate when you are enthu-
siastic, all of your energy bodies are synchronized and aligned, and a
strong intent has been generated. The mind should be attuned to your
soul, spirit, and God/Goddess within. Also, work closely with God/
Goddess within and with your High Self Spiritual Council, so that energy flow is maximized. It will be helpful for the feeling body and Love
Body to be attuned to your soul. In addition, your physical body needs
to be attuned to your emotional body. Then the following sequence
should occur: the emotional body is attuned to the mind, which is attuned to the soul, which is attuned to the Master Cell, which is attuned
to High-Self Spiritual Council and/or God/Goddess within. During
this process, keep the subconscious mind under control. If the subconscious says, *I don't think this is going to work*, then have that thought
canceled.

The whole process of manifestation involves working with Subtle
Energy through a process of transmuting one form of energy into another. The Law of Manifestation deals with the concept that energy follows thought. What you ask for already exists; you are just waiting for
its manifestation into a of physical, illusory reality. The energy change
is moving down from the higher frequencies to the lower frequencies
as manifestation proceeds.

When you add the spoken word to your request, you add power. The power of the spoken word is even greater than the power of

thought. Thus, always think carefully before you speak. Choose your words carefully. For example, assume you have been asked to assist someone with a broken finger. Rather than saying, "We are healing this broken finger," acknowledge out loud that the finger is whole, healthy, and healed. Eliminate any degree of doubt about the fact that the request has already been granted before you ask. To accelerate the process, it is desirable to build up enthusiasm as a means of increasing the vital life force that will bring the manifestation into the physical realm.

One of the great benefits of learning how to work with the Law of Manifestation is the change it brings about in an individual's well-being. As stated in *A Course in Miracles*: there is true pleasure in serving God. When one engages his feelings, subconscious mind, and emotional body, the process spiritually electrifies the whole being. With practice, these events make the manifestation faster, more efficient, exciting and in the long run more lasting. Meditation and prayer have their place within the whole process of manifestation. However, too much prayer and a lack of meditation is a sign of the lack of faith that God/Goddess has put in place the answer to your original prayer. If worry and doubt set in, then prayer may help overcome these limiting, negative effects. Realize that every thought is a prayer. Thus, monitor every thought as you pray in order to find a balance that fits your evolutionary path.

If, during "The Shift," the planet's climatic conditions result in an inability to grow food, then an alternative needs to be considered. If the food supply runs low, humans have their imaginations and creative manifesting abilities to create etheric mental food. Spirit indicates that etheric mental food can help sustain the physical body, when that becomes a part of your belief. Remember, thoughts are etheric energy and the precursors or templates to the formation of physical matter. Therefore, with a good imagination, an individual could create etheric bread and etheric beans, if he so chose. Then you could either consume the etheric food or request that the thought forms be materialized and then consume the materialized foods. Spirit indicates this procedure could be sufficient to keep the human body alive for quite awhile. This procedure will depend on your belief, confidence, and ability to work with the Law of Manifestation. A good example of manifestation is recorded in the King James Bible. Recall the story of how Jesus took bread from a boy's lunch and multiplied it to feed thousands. Jesus really did create physical food from the holographic template in the boy's lunch. Jesus also said: "Greater things will you do than I."

A word of caution: talking about your requested manifestation could dissipate your energy flow. Another problem that arises when sharing your excitement about your manifestation with others is that they may believe you're off your rocker, doubt your story, or become jealous. When this happens, they may generate negative energy which can penetrate your conscious and subconscious minds, creating doubt. The consequences of these events can be destructive to your consciousness.

It's frequently better to work quietly to create your manifestations. However, when caught up in negativity generated by others, always clear out that negativity as soon as possible. Rely on what you know is real for you. Rely upon your personal power, your subconscious mind, your High Self Spiritual Council, and all the available power from God/Goddess. This unbeatable team is always able to complete the task, regardless of what anyone else thinks.

Some ask about the desirability of working with others in the process of manifestation. Where two or more of like minds are gathered together, the creative energy is much more intense. Four unified minds can move mountains. One procedure which has worked for many is to have a small group individually write (through a process of agreement) the specific request and the approaches to be used. Each individual has an opportunity to phrase a specific request. Another possibility is to use a telephone conference call -- or to start at a prescribed time when each person is in his separate place for meditation. Then, before anyone begins, double check to make sure all group members are working together and using the same thoughts. All group members then repeat the request out loud three times. Following the audible request, each person simultaneously commands his subconscious minds take the request to his High Self Spiritual Councils for assistance in the manifestation.

After your manifestation has materialized, accept the outcome and give thanks. If you understand the Law of Manifestation, you will realize you have fulfilled the Law. Don't just believe the manifestation has occurred; rather, know it has with every cell, molecule, and atom of your being. It is finished; so be it.

Universal Law of Balancing Feminine and Masculine

One of the major prerequisites to achieving Ascension is the balancing of the feminine and masculine aspects of ourselves. This balancing involves a balancing of our intuitive right brain and our logical left brain functions. One side is not better than the other. The masculine left side provides the power and physical sensing system that masters the physical world. The feminine right side provides the ability to listen to the intuitive guidance that comes from God/Goddess and soul. Balance is an important part of all creation. There is a need to balance the creative elements fire, water, air, and Earth. For example, the four seasons of fall, winter, spring, and summer create a specific balance which allows for the growth of certain plants. Without balance there is limited growth or no growth.

When we are imbalanced, either strongly feminine or strongly masculine, we tend to seek balance outside ourselves by becoming close to a member of the opposite sex. We see this type of relationship between husband and wife, father and daughter, and mother and son.

If an individual is too energetically feminine, she will develop blind spots within her masculine side. She will likely be poor in business and mathematics and childlike in her behavior patterns. Her emotional body may take control. When the emotional body takes control, negative, ego-directed emotions and feelings can emerge. When these patterns express outwardly, it indicates the person has lost her Godliness for a period of time.

If an individual is too masculine, he will have blind spots within his social relationships and lack the ability to have heartfelt emotions toward others. One with excessive masculinity will have problems establishing healthy romantic relationships. He will have a tendency to be critical and judgmental about minor incidents. The excessively masculine personality will lack intuitive capabilities. Thus he must rely upon his physical senses for making decisions, a very inaccurate procedure. The physical world-sensing system of the left brain provides an information accuracy potential of about 10 percent, compared to an accuracy rate from Universal Consciousness God/Goddess of 100 percent.

An inaccurate sensing system reduces people's ability to relate to other parts of creation because they do not try to understand others. They lack the tools to try. As a result, they have difficulty in solving daily challenges and make poor managers of their families or businesses. The masculine personality has a very inaccurate belief system that constantly guides him down a path of extreme challenges. These individuals seldom understand what is really happening within the world around them.

The right side of the brain, or the intuitive side, has the potential to discover the remaining 90 percent of the masculine-dominant's missing sensing capabilities. However, excessively feminine personalities can also face severe challenges. With the lack of masculine personality traits, there are limitations concerning their ability to apply what they intuitively know from left brain capabilities.

The masculine and feminine traits are two distinctively different areas of awareness; both traits are required for balance. All people have a responsibility to develop both their female and male traits. The male is at a tremendous disadvantage when he fails to develop his feminine side. He loses 90 percent of his potential to understand reality. If males were to totally access their intuitive side, all their questions could be answered instantaneously. Consequently, there would theoretically be no reason for these males to remain on Earth. Perhaps this is the reason the male holds so tightly to his repeating patterns of left-brain dominance, lifetime after lifetime.

To have power without love is to become emotionally dysfunctional. The reverse is also true. To love without power is to become emotionally dysfunctional. The issue of balancing the feminine and masculine relates to balancing one's physical, emotional, mental, and spiritual bodies. In addition, you are required to balance your three local minds: conscious, subconscious and super-conscious. An important daily prayer is to ask for help in balancing your bodies and minds. Ask your God/Goddess within and High Self Spiritual Council to assist in balancing the feminine and masculine natures. This is necessary in achieving spiritual progress for graduation and Ascension. It is highly important for both sexes to realize they were designed to become balanced personalities. Therefore, everyone has a responsibility to concentrate on understanding the differences between feminine and masculine personalities. Once you understand the differences, strive for a balance with a minimum level of 45 percent to 55 percent either way. This shift in consciousness is one very helpful means of moving out of duality consciousness and into Unity/Christ consciousness. A submissive female or macho male indicates extreme imbalance and an inability to utilize all aspects of the brain. The objective is to prepare oneself to balance brain functions as a prelude to utilizing a higher percentage of the brain's capabilities. The current functional efficiency of out-of-balance individuals is around10 percent. This is unacceptable for future activities within fifth-dimensional consciousness. A minimum of 80 percent efficiency will be helpful for graduation, Ascension, and life on the New Earth.

One established method for balancing the masculine and feminine personalities is to change your sex every so often as you repeatedly incarnate on Earth. This procedure is helpful, but alone is inadequate to bring balance. Each person must accept and integrate the desirable features of the opposite sex every time they incarnate on Earth. Once balanced, the conflict between the sexes is greatly reduced. Both females and males can practice taking on the personalities of the opposite sex frequently. *Balance of the male and female attributes is very important.*

Universal Law of Integrated Prayer

Prayer is one of the most important spiritual practices known to man. The reason prayer is so important is that the God/Goddess force is not allowed to assist mankind unless there is a specific request. Humans incarnated on Earth have been given free choice to work out their challenges without interruption. The most effective prayer is one guided by a belief that when you ask, you will receive an answer. Some pray and then go through a period of self-doubt that could partially sabotage the prayer. The doubt would indicate a lack of faith in knowing that an answer will be forthcoming. The ultimate belief is that prayers are already answered before one asks. A positive attitude in all of life, including one's prayer life, is also a key to successful prayer. In order to know when the prayer is answered, one needs to utilize all sensing systems: the outer five senses, the inner sensing system, the still, small voice within, and the remembrance and interpretation of one's dreams.

The effective prayer involves an integration of the spirit body, mental body, emotional body, "Light Body," and the physical body with its many senses. These should all be in alignment with the belief and knowing that the God/Goddess force will come to answer the prayer. If you are going to pray, then why not fully believe and know that what you are asking for will in reality come to pass? Otherwise, why waste time in prayer? Other important ingredients of an effective prayer are trust and patience. This test involves trusting God/Goddess's Laws and teachings. Jesus said, "Ask and ye shall receive! Knock and the door shall be opened!" But one must be patient awaiting the answer. The prayer is made at the subtle energy level, a higher frequency than the physical level. From the subtle to the physical there is a download time for manifestation. While waiting, have patience. Hold on to the faith that an answer will come from some source. There is always the possibility of losing one's faith and trust because of a lack of patience. Having patience, faith, and trust go a long way in assisting your spiritual journey.

True prayer is a co-creation between God/Goddess and the sons and daughters of God/Goddess. All of mankind can be classified as God/Goddess's sons and daughters, since all were created by God/Goddess. Some refer to Jesus Christ as the only Son of God; this is obviously a false belief. How narrow-minded, self-centered, and judgmental it is to think God/Goddess had only one Son or only one Daughter.

The secret to hearing the answers to a prayer request involves aligning all aspects of your individual self to become involved in a co-creation with God/Goddess's energy. Put yourself in the hands of God/Goddess. Then, through a process of meditation, quiet the body and listen to the still, small voice within for the answer. This procedure has been proven very effective.

Universal Law of Integrated Meditation

While prayer is talking to God/Goddess, meditation is listening to God/Goddess within. Many people will say they pray frequently. But when asked how often they meditate and listen to God/Goddess, their answers are less definitive. In fact, some say they have never meditated. Meditation is just as important as prayer. Why pray when there is no time to listen for the answer? Some believe the reason for the lack of meditation is that many conscious minds are restless and difficult to control. Meditation takes self-control, a discipline worthy of the effort required. The ability to sit still and be quiet appears to be a major challenge for humans, especially in our Caucasian societies. The negative ego may be partly responsible for a lack of discipline; however, it can be controlled with help from your Spiritual Assistants.

There are many good books on meditation and hundreds of suggested meditations available that could be helpful. Different types of meditation have been developed for different purposes. The secret to good meditation is to find a place and time when one can quiet the body and mind. The meditation could either be active or quiet. An active meditation would involve repeating some word or phrase that speeds up the activation process. Channeling could be considered a form of meditation in which a spirit is contacted and information flows to the receiver. Remember, you can channel God/Goddess with practice. Soul travel and bilocation are also meditation techniques capable of assisting you in contacting the spirit realm.

Self-hypnosis can also be used for the purpose of preparing oneself for meditation and communication with God/Goddess. This is considered a quiet meditation, where all chatter of the mind is eliminated and one listens within. The presence of God/Goddess resides in the heart and, if we can learn to move into the null zone between thoughts in a quiet place, we can experience a peace that passes all understanding within the null zone, and we can pick up spiritual thoughts.

In reality, every moment of life could and should be be a meditation, since every moment could be spent finding our spiritual paths. Our goal should be to make life a beautiful meditation where we live in synchronicity, awaiting the hand of God/Goddess and his servants to help us incarnated human spirits set up a series of events that make life a joy. By living in the "Now," you bring into your reality all of your past and future lives (and for some, your parallel lives). All lives are taking place in the "Now." Thus your past, present, and future are all present "Now" with you in your every moment. As a result, you can not only control your current "Now," but also you can control your past and future "Now." Therefore, you are in charge of your past "Now" and your future "Now."

Universal Law of Dreams

Our dreams are in part a mirror of our lives, originating from either the subconscious or the super-conscious levels of mind. Dreams reveal how we think and act during our conscious, awake periods. Night dreams are like receiving a newspaper every night, since most humans have seven to ten dreams per night. Dreams can be run on automatic pilot, or you can have some control over your dreams. Your dream feedback mechanism is a very important part of life on Earth. When you learn to work with the feedback dreams provide, the information can provide you with daily guidance.

To remember dreams requires some effort. First, one must request to remember the dream before taking on a sleep state. Then at the end of each dream when the mind approaches a waking state, brain frequency increases and rapid eye movement (REM) occurs. When this happens, "Wake Up" just enough to record a few key points about the dream in a dream notebook. This will help you remember other portions of the dream. After fully awakening, record the dream details in your notebook. After a series of recorded dreams, it will be helpful to review them to detect a pattern. Over a period of time, one can study the dream notebook and detect trends that help the dreamer understand the most efficient path to follow. Based on dream interpretations, you can make attitude adjustments to align the conscious, subconscious, and super-conscious so they can become synchronized and work as a team.

Dreams contain a universal language of symbols. Obtain a good book on dream symbols and interpretation and work through the symbols revealed in your dreams. Avoid some dream books with limited accuracy concerning the symbolic meanings. During your interpretations always work within and ask what each symbol means to you for a more accurate understanding. By working through this process, you can gain insight into the understanding of the thought patterns that are daily manifesting themselves in your dreams.

Each group of symbols gives insight to the lessons currently in progress. That is, every symbol represents an aspect on one's self. Frequently, the symbol means something very specific to the dreamer. Thus, the dreamer's interpretation is generally more accurate than the universal interpretation of a symbol. Exercise caution to keep the negative ego from making inaccurate interpretations of dreams. Ego can interpret a dream so that it reinforces a false belief system, a method of maintaining the status quo. False interpretations can result in improper guidance and stall the Ascension process. As you proceed along the spiritual path, some dreams will be spiritual in nature. These dreams can be inner-plane spiritual encounters where the individual recalls attending spiritual classes. Some dreams can be precognitive; future events are played out in the present "Now." These dreams can prepare you for significant upcoming events and give you insights as to how to best work out the details. Some dreams may be actual encounters with those within the spiritual realms, such as Ascended Masters, members of our Spiritual Councils, or one of the Archangels. Some dreams are hardly worth working with because of the difficulties required to make clear the interpretations.

Do not let dreams control your life. If you don't like the way a dream turned out, request changes. The next night, just before bed, reprogram the dream as you like. When you wake up before a dream is complete, the next evening, just before going to sleep, ask that the dream be continued so you can better understand its meaning.

Keep in mind that many dreams originate from the subconscious, which has no reasoning power. What your subconscious mind is doing is reflecting on the thoughts, feelings, and behavior patterns that have occurred during the day. The dreams are not telling you what to do. They are showing you what you are doing and providing possible alternatives for change. By recording your dreams and working with the interpretations, you can adjust your conscious activities as a means of assisting the soul along its spiritual path.

Universal Law of Temptation

Temptation is the end result of the negative ego trying to guide us off the straight and narrow Ascension pathway. Negative ego has a tendency to both misinterpret reality and direct us to indulge in pleasure-seeking and overindulgence. In general, temptation pulls you down into what is termed your carnal self. This process initially takes the form of a desire to indulge in an activity that will provide some form of temporary pleasure as a means of escaping reality. For example, the desire to watch television, when there are many more important activities that need your attention, can be a big temptation. Video and television addicts escape into a make-believe world as an alternative reality to self discipline and control of their ego. This escape allows a person to avoid all kinds of responsibilities.

One major interest of the negative ego is the pleasure it receives by taking control. The negative ego utilizes bad habits to provide the energy in thought to pollute several of the thirteen bodies with thought forms from the lower realms. These lower realms are the opposite of the love of God/Goddess. They are part of the negative polarity within the third dimension that is used by humanity to know the difference between the illusion of good and evil. We all have gone through these lessons. Therefore, we need to be patient with ourselves and our brothers and sisters as we learn the importance of communing with God/Goddess and the understanding of unconditional love. Sexual love has its place when conducted with a proper attitude. When used for selfish pleasure, it is destructive. Many marriages and relationships have been damaged by this form of negative ego activity. In Christianity, these temptation thoughts are referred to as originating from the devil, or Satan. The cop-out is, "The devil made me do it." Hogwash! The ego self sought the pleasures of lower types of behavior, below what the animal world would ever consider. In reality, the terms "devil" and "Satan" are nothing more than man's symbols for illusions about the individual's negative ego that is out of control. In Hinduism, the negative ego is termed "illusion." Even though they are illusions, they still exist, just as all of the other illusions exist in the lower dimensions. These illusions exist as creations of humans. Humans create illusions as a feedback mechanism for the third dimensional lessons and associated challenges.

Thus illusions relate to the perspective of their value in learning how to create and un-create within the school room called Earth.

Temptation is designed to pull you away from the Ascension path. One important way to avoid such a pull is to make a concerted effort to get back on the Ascension pathway. God/Goddess can help you stay on or return to the Ascension path if you but ask. However, the God/Goddess within expects you to control your reactions to temptation. All humans have free will to destroy themselves. God/Goddess will not take total responsibility for controlling your reactions to temptations.

There are several methods that can help control temptations. One is to pray to God/Goddess. Ask for the strength and intelligence to know how damaging temptation is to the overall energy system. Also, you need to ask your guardian angels and spirit guides for help in keeping the negative ego under control. The use of positive affirmations, such as repeating certain mantras (e.g., "ohm") is helpful. Many other procedures are available and discussed in self-help books.

When you are busy serving others, you have a limited amount of time to fall into the pit of temptation. Thus serving others is a means by which you can overcome temptation. You can take your eyes off self when serving and realize we are all connected as brothers and sisters, and we need to help each other. An idle mind is ripe for a fall into negative ego, dark force illusory workshop, and a dirty-dark place. The Light of God/Goddess can clean out such an illusory place. There is no sin other than being self-centered. By becoming self-centered and controlled by the ego, you have missed the mark. You have sinned against self. All so-called sins are a self centered weakness associated with believing that you are separate self centered. When you believe you are separate, your primarily focus is on self. What is termed "sin" originates by acting on a temptation, either mentally or physically. Mental energy becomes physical activity. As a man thinks in his heart, so is he. You can miss the mark through your thoughts and actions.

The key is to become conscious when starting to indulge in negative ego thinking. Direct your attention towards making a positive response to the temptation. At this point, just stop without judgment and ask for forgiveness to help cancel all negative ego thinking. *Perfection is avoiding making mistakes.* God/Goddess does not expect perfection at any level of consciousness. Even if we give into the negative ego or to temptation, it is not the end of the world. It is just a mistake, and by making mistakes we can learn. Righteousness, in the eyes of God/ Goddess, is trying. One major secret to overcoming temptation is to take control of your personal power. When we learn to take back our personal power, we will indeed be moving towards Ascension.

Some individuals, aware that they are giving into temptation, make the mistake of listening to the negative ego when it says. *You have already totally blown it, so you might as well just continue.* Wow! Keep alert; *do not* compound a small mistake by making it a bigger one. To become a conscious victim makes it even worse. The key is to forgive your-self for missed opportunities. Once you have forgiven yourself, you have moved beyond that specific lesson to the next lesson. At this point in the sequence, you can choose unconditional love for yourself and learn from your mistakes. One theory is that incarnated humans make mistakes in order to set up new challenges from which to learn. However, to continue making the same mistake over and over is ridiculous. *Some would define these repetitious behavior patterns as a form of insanity, expecting a different outcome when we keep doing the same thing over and over again.* However, always remember that God/Goddess is faithful and will not let you be tempted beyond what you can bear. God/Goddess will provide a way out. Once out of the trap, you can head back on the graduation and Ascension path.

Universal Law of Service

The best way to find your-self is to lose your-self in service to others (STO). This statement has unlimited potential for understanding why we are here. As you examine the Law of Service, this ancient proverb has merit. "One who is pure in heart has the strength of ten." Similarly, in *A Course in Miracles*, Jesus asked the question of man," Is there anything more exciting than serving the One who created and embodies all of Creation, Isn't serving God the most glorious thing in the Universe?" Jesus stated at another time, "If any man desires to be first, the same shall be the last of all, and servant of all!"

Regardless of what one does in life, the most important thing is the attitude and perspective one has towards one's job responsibility.

I remember when I was living in Wichita, Kansas, years ago, and our garbage collector said, "My greatest joy in life is doing the best I know how in picking up the garbage on my daily routes."

That comment has stuck in my mind for more than forty-five years. He was the best garbage collector I have met in my eighty years on Earth. Mother Teresa once said "Love cannot remain by itself; it has no meaning. Love has to be put into action and that action into service. Another has stated, See each customer as God/Goddess, which is who they are, and treat them as such." See your-self as God/Goddess! See your interactions with other humans as relationships within a family where each is a son or daughter of God/Goddess serving other sons and daughters of God/Goddess.

Some people are trying to serve from a place of not being right with self, but from trying to be right with God/Goddess. It is a noble thing to want to be of service, but service begins with self. You must first stay centered, whole, and complete within—then you are ready for service towards others. Each person is to love self first. Taking the attitude of self-love into service for others makes work a pleasure and a joy. Serving self and others becomes a spiritual practice, which is the joy of serving God/Goddess. When we are serving the God/Goddess within ourselves, our brothers, and our sisters, we can grasp the concepts of Oneness.

As you serve from a pure heart and with pure motivations, you bring the love of God/Goddess to Earth and help make the world a better place. Some individuals may guard against serving others for the purpose of retaining their individual power, fame, self-love, self-worth, approval, or praise. You can serve others as you realize that there is true pleasure and joy in serving. Joshua 24:2 says, "As for me and my house, we will serve the Lord."

Universal Law of Unconditional Love

When another person's life and welfare means more to you than your own, you can say you have love. Anything less than willingness to serve others with love is just business as usual, the world of give and take. Scientists researching the influence of love on the human body have discovered that love heals. Love can improve a person's metabolism and change the DNA within the genetics of a person. The power of love is the greatest power on the face of the Earth. There is only one condition for loving: to love without conditions.

The foundation of such a belief system is that when one loves unconditionally, there are no judgments, no conditions, no attachments, no boundaries, no restrictions, and no attitudes that interfere with recognizing the God/Goddess within others. Jesus said in John 13:35, "By this shall all men know that ye are my disciples, if ye have love one to another." He also said, "The whole Law could be summed up as, Love the Lord thy God with all your heart and soul and mind and love thy neighbor as you love yourself." Yes, the male translators of the Bible purposely left out the Goddess aspect of God/Goddess in order to establish a male-dominated society.

In reality, each person on Earth is an expression of One spirit, God/Goddess and their thoughts, feelings, actions, and behavior patterns should be demonstrating that. What we give, we get back. If a person desires to have love, he must give love. Earth is a school where we are learning to love unconditionally. In our daily walk of loving self and others, we demonstrate by our actions what Unconditional love really looks like. The process of loving takes patience and practice. We have been brainwashed to believe in conditional love, which means that another person must meet some requirement to deserve our love. When we are demonstrating conditional love, we are unconsciously attacking. Someone who is sensitive or aware can realize there is an attack underway somewhere. All of humanity is connected at the thinking level; consequently, all humans are sensitive and can become aware of those attacks a self centered person sends out.

As soon as you think of someone, you have made a connection to that person's energy field. If you attack, then you become fearful because you expect the other to attack back. Conditional love is guided by ego. To truly love, you will need to work with and control your ego first.

Unconditional love is guided by God/Goddess. I repeat: unconditional love means loving one another unconditionally with the understanding that every component of creation (animal, plant, rock, bird, tree, and human) is a part of God/Goddess and Universal Consciousness. Unconditional love extends out to include all parts of creation. In a true sense of the meaning, humanity's love occurs because we *are* love. We were created in love with guidance from the Creator of Love.

One helpful practice that everyone can use in their relationships is to let anyone who comes in contact with you leave happier and thankful they made that contact. Shed a little bit (or a lot) of kindness on all those around you during your daily activities. Share kindness in your smile, kindness in your eyes, kindness in your face, and kindness in your warm greeting while walking the street, in person, on the telephone, or on the Internet. Love has many desirable attributes. 1st Corinthians 13:4 says, " Love is kind, love is patient, love does not boast, love is not rude, love is not self-seeking, love always protects, trusts, hopes, and cares."

One of the most important aspects of unconditional love is love for our-selves. To love ourselves conditionally, we must meet certain conditions. Unconditional love is based on an understanding that we are worth loving because God/Goddess created us as loving beings. God/Goddess creates that which is worth something, and that something is very special. Because of who you are, a child of God/Goddess, you have no need to base your love on what you have done or what you will do. Focus on all the wonderful things you have done; emphasize the positive rather than the negative. As you focus on your victories, the defeats fade away. You have no need to judge, make comparisons with others, or compare those around you to anyone else. None of us have to come up to a standard that will qualify us as one of God/Goddess's children. Matthew 7:1 says, "Judge not lest ye be judged." Likewise, none of us have specific belief systems that will better qualify us to be the chosen one. We all qualify to be on a direct evolutionary path back to God/Goddess. We qualify, not based on any form of judgment or belief, but on the basis of love because God/Goddess created us in Love. You are love, thus you qualify to be on your spiritual path, because "You are love."

As you learn to connect with and accept God/Goddess's love, you have a greater capacity to love yourself. All humans need love; it is a survival requirement. A child growing up without love is incomplete mentally and emotionally. You can receive love from God/Goddess and channel love to those who lack it, and they in turn can channel that love back. When humans break the love connection with God/Goddess, we tend to seek out others to provide us with love. By seeking acceptance, we have turned our power over to others. We then depend upon them, and they become our programmers. They can then have an undesirable impact on our reality. We have lost our freedom, lost our power, and given control of our lives to someone else. One challenge we all face is that a majority of our belief systems are built on society's beliefs rather than being built on God/Goddess's foundation of beliefs about love.

In order to achieve unconditional love for ourselves, we must own 100 percent of our personal power. As we take our personal power back with the realization that God/Goddess has given us all the wisdom we need, then our self-worth can gradually increase to a higher level. To accomplish this task, it will be helpful to demonstrate God/Goddess's love flowing through you by serving others. You can do your best to channel God/Goddess's love when you take your eyes off yourself (eliminating the "woe-is-me" attitude) and focus on helping those who need your love. Even if you are making mistakes, that's OK with God/Goddess, as long as you are trying to practice the presence of God/Goddess's love flowing through you. God/Goddess is totally pleased with your soul progress here on Earth. Everything you go through is one of your lessons. As we see the Universal Law of protection around us and seek God/Goddess's assistance, we can develop 100 percent self-love and self-worth. Then we can love our neighbors as ourselves—unconditionally.

Universal Law of Integrity

The Universal Law of Integrity starts with your doing what you said you would do. A challenge comes when there is a lack of integrity and harmony among your Higher Self, conscious mind, subconscious mind, emotional body, and the physical body. What sometimes happens is that the conscious mind sees the situation one way and the subconscious sees it another way. Sometimes the conscious mind wants to do something and the physical body does something different. Your task is to discipline the conscious and subconscious minds, and when you speak, speak the truth. Be someone who is dependable and has integrity. Even if you lack material possessions, seek integrity. Jesus Christ said, "Heaven and Earth will pass away, but my words will not pass away." Those who fail to do what they have promised have placed a tremendous burden on their shoulders. Deep within themselves, they remember their false words (they have not passed away), and it restricts their ability to have faith in themselves. Some may wonder if they are capable of having integrity. To develop integrity, allow your speech to flow from God/Goddess, through Spirit, and out through your conscious voice. Avoid using thoughts and speaking words taught to you by parents, teachers, and friends who lack spiritual integrity. Listen to the thoughts of God/Goddess within, that still, small voice; from those thoughts, you can speak with integrity and from your heart.

Watch out for excuses such as, "I am just human," or, "I can't help it; that's just the way I am." This is a false belief pattern promoted by the negative ego. There is no need to try to cover up for your lack of integrity. It is a misconception of what it means to be human to come up with excuses. Human souls are the highest creation of God/Goddess. As you identify yourself as a Spirit living in a physical body, you can acknowledge that everything is a creation brought into existence by the Creators and God/Goddess. Then you realize there is no justification for excuses. To procrastinate, give in to fatigue, or give excuses for your lack of integrity is laziness. Laziness is the path of least resistance. Your word is, and should be, Law. Your word creates your reality. Thus, as you align yourself with God/Goddess, allowing The Word to flow through you, all good will flow from your thoughts and voice. The key in walking upon the Earth is to walk in an upright position with integrity. Avoid slumping over and trying to hide. Be consistent at all times with your thoughts, words, and actions. Integrity is a part of the path to Ascension. An Ascended Master is "One" who lived the Universal Law of Integrity before graduating from Earth school.

Universal Law of Compassion

As you follow along on your spiritual path, compassion is one of the most important qualities to develop on the Earth plane. The Universal Law of Compassion recognizes that we are all connected to each other. Another's pain is our pain. Another's suffering, anywhere in the world, is our suffering. However, we are required to walk a thin line and be careful not to take on another's lessons or pain. It is possible to allow another's energies to enter your energy system and develop within you. These manifestations could develop physically, mentally, or psychologically. That fine line between knowing the difference between compassion (non-attachment) and attachment is very important. Knowing when you have actually attached yourself to another, taking on their lessons or a part of their soul, is critically important. Taking on the suffering of others is very debilitating and can damage all your bodies. You can briefly sense what others are experiencing. Then, once you understand, pull away and ask for guidance as to how you can help. Anyone can have the utmost compassion for others' suffering without taking on their lessons. Your compassion shows as you assist in lessening their suffering by being of service—that is, after you have been asked, or when their Higher-Self and your Higher-Self senses a need. Then Spirit can guide you in helping them resolve their own lessons. Remember, you cannot live someone else's lessons. Buddha, one of the world's great religious leaders, on http://www.buddha.com said: "All beings long for happiness; therefore, extend thy compassion to all." These are words of wisdom.

Universal Law of the Twelve Signs of the Zodiac

The Twelve Signs of the Zodiac relate to the stars and their positions in the cosmos. The positions of those heavenly creations have an influence on all of life forms on the Earth plane. If you are a victim in life and have given your personal power away, the stars will influence the type of choices you make. Even when you have a large number of negative aspects in your horoscope, you can still be in charge. God/Goddess created the stars; the stars did not create God/Goddess. Consequently you, being a part of God/Goddess, have ultimate control. There is no force in the Universe that is more powerful than your will. You are the total master of all astrological patterns once you're connected to Source and have developed the higher aspects of yourself.

The keys reside within the higher aspects of each Zodiac Sign. The fact that in this life we are born under a certain sign creates an energy pattern that can have a predominant influence on our lives. However, in our evolution we are required to integrate and master all twelve signs of the Zodiac. We spend many lifetimes incarnating on Earth under each of the signs until we master each sign's lessons. Living under each sign gives us a specific perspective on each phase of our evolutionary pattern.

Is Astrology a science? Yes! It is definitely a science! Scientific studies indicate that the position of stars and the moon have significant influences on all activities on the Earth plane. *The Old Farmer's Almanac*, published for many years, has been a guide to living productive lives, planting crops at the appropriate time, and living with the Zodiac. As scientists study subtle energies, an understanding of Astrology is emerging. Astrology is one of the oldest sciences on Earth. Its history goes back beyond Greek, Egyptian, and Chinese cultures. Hipparchus, one of the world's greatest historical scholars, and many other leading historians have supported Astrological science. Astrology was damaged by the limiting belief systems introduced with the acceptance of Copernican science, based on the physical concepts of astronomy.

Traditional science, based on what the senses can observe, purposely removed spiritual concepts from its view of reality. Astrological studies go beyond traditional science into realms of subtle energy, an area most scientists either ignore or have no way of studying. Their scientific method is currently based on developing a hypothesis, setting up an experiment, and using the five senses to prove or disprove the hypothesis. Most scientists unknowingly fail to realize that the energy of their thoughts have a direct effect on their experimental observations. A belief system that states *truth comes from proving something scientifically* is extremely limiting. It separates humanity from reality and makes science a God. This scientific system of developing theories to prove or disprove something is tragically utilizing a series of limiting false beliefs.

As a result, science has limited humanity's evolutionary and spiritual development. As man evolves to become more spiritual, Astrology will again take its rightful place. The spiritual path involves creating a new "Light Body" and shifts in consciousness. Then old, false beliefs fall away; new, more accurate beliefs are instilled; and one's consciousness is raised to a higher level of reality. Astrological research can assist by discovering new concepts about reality, bringing new understandings. These new Astrological understandings will help humanity synchronize with the newly developing paradigms within spiritual dimensions and many other parallel realities.

Universal Law of Channeling

Channeling is considered a method whereby humanity can make contact with the spiritual realm. However, a host of factors influence the ability to accurately make contact and become a clear channel. Because of the nature of channeling, it is influenced by an individual's belief systems, personality, philosophies, and the personal agendas of both the source and the channel through which the information flows.

The use of accurate dowsing techniques reveals that channeling accuracy varies from 20 percent to 100 percent. Therefore, it is wise to verify the accuracy of any channeled material before integrating it into your consciousness. Many people think that if the material is channeled, it is true. Nothing could be further from reality. Some channelings that come from the Mental and Astral planes are very inaccurate. Channelings coming from the Ascended Masters, Extraterrestrials, and Archangels (spiritual realms) are generally more accurate. Again, always use discernment and accurate pendulum dowsing to determine the accuracy of any channeled material—even portions of the Bible and other Holy books have been purposely altered and are thus inaccurate.

The accuracy of the channeling is directly related to a person's consciousness development. If a person's belief systems and consciousness are not developed and balanced sufficiently, the channelings or psychic readings coming from that person will reflect limiting belief systems, and the negative ego of the channeler becomes a part of the information supplied. Those who accept information from a corrupted channel become contaminated themselves.

This is the reality of channeling, not a judgment on all channels. Many channels give accurate psychic readings or are channeling from the spiritual realms. Have someone dowse the accuracy of the channel or the accuracy of the material received before accepting any information. This is true of all written and voiced information. With so many false beliefs floating around, one must be very careful lest you be led astray. You can even be led astray by inaccurate dowsing procedures.

Channeling should be carried out with love and from a perspective of securing spiritual wisdom from beyond the physical realm of the five senses. The reality of channeling is influenced by how you think, because that becomes your reality. What you think manifests in your DNA and your chakra system. That is, our thinking determines the functional features of our genetic codes and the function of our chakras and their associated glands. The overstimulation or under-stimulation of any chakra will influence the channeling process and its accuracy.

Every thought we energize and bring into consciousness has a direct influence on the function of our chakras and glands. For those interested in channeling, it is very important to become as integrated and balanced as possible. Those interested in channeling should make sure their chakras have gone through an energetic repatterning, a process you and your Spiritual Assistants can work on. Every negative ego thought will adversely affect specific chakras. Likewise, every positive thought of love, patience, and understanding of self and others will help balance the chakras and improve the health of body organs. Perfectly balanced chakras are the byproduct of becoming integrated with Unity/Christ consciousness. The qualities of those who are open-minded and receptive to improving their belief systems are moving on the Ascension pathway to the higher dimensions. Energetic repatterning will help balance the external grid and overlay, the major chakras, meridians, energy gates, core star, collaterals, aura, etc. This in turn helps improve the accuracy of the channeled material. The key is to be open to divine order in our lives. Each channel will have its own unique gift; no two channels will function by using similar channeling patterns, and that is the way it should be.

A word of caution is in order as one picks up on the many channelings being published in books and magazines and on the Internet. Many Light Workers are being asked by the Spiritual Hierarchy, cosmic and planetary entities to become channels. One should be very cautious and use considerable discernment in responding to any channel request until it is proven beyond any doubt that the entity is truly who it says it is. In truth, there is no such thing as channeling. What is really happening is that people are receiving messages, insights, or visions that are passing through their conscious belief systems—their own filters, lenses, and subconscious programs. Consequently, distortions can take place as they pass through the receiver. Take all external channeling with a grain of salt, and trust your internal guidance by listening to the still, small voice. When that voice comes from spiritual sources with highly accurate belief systems, it will be more closely connected to God/Goddess. For helpful channeling guidelines see www. God/Goddess.com. Use accurate pendulum dowsing to check all channeling requests in order to keep from giving away your power.

Universal Law of Giving

Giving to others in a cheerful manner with a smile and a sincere desire to love God/Goddess and your brothers and sisters is one of your highest callings. That which you hold back from giving to your brothers and sisters throughout the world is, in truth, a holding back in giving to yourself. All humans are incarnations of God/Goddess as spirit, and we are all connected to each other. We all came from the same source. When you give, you are not giving to a physical body; you are giving to a spirit that is a part of God/Goddess and a part of you. We are all interconnected components of creation that came from God/Goddess. All humans are your brothers and sisters; each is literally a part of you. So when we hold back giving to another out of fear, competition, comparison, jealousy, envy, selfishness, or any other negative, ego-based duality, we are hurting ourselves.

When you hold back from giving, you think you are helping yourself. The negative ego will tell you that when you give, you will be losing. This concept is also true regarding stealing. If you steal from one of your brothers or, you are stealing from yourself. But you are also stealing from God/Goddess, since God/Goddess is in everyone. Giving, and respecting others' possessions, is a win-win situations. *The second you stop giving, you have not lost God/Goddess; however, you have lost your realization of God/Goddess's holy presence in everyone.*

This does not mean you are not to take care of yourself and set proper boundaries in your giving activities. The choices can become a delicate balance. They can require guidance from your Higher Self Spiritual Council. The art of giving is an essential lesson to master on your spiritual journey. We all need to constantly avoid the pitfalls of selfishness, greed, narcissism, self-centeredness, competition, jealousy, envy, and comparing.

Remember to judge not, lest ye be judged. God/Goddess or your High Self will judge you at the appropriate time, but that judgment may not be what you have been led to believe. God/Goddess's due time is beyond any human's comprehension and has been said to be hidden from the hearts of man. During judgment time, we will be recognized by High Self and God/Goddess for the extent to which we have given help to our sisters and brothers. It takes a pure heart and spiritual discernment to know when and how to give. The Universal Law of Giving is based on the concept that what you send out, you receive tenfold. That's good pay in anyone's ledger.

Universal Law of Discipline

It is time to stop listening to the negative, ego-driven mind and all its excuses (I can't; I'm too busy with my job; I'm too tired; Find someone else; I'll do it tomorrow; I'll do it just this one time; What's the use?; I give up!).

Life on Earth is an ongoing schoolroom where you are constantly in class and working on the next lesson. It is a marathon we continue to run, lifetime after lifetime, until we get it right. It's time to become physically fit, emotionally fit, spiritually fit, and enjoy workouts in each other's gyms. Shape up and get with the program. Complete each lesson and move on. The alternative is to keep using the old, worn-out patterns you have always used, until frustration sets in. Then maybe you will finally decide that self-discipline is easier in the long run.

Why take the same classes over and over, lifetime after lifetime, and not make an attempt to graduate some day? With no judgment towards others, the question is, "Where am I on my Ascension Path in terms of self-discipline? Can Self Discipline accelerate my evolutionary process? If so, how can I develop the qualities of self-discipline?"

Other important questions are, "Do I want my lifetime program to be in alignment with God/Goddess's ultimate plan for me? Can I develop order in my life, and can I dedicate myself to the task at hand every moment of the day, regardless of the sidetracks and roadblocks?" The Higher Self can reveal to us, when we ask, the strength from the Creator of Love, the strength we need to develop Self Discipline. The Creator of Love, the "One" who cares for us, would truly like for you to graduate from Earth's low-frequency school as soon as possible. You are here on Earth to learn to become a Creator. An important part of your school classes is learning self discipline.

By applying the Universal Law of Discipline to your life, you can make significant progress in passing classes. You can graduate from Earth school and move on to the New Earth classes.

* * * * *

23

My Spiritual Mission on Earth in Relation to Universal Law

All of humanity is faced with the following question: "What is my mission on Earth, and does that mission in any way relate to the implementation of Universal Laws?" The indwelling desire of all souls incarnating anywhere within the Universe is to learn to serve others. In order to accomplish that desire, it is critical to see everything and every person as yourself, or as a part of yourself. This will require an open heart that has the capability to love unconditionally. The overall objective is to aid you, aid others, aid the planet, and aid all other creations to achieve their missions. That objective will, of necessity, require that you shift to the higher states of dimensional consciousness. You must increase the amount of light you have available so you have the willpower to live up to all Universal Laws. As you become a light to the world, allowing source energy to flow through you to all of creation, you have mastered one important lesson in creating.

As your light increases, it will become available to raise the light of the planet. As a result, you will have helped create the New Earth. You will have moved your consciousness to the fifth-dimension state or higher—into Unity/Christ consciousness. Those accomplishments will be the direct result of knowing and living by Universal Laws.

Acceptance of the events on Earth involves an understanding that there is nothing absolute in this reality realm called planet Earth. Everything is an illusion. Thus I do not claim that anything in this book, or in any other source I've noted, is absolutely accurate. Reality is full of contradictions, and life on Earth is a paradox. Realities and perceptions will constantly change as creation evolves spiritually. It is impossible to be totally accurate about anything. Apply your own spiritual insights and mastery of the subject, and allow the divinity God /Goddess in your heart center to guide you with its knowingness and feelings. This is the most

> **Acceptance of events on Earth involves an understanding that everything is an Illusion humans have created.**

reliable source of knowledge, awareness, and realization in creation. If you want to know if something is worthwhile, truthful, or accurate, including spiritual teachings and predictions, spirit recommends finding out for yourself. Use your own discernment, your own intuition, and the internal knowing from your God/Goddess within. Yes, accurate pendulum dowsing, when connected to Universal Consciousness for the answers, is one spiritual pathway worthy of your consideration. However, such a practice requires skill, a healthy body, a belief in the system, and the removal of a multitude of interferences that can influence the results. In order to pendulum dowse, it is best to work with others who are skilled dowsers. Make sure each person involved in the dowsing process is on the same time line in which the question is based, phrased, and directed. Two individuals dowsing on different time lines can receive accurate answers, but those answers may be different. The American Dowsing Society has many books, workshops, and courses available on how to pendulum dowse. It is obvious that pendulum dowsing takes a lot of faith, practice, and hard work.

Once you have chosen to proceed to prepare for graduation and Ascension, you may notice that those who have chosen to continue their third-dimension lessons on Earth or another third-dimension planet are having difficulty understanding what you are up to. You will notice that these individuals are having difficulty accepting the new, high-frequency energies arriving on Earth. Their low-frequency bodies are having difficulty adjusting, and they have all types of imbalances. They have been programmed with low-frequency duality programs, many of which are founded on false beliefs and limiting illusions. Those tied to the third-dimension duality continue to function within a mode of self-protection and survival. They are burdened with many different challenges and have difficulties dealing with negative emotions.

Some individuals who have chosen to continue their third-dimension lessons actually fear that their survival would be at stake if they were to accept your Spiritual Pathway, and rightfully so. They are frequently caught up in a state of consciousness that emphasizes STS, a feature of third-dimensional duality consciousness. Spiritual evolution to the fifth-dimensional state of consciousness emphasizes STO and Unity/Christ consciousness. Individuals trapped within the third-dimensional state of consciousness will have difficulty understanding the importance of Universal Laws and as a result, they may choose to ignore them. Their inability to maintain an attitude of unconditional love, when faced with a perceived threat to their established, duality way of life, frequently creates confusion in their thoughts. They may even argue with you and exhibit warrior tendencies. By all means, move away from such behavior patterns lest they draw you into a lower frequency.

Gradually, those clinging to duality consciousness are experiencing a mismatch in vibrations that relate to time-space as compared to space-time. Within the third-dimensional state of consciousness, in "time-space," time is fixed to sequential clocking periods and space is continuous to infinity. Within the fourth-dimensional state of consciousness, in space-time, space has no limitations. Movement from point A to point B is instantaneous because there is no space in a spiritual sense. Also in space-time, time is fixed at the zero point (there is no time).

As the Earth and a large portion of humanity shifts into the space-time continuum, the choice-making activity of the brain is increasing. As a result, it is becoming more difficult to feel comfortable with the increased brain activity. This experience of discomfort is increased by making unwise choices, such as continually purchasing gadgets to satisfy self. Discomfort is also increased as one continues to listen to and buy into the thoughts disseminated by the communication media and by rushing around to meet artificially created third-dimension deadlines. When one fails to let go of these destructive behavior patterns, stress, uneasiness, or even depression sets in, further compounding the discomforts. Those individuals interested in following the graduation and Ascension pathway have a choice to avoid all of these discomforts. Detach yourself from time-space, shift your consciousness into space-time, and make sure all of your choices are wise and guided by the God/Goddess within. Shift away from lifestyle patterns that emphasize duality consciousness, and shift into lifestyle patterns that emphasize Unity/Christ consciousness.

Thus, when you are considering your spiritual mission realize that the above described mismatch has a dramatically different effect on each soul. Those who long for the opportunity to graduate and Ascend out of the third-dimensional state of consciousness create a desire to keep that infinite Love flowing through their energy bodies. This spiritual energy has a tremendous impact upon the space-time spiritual continuum, rather than the time-space of the third-dimension continuum of separation and duality consciousness.

By seeking to follow the Universal Laws one is preparing to graduate and transition to the fourth-dimensional state of consciousness. The goal is not perfection, but the returning to and remembrance of unconditional love. You will dwell in a reality realm free of danger where you're every wish and desire is granted. The process of moving from the third-dimensional to the fourth- and fifth-dimensional states of consciousness is based in part on accepting the belief that Oneness is more spiritually real than the beliefs associated with duality illusions.

Also, as you strive to understand your mission on Earth in relation to the Universal Laws, realize that you did not come into this incarnation merely to escape physical death, nor to save self. You came to reach out a hand to others so that, as each hand reaches out, hands begin to connect one to another. Then others begin to have hope and become a part of the rhythm and flow towards graduation and the New Earth.

The harvest of souls can be greatly increased at this time because so many souls are very close to "Waking Up." Many souls know something is happing but await your help in understanding what effect the upcoming Earth changes and dimensional shifts will have on them and all parts of their world they have become so familiar with.

Accumulating evidence indicates there is "Now" an Earth Christ Grid around the planet. Scientists have now discovered a new grid and are in the process of trying to understand the portals and grid points associated with its structural features. Thus one channel of service you can take is to strengthen and tweak the Earth Christ Grid, located within the fourth-dimensional state of consciousness. By visualization of the Violet Light, you can have that light infuse and purify the new Earth Christ Grid. Those of you planning to Ascend can look forward to passing through portals (Star Gates) in the Earth Christ Grid to the New Earth.

Spirit has long ago indicated that spiritual evolution is all about change in consciousness. Change, by nature, is a condition that biases and disrupts the consciousness toward a feeling of discomfort. Avoid such discomforts as you travel the road ahead by being gentle with yourself. Avoid any form of self-punishment and emphasize love in all of your endeavors. Then remind yourself and others that to be of service, one must first love self. Loving one's self requires considerable effort and forgiveness. Search for help from your High Self Spiritual Council the God/Goddess within, and keep your expectations in line with the heart. Clear the mind of less-than-desirable thought forms, and be open to receive guidance from within. Make regular use of meditation, whether it is done in solitude or in a group. Group meditations have advantages in that they are safer and one can meditate for longer periods of time without becoming imbalanced. Group meditations are also more energetically powerful.

* * * * *

24

Integrating Energy Patterns Required to Create Balance

For complete integration of your third-dimension energy system, various energy-carrying paths, centers, or circuits will need to be brought into your conscious attention and tuned up. You do not have to understand the characteristics of each of these energy paths to ask for their attunement and balance. Just ask your Spiritual Assistants, High Self Spiritual Council and God/Goddess within to meet your request. Some of these energy systems are: the grid surrounding the body; the upgraded holographic template; the reality vessel, Buddhic net, core star, and prana tube; the chakras, chakra cords, meridians, and acupuncture points; collaterals, slip strings, brain strings, and axiatonal lines; the silver cord, implants, implant cords, imprints, and overlays; and the emotional storage sites, spiritual tunnels and clusters, and brain and nerve function synapses. Other important energy concepts include: light flow quotient, connection to source, available energy complex, and love flow intensity, degree of polarity point balance, electrical flow efficiency, DNA energy code storage and transference, and essence, prana flow, and photon energies.

You can begin your integration activities by internally integrating the twelve items listed below. After each item is integrated separately, integrate it with the previous item. Once all items are integrated together, you can request for a total integration of these energy patterns. The integration sequence evolves these energy groups: (1) All physical body components, (2) All spiritual bodies, (3) All brain and nerve energy circuits, (4) All mental and emotional bodies, (5) Core star and prana tube energy patterns, (6) Buddhic web energy net. (7) DNA energy patterns in all bodies, (8) All grid, chakra, meridian, and energy circuits, (9) Reality vessel energy patterns, (10) Connect all energy circuits with your reality vessel, (11) The upgraded hologram of all physical body parts and (12) Ideal chemical makeup of all catabolic and metabolic systems. Use accurate pendulum dowsing connected with

Universal Consciousness to measure the extent to which each integration process has been completed.

The objective of this integrative sequence is to bring together all of these human energy patterns in one unified, functional system. Start by integrating each item in sequence until it is at least 50 percent integrated and has been integrated at least 50 percent with the previous item. Then move on to the next item. Continue to work down the list until each item is internally integrated to register close to 100 percent of its potential. As you continue, obtain a high percentage of integration with all previous items, taken in sequence. The objective is to eventually integrate all items to 100 percent compatibility. The whole process will require considerable clock time; however, it can pay great dividends in the functional efficiency of your energy makeup. There are many possible signs that can help you sense that you have integrated your energy systems and obtained a degree of spiritual awakening.

As you shift your consciousness from the third dimension to the fourth- and fifth-dimensional states of consciousness, a whole_new group of energy systems will be created and available for creating your new reality.

* * * * * *

25

The Power of Acceptance and Making Spiritual Adjustments

In the "Messages from The Hosts of Heaven" posted on the Web site www.operationterra.com, it is pointed out that all people on Earth are simply striving to follow the evolutionary path for their lives. Each individual soul has chosen that path before they incarnated on Earth. Quoting their messages:

> Everything you are, everything you have done, is all within the plan for your life. The place you *can* be responsible is for your own *responses* to the situations. Your own responses are your own processes of working out who you are, why you are here, and where you are going. You are one aspect of the Creator, providing the Creator with a particular experience through the focus of your perception as an individualized aspect of the Creator. If you must blame anyone, you must blame the Creator. If you must be angry, you must be angry at the Creator. When you look, everything you observe is the Creator-in-expression. The people who die are the Creator. The people who kill them are the Creator. If you can just get this, you will have peace, you will transcend the phenomenal reality, and you will be that much closer to home.

Some level of understanding is needed when one contemplates the evolutionary path of the soul within this Universe and all of its multidimensional aspects. The incarnated part of your reality has very limited understanding because of the many veils and the loss of memory. Your soul has not evolved to a high enough vibrational level of consciousness to realistically guide your consciousness along the spiritual path back home. Thus you need considerable spiritual help to follow the most appropriate path (time line). Obviously, connection to the God/Goddess within is a very important spiritually. Beyond that connection are many more opportunities.

In the past when an individual soul allowed its physical body to die, the sprit form passed into the lower overtones of the fourth-dimensional state of consciousness. Here each soul was given the opportunity to reassess its last incarnation and decide what new experiences would best serve for its future experiences for spiritual and soul growth. However, this reassessment is unconscious to the personality because of the soul's low state

> **Bardo, the state between physical lives is where your soul reviews your past lives and creates a new contract for the next life.**

of dimensional consciousness. If such a large amount of information was available to your consciousness, it could overwhelm the limited capabilities of the mental and emotional bodies. Thus, the veils of protection were created so you would not remember all your other experiences.

Keep in mind that throughout all of your evolutionary experiences, there was never any judgment about your activities. Judgment is a human concept, an illusion of the lower dimensions, and does not exist in the higher spiritual reality realms.

Bardo, the state between physical lives (where the review takes place), was designed to determine the evolutionary status of the soul in relation to the path it had chosen. That's all; just the current status of your soul at the time of review. When you think back to your last reassessment while in Bardo, you realize that you have almost no memory of the process, nor do you generally remember that your other lives were reassessed. Each time you pass through Bardo (during your fourth-dimension reassessment); your memory slate is cleared. Then, as soon as the memory is cleared, a veil is installed to block memory from past, future, and parallel lives so that you can begin each upcoming incarnation anew. One misfortunate aspect of completing the reassessment and creating a new contract is that very few humans remember the contract they agreed to carry out. That contract for the upcoming incarnation was designed to accelerate the soul's spiritual evolution. However, if the soul is unable to remember what it agreed to carry out, then how can much progress be made during the upcoming incarnation? Thus, humans struggle and are constantly faced with asking their High Self Spiritual Council and God/Goddess within to gain some insight about their contracts.

Everyone is interested in choosing the most appropriate activity to propel them forward on their spiritual path. The question is; what are the most appropriate choices to make each day? And what conscious decision is required to make the appropriately choose? The solution is to make sure you are in contact with your Spiritual Assistants and God/Goddess within. When an individual loses contact with their spiritual guidance systems, they have a tendency to just drift through life. Then they reincarnate again with the same broken record. Thus there is value in keeping in touch with your God/Goddess within so you can know how to continue to progress forward spiritually.

The pace of spiritual progress for each soul incarnated on Earth has been very slow the past twenty-six thousand years. Humanity within the lower, third-dimensional state of consciousness has been caught in a repetitive pattern of returning to a third-dimensional planet lifetime after lifetime. This repetitive pattern continues until the spirit "Wakes Up" and finally gets the cosmic absurdity of this trap on the third dimension Earth. The absurdity was that we believed we were separate from God/Goddess and other parts of creation. There is no separation of anything in the Universe, and life on Earth is just one big game of illusions. Some call these illusions a play and we are the actors.

When we volunteered to come to Earth, we humans created the illusion of separation and the illusory (though real in a physical body sense) forms of pain and suffering. We chose this pattern so we could solve these challenges, thereby accelerating our spiritual evolution. Frequently, when souls allow their physical bodies to die on Earth and the souls arrive within the lower overtones of the fourth dimension, they may "Wake Up" and respond to their current situation.

When the soul "Wake Up" occurs, that soul will realize that an additional incarnation within a third-dimensional reality will not be of karmic value, nor will such an incarnation likely provide any new or helpful experiences for soul growth.

Thus, these souls may choose to request a holding pattern in the fourth dimension. In fact, it has been established that some, who are tired of Earth and the associated lessons, choose to rest for a period between incarnations. Following the rest and additional consultations, they may then be able to make an alternate choice of how and where to proceed. Others may remain within the spiritual levels of the fourth dimension indefinitely for various reasons. Some souls evidently realized that at an appropriate point, they can choose to resurrect their spirit to obtain Light -Body status. From that new vantage point, other choices become available for spiritual evolution.

This above procedure is described biblically as: *The dead shall rise.* Those souls classified as the dead are in reality living within their spirit bodies within the fourth dimension. When those souls within the fourth dimension make a decision to Ascend and they have met the qualifications, then they have in a sense decided to create a new body and Ascend to the New Earth. Thus in a way they will be resurrected from the fourth dimension or from the dead. This possible option, in the sequence of spiritual evolution, is related to the dimensional consciousness of the planet, in this case, Earth. When the planet Earth Ascends to the fifth-dimensional state of consciousness, there will be no more third-dimension activities at that frequency until the planet is cleansed and renews it, a lengthy process. That soul which is unprepared to graduate will be unable to incarnate upon the third-dimension Earth. Thus the soul in fourth dimension Bardo is faced with several possible options.

As mentioned, one option is for a soul to Ascend from the astral plane (fourth dimension) to the fifth-dimension New Earth. Another option for some souls is to transfer to another planet with the dimensional state of consciousness that is compatible with their evolved state. Obviously, there are other options or choices.

Regardless of what option you have chosen, you have only a few years left before all man-made, illusory creations, characteristic of third-dimension Earth will be swept away. When you have made the decision to Ascend with a new body in this incarnation, all of your personal experiences through many lifetimes will continue to be revisited and cleared. They will come crashing back from all "Now times" into your current incarnation to be cleared, so you can move to the New Earth with a clean slate. Spirit indicates everyone on Earth will experience these cleansing experiences. Mother Earth has taken on many of these adverse experiences and is "Now" releasing them back to those who created them. As they manifest or are revisited, seek Spiritual Assistants to help facilitate these clearings.

So what would you do if you sensed from your God/Goddess within that you had thirty-two months left to live on Earth? How important would it be to plan anything? What would you do in your last remaining months? Is there some unfinished business in your life? Are there some people you need to talk to? Is your home in order, and does that matter? Spirit has revealed to me that everyone needs to start thinking in these terms. Begin to analyze and sort out activities within your life to know where you are and where you are headed. Your goal should be to detach from all of the chaotic events surrounding you. Release all your material possessions and so-called remaining treasures. They will have no real meaning on the future New Earth.

However, be prepared for and ready to accept all types of changes during your remaining thirty-two months. All signs indicate that before "The Shift" there will be a gradually reduced food supply, economic hard times, extreme weather conditions, political unrest, a possible pole shift, Earth changes, and many other events too numerous to mention.

Take a look around. Spend extra time with your family and friends. Enjoy the beauties of nature, and feel your connection to the sunset, the birds, the stars, and Earth. Enjoy the good things available, find balance in all activities, be good to yourself, give the trees a hug, send love to all the animals, and take time to really appreciate the third-dimension world you have enjoyed for many lifetimes. Give appreciation to all those around you who have helped make your life meaningful. Soften your walk, soften your talk, and appreciate a time of quiet meditation.

Then look around at everything that you have come to accept as real. You have often heard of the concept of a homecoming. However, there is also a "home leaving" in your near future. All of humans on third-dimension Earth are going somewhere else. So as you look around, know that you will soon be leaving all of the familiar activities and places. "Soon" is relative, since no one knows the exact timing of ""The Shift" and all the events leading up to it. However, "soon" could come at any time, and it is sufficiently close that you will be wise to continue your preparation. Just as all things shall pass away in their due time, so also will you eventually pass along on your spiritual path—through a host of experiences within this and other Universes.

After the world you have known fades away, realize that everyone is an eternal creation. Everyone will resume their opportunities as they travel down their time tracks and time lines toward their chosen destinations. So why not start "Now" to wipe away any tears you may shed concerning leaving? Relax as you use peace and love to help create your new reality realm.

Spirit has led me to the following message while I was sitting at the computer as a means of approaching the closing of this book. This is a reminder from spirit of the choices you have had available and the opportunities you have "Now." By accepting your chosen path (time line) and coming opportunities, you will be heading back toward your real home. The accuracy of the following message is for your own discernment, since the accuracy or reality of anything occurs within each individual's perception and consciousness.

> From a spiritual perspective there is no difference between living and dying, since both of these experiences are illusions. Since living and dying are illusions they can be uncreated and created. Thus one helpful internal change that will facilitate the Ascension process is to release all false illusory programs and false beliefs. For example: the false belief that physical death is natural, inevitable, and real. Physical death was and is an illusion humans created because they believed they were unworthy of eternal life. To facilitate this false belief about death, humans on Earth created a hormone called the death hormone that helps age the body and brings on death. As these humans created the death hormone they simultaneously uncreated the rejuvenation hormone to shorten their life span. In order to extend your life span you must deactivate the death hormone and reactivate the rejuvenation hormone to create a new physical body.
>
> The last chance for a soul to incarnate on the third-dimensional Earth during this Galactic cycle is coming

313

to a close in the very near future. Anyone who does not remember who they are by then will have a choice to die and go to the spiritual waiting room in the fourth dimension. There they can sit and look at old magazines until they face a decision time. If you don't remember who you are, and desire to continue playing the games of separation, control, manipulation, power, etc., then you can go play on another planetary school that is still densifying within the third dimension. There you can continue your third dimension lessons as long as you so desire, rather than Ascend to the fifth dimension.

Sometime following "The Shift," within the period from 2010 to 2014, planet Earth will be inhabited by those souls embracing Unity/ Christ consciousness within the fifth dimension. Those souls who have incarnated on the New Earth will have accepted the opportunity to Ascend. They will realize they cannot die, because their new fifth dimensional body is an eternal creation. In contrast, the human physical body on third-dimension Earth is a mortal illusion because it can be uncreated. Anything that can be uncreated is an illusion characteristic of the lower dimensional states of consciousness.

Recent social, political, and economic events on Earth in the early part of 2009 will be under review by the Hosts of Heaven concerning the possibility of dramatic Earth changes.

When and if a state of emergency is detected, the Creators of the Universe have requested all parties to stand by for a change in plans. These possible changes in plans could create a sensation of jitters and butterflies in the stomach and an associated mixture of anxiety and anticipation by those who plan to graduate. As you sense the possibilities of an acceleration or deceleration in plans, keep your attention on your God/Goddess within. Calm yourself by deepening your breathing, closing your eyes, and trusting those who are orchestrating the whole transition event. These procedures will lessen the discomfort. Detach from the drama around you by eliminating or dramatically reducing your communication intake. If and when the Extraterrestrials take control of the communication systems, then listen for their instructions. Yes, they have the technology to take over all communication systems worldwide.

Currently, your objective is to avoid all fear and anxiety and exercise complete trust. No one, not even the Hosts of Heaven, knows for sure what will happen in the near future. Thus prepare for anything conceivable and release all concern, turning everything over to your God/Goddess within.

The Hosts of Heaven and benevolent Extraterrestrials will be closely observing each of you in the upcoming days. One possibility is that additional conflicts could break out in the Persian Gulf region. If so, those conflicts could spread to other parts of the Earth. As a result, there could be a financial collapse and all kinds of chaos.

In order to ensure that those who plan to Ascend within their new physical bodies are safe from these possible events, plans are being revised to possibly lift you up into one of the Mother Ships before conditions on Earth become unbearable. Keep your inner radio tuned to the God/Goddess within for specific instructions. Then pay attention to those instructions regardless of what others say. Spirituality is about seeking to express your desires fully, without limitations imposed by anyone or the need to seek permission from anyone to follow your inner guidance system, always using discernment.

There will always be those who seek to dampen your enthusiasm for spiritual progress. It is time to create your spiritual foundations upon the spiritual enthusiasm that is building all over the Earth. Your soul journey comes from and through the heart. The heart receives guidance to help you make the most appropriate choices. However, it is important to process the heart's message with a clear mind. By first listening to the heart, you can begin to use your mind more constructively. The heart is the female, feeling side of life that needs to be in balance with the intellectual male side. This means balancing your ego and living from the heart, as previously discussed.

Your consciousness has been energized to "Wake Up" to who you are so that you can remember your divine nature. There is no more need to walk the extreme paths of challenge. In past lives you have sacrificed to be the robber, killer, drunk, priest, shaman, monk, or lama. You have experienced all the challenges of sickness, war, crime, and

> **Open the door of your heart. Change your perspective. Release all negative emotions. Align with your Divine Self.**

315

poverty. "Now" is the time to fully "Wake Up" and let your life become spiritual in all aspects of living. Becoming spiritual is not about going to a seminar, following a spiritual leader, reading a certain book, or going to church. It's about recognizing a need to shift your consciousness so that everything in your life is on a spiritual path. You will need to change your perspective, shift your attitude, release all negative emotions, and carefully monitor all your thought patterns. What is right for you may be totally different from what is right for someone else. Install those changes in consciousness that direct your attention towards your heart and the Master Christ within. There never has been a Master who has Ascended without calling upon the Master Christ within for assistance. It is your responsibility to open the door of your heart, request assistance, and bring forth your Ascended Master waiting therein. For those who plan to Ascend, you came to Earth at this time to immortalize a physical body for yourself and take it with you to the New Earth. Your path of salvation is to align with the God/Goddess within. The "I-AM That I- AM" is the divine self of the fifth dimension and beyond. The Supreme Being of everyone on Earth is called "I-AM-That-I Am." Alignment with your divine self is what Ascension is all about. The God/Goddess within will help you understand and apply what will be the most helpful path and time line for your spiritual journey.

Spirit provided the closing prayer:

> **May my journey to the New Earth be filled with love, joy, fun, and excitement as I travel my chosen path and time line. May the Love of the Creator Source (God/Goddess) guide me from within at all times as I experience this dramatic shift in consciousness and the beautiful transformations. Assist me to set aside quiet times to enjoy my transformation as the still, small voice within guides me to accept my multidimensional nature with a sense of wonder and awe about its magnificence.**

* * * * *

Epilogue

Many humans sense the coming changes on Earth ("The Shift") and realize they will soon need to make some very important choices. The choice to remain on third dimension Earth is not a choice (option) since it will not support human life shortly after 2012. Those who prefer to avoid "The Shift" have several options. For example, they can physically die and return to their home planet, choose to go to another third dimension planet, or go back to the Creator. Those who qualify to ascend can physically die now so that they can be of assistance on the New Earth after "The Shift." Others who qualify to ascend can physically remain on Earth, consciously leave their bodies at night, help prepare the New Earth for inhabitation, and return each morning. These souls are preparing to experience "The Shift" and go to the New Earth.

A more complete description of these options and events has been communicated from the Master Guide Kirael through Kahu Fred Sterling. They are available at www.kirael.com, in Kirael's books on "The Shift," and within articles in the *Sedona Journal of Emergence*. As you prepare to go through "The Shift" maintain your Mer-Ka-Ba magnetic field so you can retain your memory, e.g. remember who you are. Following is a brief summary of messages from Master Guide Kirael about "The Shift" and the associated three days of darkness.

Every human physically remaining on Earth up to "The Shift," will experience the three days of darkness and will go into a deep sleep-like hibernation. During hibernation your pulse will be slowed to one beat for every two to three hours. Also for those who plan to ascend many internal molecular changes will take place. For example, your low frequency carbon-based molecular design will be replaced with a higher frequency silica-based crystalline molecular design.

Immediately after awakening from the three days of darkness you may wonder what just happened? The third dimension landscape will be akin to what you have seen following some hurricanes or typhoons where many physical structures were completely leveled. Humans should understand that all physically man made creations depend upon human consciousness to maintain their structural features. Thus without that human consciousness energy, during the three days of darkness, these manmade creations will begin to disappear. Besides the loss of your man made physical possessions and the associated devastation, you will observe portals (dimensional doorways) that you must pass through to enter the fourth dimension.

As a result of these changes some individuals will become confused and frightened. They will most likely be unaware that the planned Shift is taking place. Thus it would be wise to consider their needs. If you qualify and plan to ascend through the portals be patient and wait your turn. Those who have chosen not to ascend have an option of going through the portal first. As these individuals enter the portal their physical energy will dissipate and they will return to the Creator's Light. Note; *About two thirds of the population, or four billion souls, currently have chosen not to graduate and ascend to the New Earth. They will be leaving third dimension Earth, by dissipating their physical body, by physical death, or by other choices.*

The remaining two billion plus humans will qualify to ascend and pass through the portals to the New Earth. Those who qualify will receive guidance from the "Senders of Light." That information will help guide them though the portals to the "New Earth" and help them during several trying days on the other side of the portal. The "Senders of Light" will also guide the portal workers. The portal workers on this side will assist those who are unfamiliar with passage through the portal. The portal workers in the 4th dimension will know truth and teach classes. These classes will help the ascenders adjust to the New Earth. These workers can also discern those who barely slipped through the portal without adequate qualifications and have them sent back. To remain within the fourth dimension that individual's consciousness must vibrate at the frequencies of unconditional love and unity (Christ) consciousness.

Ascenders keep in mind there is nothing about "The Shift" to fear. Relax and know that everything is in divine order. Then promise yourself that you will hear the messages of the "Senders of Light" in order to know what to do. Your mental capacity will be greatly increased and your physical body will be cleansed of most imbalances. You will notice that your physical features have changed. Your brain may increase in size and your ears will become somewhat larger allowing you to hear distant sounds. Your heart rate will slow and your lung capacity will shrink because of breathing changes. If you tell a lie your eyes will flash. You will be able to exist without food or water for several months, because you can survive on prana (photon) energy, received through prana breathing techniques. Making love will be beyond your wildest dreams and simply involve putting your hands together. There will be no need to take money with you because it will not purchase anything anywhere in the 4th Dimension. Your new home will be simple and made of beautiful natural local products.

If you are a Lightworker, you currently have an obligation to get the word out about "The Shift." Many people will not want to listen when you first attempt to explain "The Shift," but that doesn't matter because they will remember your words when their time comes. Thus it would be wise to tell your family and friends of the anticipated graduation and "The Shift." You do not have to tell them about the three days of darkness unless they ask. You may help them by stimulating their interest in staying upon Earth until graduation time. Many of your associates will make the transition, at least into the lower levels of consciousness within the fourth dimension. Limit your concern about others, because by the time "The Shift" occurs many of you reading will cease to be concerned about who will make it through. Why? Because everything is in absolute perfection and each individual has free will to make choices. Thus each Soul will make the most appropriate choice for their spiritual evolution.

Following The Shift and passage through a portal into the fourth dimension you can discover there are seven levels of consciousness. Within each level there are seven more levels for a total of forty-nine possible levels or reality realms. It would be best to avoid going to any level one realm for several reasons outlined on the website. The best level to begin with is level four, because there you are fully enlightened, have a spiritual awareness, and still have a conscious presence, somewhat like Earth. Level five of the fourth dimension is similar to the fifth dimensional like state of consciousness. It is like living in a luxury hotel where you are waited upon and can receive your every wish. This "heaven like" level can be defined as being within the Light of the Creator. Here you will have opportunities to travel to other planets aboard various spacecraft and make many new friends. Level seven is where you spend very little time in Earth like activities and can transcend to do anything you desire. You will have perfect coordination and thus may decide that this place is where you would like to stay for awhile.

If you have a sincere desire to graduate and ascend the answers to the following question may be helpful. Someone asked Master Guide Kirael: "In preparing for "The Shift," is there anything we can do besides practicing prana breathing?" His answer was:

> The first step is to keep you body as healthy as you can now, so you have less straightening out time once you get over there. Learn your lessons. Do what you know you are required to do, because every lesson learned assures you of a higher vibration during "The Shift." If you are in a wheelchair and you wind up in the fourth level, you can run around in circles, but if you end up in the second level, you will have to work yourself out of that situation.

> Focus on the Now and you will have no need to consider the past or the future to figure things out. What you do Now will affect what you do later on. Ask yourself, "What can I do today to make tomorrow better?" Stay in the present moment.

Section VI: References Used and Suggested Readings

References Used In the Text and Suggested Readings

Ascension Guidelines - Web Sites: www.operationterra.com/News, www.channel.com, www.lemureanconnection.com, www.matthewbooks.com, and www.masterdk.com

Achterberg, Jeanne, Barbara Dossey and Leslie Kolkmeier. Rituals of Healing. Bantam Books, 1994.

A Course in Miracles. Foundation For Inner Peace Pub., 1975.

Akasha and Asun. The Greatest Power in the Universe. Angelic Encounters Pub., 2006. See also: www.akashaonline.com.

Alien Shift Disclosure Project. Reports about 2012, UFOs, Aliens, HARRP, Earthquakes, Area 51, and related subjects. For Details See Web Site www.alienshift.com .

Amen, Daniel G. Change Your Brain, Change Your Life. Random House, 1998.

Arcturian Connection (information about fifth-dimensional consciousness): From Commander Adama (High Priest of Telos within Mt. Shasta). www.tribes.net.

Ascension Research Center. Teachings of Ascended Masters; Teachings, Messages and Activities. www.Ascension-research.org.

Ashtar Command. (Current Information from the Extraterrestrial Intergalactic Fleet). www.ashtarcommand.hylava.

Azevedo, Jose Lacerda de. Spirit & Matter. Reno, NV: New Falcon Publications, 1979.

Bacon, Summer. "This school Called Planet Earth Channeling Dr. Pebbles" www.summerbacon.com.

Bartlett, Richard, D.C., N.D. Matrix Energetics: A Hands-on Guide to Subtle Energy and Radical Change. Hillsboro, OR: Beyond Words Publishing, 2007.

Baumgartner, Bonnie. Expanding Into Other Dimensions: The Ascension Process. Book Surge Publishing, 2007.

Becker, Robert O, MD. Cross Currents: Perils of Electropollution. New York, NY: Jeremy P. Tarcher, Inc., 1990.

Blue Star Web Sites. The Pleaiadian Speaks. 1997-2008. (Transmissions through Celestial and David to help spiritual evolution): www.God/Goddessmentary.com, www.awakenedhearts.com, and www.bluestarspeaks.com

Braden, Greg. The Divine Matrix: Bridging Time, Space, and Belief. Carlsbad, CA: Hay House, 2008.

Braden, Greg. Walking Between the Worlds: the Science of Compassion. Bellevue, WA: Worlds Radio Books Tore Press, 1997.

Braden, Greg. Awakening to Zero Point: The Collective Initiation. Ann Arbor, MI: Braun-Brumfield, Inc., 1993.

Braden, Greg, Peter Russell, Daniel Pinch and Geoff Stray. Mystery of 2012: Predictions and Possibilities. Louisville, CO: Sounds True, Inc., 2007.

Brennan, Barbara Ann. Light Emerging: The Journey of Personal Healing. Bantam Books, 1993.

Bryce, Sheradon. Joy Riding the Universe; Snapshots of the Journey. Rio Sabe Loco Publishing, 1993.

Cannon, Dolores. The Convoluted Universe - Book Three. Huntsville, AR: Ozark Mountain Publishers, 2008.

Cannon, Dolores. The Convoluted Universe - Book Two. Huntsville, AR: Ozark Mountain Publishers, 2005.

Cannon, Dolores. Between Death and Life. Huntsville, AR: Ozark Mountain Publishers, 1993.

Carrol, Lee. (Channeling Kryon in eleven books). Published by Kryon Writings and Hay House. www.kryon.com and www.amazon.com

Cayce, Edgar Evans. Edgar Cayce on Atlantis. Grand Central Publishing, Hachett Book Group USA, 1998.

Chapman, Cathy. Change Your Encodements, Your DNA, Your Life, Light Technology Publishing, 2005.

Cheery, Joanna. Ascension Mastery International. Mount Shasta, CA: 2002-2008. See Web Site for details. www.Ascensionmastery. com.

Chopra, Deepak. The Book of Secrets: Unlocking the Hidden Dimensions of Your Life. New York: Three Rivers Press, Random House, 2005.

Clow, Barbara Hand. The Pleiadian Agenda: A New Cosmology for the Age of Light. Santa Fe, NM: Bear & Company, 1996.

Cotterell, Maurice. The Tutankhamun Prophecies: The Sacred Secret of Maya, Egyptians, and Freemasons. Santa Fe, NM: Bear & Company, 2001.

Cotterell, Maurice. The Supergods: They Came on a Mission to Save Mankind. Thorsons New Ed, 1998.

Cotterell, Maurice. The Mayan Prophecies: Unlocking the Secrets of a Lost Civilization. Auburn, MA: Element Books Ltd, 1996.

Detzler, Robert. Soul Recreation: Developing Your Cosmic Potential. SRC Publishing, 1999.

Dyer, Wayne. The Power of Intention. Carlsbad, CA: Hay House, 2005.

Eloff, Michelle. The Ascension Process. (Channeling Kuthumi and the Ascended Masters): See Websites www.thelightweaver.com.za ; and www.lightweaver.org.

Erb, John E. and T. Michelle Erb. The Slow Poisoning of America. Boulder, CO: Paladins Press, 2003.

Essene, Virginia and Sheldon Nidle. You Are Becoming A Galactic Human. Oxford, GA: Spiritual Education Endeavors Pub. Co., 1994.

Essene, Virginia. New Cells, New Bodies, New Life: You're becoming a Fountain of Youth. S.E.E. Pub Co. 1991.

Free, Wynn and David Wilcock. The Reincarnation of Edgar Cayce? Interdimensional Communication and Transformation. Frog Book Pub., 2004.

Gerber, Richard, MD. Vibrational Medicine: New Choices for Healing Ourselves. Bear & Company, 2001.

Gibson, Mitchell. Your Immortal Body of Light. Reality Press, 2006.

Gibson, Mitchell. Living Soul Seminars and Spiritual World Insights. www.tybro.com.

Gilbert, Maurice M. The Mayan Prophecies: Unlocking The Secrets of a Lost Civilization. Element Books Limited, 1995.

Gilbert, Adrian. 2012: Mayan Year of Destiny: Appointment With Destiny & Global Change. Virginia Beach, VA: A.R.E. Press, 2006.

God/Goddess Messages. The Universe as Revealed by God: (channeled by Celest and David). www.Godchannel.com; and http://www.healingtowholeness.com.

Goldberg, Bruce. Protected By The Light. Llewellyn Publications, 1998.

Goldberg, Bruce. Complete Book of Psychic Self-Defense, 1998.

Goldberg, Bruce. Time Travelers from Our Future: An Explanation of Alien Abductions. St. Paul, MN: Llewellyn Publications, 1998.

Goldsmith, Joel S. Beyond Words & Thoughts. Fort Worth, TX: Citadel Press, 1974.

Green, Glenda. Love Without End: Jesus Speaks. Crozet, VA: Heartwings Publishing, 1999.

Greer, Steven M., MD. Hidden Truth: Forbidden Knowledge. Quality Books, Inc., 2006.

Hawkins, David R., MD, PhD. The Eye of the I. Veritas Pub., 2001.

Hawkins, David R., MD, PhD. Power vs. Force. Carlsbad, CA: Hay House, 1995.

Hopkins, Budd. Intruders. Ballantine Books, 1987.

Hornecker, John. Cosmic Insights into Human Consciousness. 1996. book at www.earthscape.net.

Hurtak, J.J. The Book of Knowledge: The Keys of Enoch. The Academy for Future Science, 1977.

Icke, David. Tales from the Time Loop. Wildwood, MO: Bridge of Love Publications, 2003.

Inove, Alice Channeled. Lemuria: What Was It? And Where Was It? www.peleoflemuria.com.

Jones, Aurelia Louise. Telos Volume 3: Protocols of the Fifth Dimension. Mount Shasta, CA: Light Pub., 2006.

Jones, Aurelia Louise. Telos Volume 1: Revelations of the New Lemuria. Mount Shasta, CA: Light Pub., 2004. See also: www.onelight.com/telos.

Jones, Aurelia Louise. Telos Volume 2: Messages for Enlightenment of a Humanity in Transition. Mount Shasta, CA: Light Pub., 2004. See also: www.lemureianconncetion.com.

Karagulla, Shafica, MD and Dora Van Gelder Kunz. The Chakras: Human Energy Field. India: New Age Books, 2002.

Kenyon, Tom and Virginia Essene. The Hathor Material. Santa Clara, CA: Spiritual Education Endeavors, 1996.

Khul, Master Djwhal. From the Spiritual Plane to the Earth Plane. www.masterdk.com.

King, Soluntar. (Communications from within higher consciousness; connections with Councils of Light & the Galactic Federation): www.evenstarcreations.com.

Kingdom, Kathlyn. The Matter of Mind: An Explorer's Guide to the Labyrinth of The Mind. (Channeled from Tibetan Master Djwhal Khul): The Tibetan. See: www.masterdk.com.

Kroger, Hanna. God Helps Those Who Help Themselves. Hanna Kroger Publications, 2004.

Levine, Barbara Hoberman. Your Body Believes Every Word You Say. Work Press, 2000.

Lewis, Pepper. Wisdom for An Awakening Humanity. Channeled from Mother Earth): www.thepeacefulplanet.com; and www.http://spiritlibrary.com

Light Workers Free Energy Web Site. (The Race to Zero Point, Data Base for Spirit Directory with Guides). See website: www.lightworkers.com.

Lightworkers' Spiritual Network. http://lightworkers.org Spiritual channelings from the masters.

Marciniak, Barbara. Path of Empowerment. Inner Ocean Publishing, 2004.

Marciniak, Barbara. Family of Light: Pleaiadian Tales and Lessons in Living. Santa Fe, NM: Bear & Company, 1999.

Marciniak, Barbara. Pleiadian Keys to the Living Library. Santa Fe, NM: Bear & Company, 1995. See also: www.pleiadians.com.

Mc Moneagle, Joseph. Remote Viewing Secrets. London, England: Hampton Roads Publisher, 2000.

Mc Taggart, Lynn. The Field. New York: Harper Collins, 2001. See also: www.harperperennial.com.

Mc Taggart, Lynn. The Intention Experiment: Using Your Thoughts to Change Your Life and the World. New York: Simon & Schuster, 2007.

Megre, Vladimir. Anastasia, The Ringing Cedar Series-Books 1-8. Original in Russian: English Translation. Paia, Hawaii: Ringing Cedar Press, 2008. Important books – Visit www.RingingCedars. com, Over ten million copies sold worldwide in 20 languages.

Melchizedek, Drunvalo. Serpent of Light: Beyond 2012. Weiser Books, 2008.

Melchizedek, Drunvalo. Living In The Heart. Light Technology Publishing, 2003.

Melchizedek, Drunvalo. The Ancient Secret of the Flower of Life, Volume 1. Sedona, AZ: Light Technology Publishing, 1990.

Melchizedek, Drunvalo. The Ancient Secret of the Flower of Life, Volume 2. Flagstaff, AZ: Light Technology Publishing, 2000. See also: Drunvalo Web site: www.floweroflife.org.

Milanovich, Norma. The Light Shall Set You Free. Athena Publishing, 1996.

Milanovich, Norma. We Are the Arcturians. Athena Publishing, 1990.

Miller, David. Connecting With the Arcturians. Planetary Heart Publications, 1998.

Miller, David. Teachings From The Sacred Triangle: Tools For The Ascension, Volumes 1 and 2. Mount Shasta, CA: Heaven on Earth Project, 2004.

Modi, Shakuntala, MD. Remarkable Healings: A Psychiatrist Discovers Unsuspected Roots of Mental and Physical Illness. Charlottesville, VA: Hampton Books, 1997.

Morgan, Marlo. Mutant Message from Forever. Thorsons Pub., 2000.

Mulford, Prentice. Thoughts Are Things. 1889. Republished by Barns & Noble, Inc., 2007.

Newton, Michael, PhD. Destiny of Souls: New Case Studies of Life Between Lives. St. Paul, MN: Llewellyn Pub., 2002.

Newton, Michael, PhD. Journey of Souls: Case Studies of Life Between Lives. St Paul, MN: Llewellyn Pub., 1994.

Nichols, Preston B, and Peter Moon. The Montauk Project: Experiments in Time. Sky Books, 1992.

Pearl, Eric. The Reconnection: Heal Others, Heal Yourself. Carlsbad, CA: Hay House, 2001.

Perala, Robert and Tony Stubbs. The Divine Blueprint: Roadmap for the New Millennium. Campbell, CA: United Light Publishing, 1998.

Peterson, Scott. Native American Prophecies (Does not discuss Native American Prophecies). Continuum Publishing Group, 1999.

Quan Yin, Amorah. The Pleiadian Workbook: Awakening Your Divine Ka. Santa Fe, NM: Bear & Company, 1996.

Ra, A Composite Soul. Channeled the Law of One, Books I, II, III, IV. See Also: www.llresearch.org.

Raphaell, Katrina. The Crystalline Transmission: A Synthesis of Light. Santa Fe, NM: Aurora Press, 1990.

Renard, Gary R. The Disappearance of the Universe. Fearless Books, 2002.

Renard, Gary R. Your Immortal Reality: How to Break the Cycle of Birth and Death. Carlsbad, CA: Hay House, 2007.

Revelatorium 2008. (The cosmic plan of the Creator.) An e-book at www.revelatorium.com.

Rhodes, Michael J. Journey into Oneness: A Spiritual Odyssey. J. H. Kramer Inc., 1994.

Robbins, Dianne. Messages from the Hollow Earth. Trafford Publishing Co., 2006. See also www.diannerobbins.com.

Rogers, Sherry A., M.D. The High Pressure Blood Pressure Hoax. Sand Key Co., 2005.

Rogers, Sherry A. M.D, Detoxify Or Die. Sand Key Co., 2002.

Rose, Kalina Raphael. The Melchizedek program and related procedures: See Web Sites www.roseofraphael.com; and www.bethcoleman.net

Rosek, Cathy and William Rosek. Who Am I and Why Am I Here? Monument, CO: Universal View Pub., 2001.

Rother, Steve. Welcome Home: The New Planet. Poway, CA: Lightworker Pub., 2002. See also www.lightrworeker.com.

Royal, Lyssa and Keith Priest. Visitors from Within: Extraterrestrial Encounters & Species Evolution. Wildflower Press, 1999.

Russel, Craig. Journey to Self Realization. Angelic Encounters, 2005.

Russel, Craig. Ancient Wisdom Revealed: The Soul Journey Discourses. So Be It Publications, 1999.

Scallion, Gordon Michael. Notes from the Cosmos. Matrix Institute, 1997. See also: www.matrixinstitute.com.

Schorn, M. Don. Elder Gods of Antiquity. Ozark Mountain Publishing, 2008. See also: www.ozarkmt.com.

Sedona Journal of Emergence (Monthly channeling reports). Sedona, AZ: Light Technology Pub. Visit the website www.sedonajournal.com for information.

Shapiro, Robert. Explorer Race. Light Technology Publishing, 1997. See also: www.lighttechnology.com and www.thepeacefulplanet.com

Shealy Norman C., MD. Life Beyond 100: Secrets of the Fountain of Youth. Jeremy P. Tarcher/Penguin, 2006.

Smith, Jerry A. HAARP. High-frequency Active Auroral Research Program. The Ultimate Weapon of the Conspiracy. Kempton, IL: Adventures Unlimited Press, 1998.

Steiner, Rudolf. Knowledge of the Higher Worlds and Its Attainment. Murine Press, 2008.

Steiner, Rudolf. Cosmic Memory. San Francisco: Harper & Row, 1959.

Sterling, Fred. Kirael: Volume II - The Genesis Matrix. Honolulu, Hawaii: Lightways Pub., 2001.

Sterling, Fred. The Great Shift. Honolulu, Hawaii: Lightways Pub., 2001. See also: www.kirael.com.

Stone, Joshua David and Gloria Excelsias. The Universal Laws of God, Vol. 1. Writers Club Press, 2002.

Stone, Joshua David. Hidden Mysteries. Ascension. Light Technology Pub., 1995.

Stone, Joshua David. Beyond Ascension: How to Complete the Seven Levels of Initiation. Light Technology Pub., 1995.

Stone, Joshua David. The Complete Ascension Manual: How to Achieve Ascension in This Lifetime. Light Technology Publishing, 1994.

Stubbs, Tony. An Ascension Handbook. New Leaf Distributing Co., 1999.

Talbert, Michael. The Holographic Universe. New York: Harpers Collins, 1991.

Tiller, William A., PhD. Science and Human Transformation: Subtle Energies, Intentionality and Consciousness. Pavior Publishing, 1997.

Tobias Materials A series of useful channelings: http://crimsoncircle.com/channel.

Tolle, Eckhart. A New Earth: Awakening to Your Life's Purpose. New York, NY: Penguin Group, Inc., 2005.

Tolle, Eckhart. The Power of "Now". Novato, CA: New World Library, 1999.

Truman, Karol K. Feelings Buried Alive Never Die. Las Vegas, NV: Olympus Distributing, 1996.

Von Ward, Paul. God, Genes, and Consciousness: Nonhuman Intervention in Human History. Hampton Roads Publishing Company, 2004.

Vrenios, Rick. Extraordinary Living through Chakra Wisdom. Reiki Council Publishing, 2004. www.reikicouncil.com.

Walsch, Neal Donald. Tomorrow's God: Our Greatest Spiritual Challenge. New York: Atria Books, 2004.

Walsch, Neal Donald. Conservations with God: An Uncommon Dialogue, Book 1. Putnam Publishing Group, 1999.

Walsch, Neal Donald. Friendship with God. G. P. Putnam's Sons, 1991.

Ward, Suzanne. Voices of the Universe. Matthew Books, 2004. See Also www.matthewbooks.com

Ward, Suzanne. Illuminations for a New Era. Matthew Books, 2003.

Ward, Suzanne. Revelations for a New Era: Keys to Restoring Paradise on Earth. Matthew Books, 2001.

Waters, Owen. "The Shift": The Revolution in Human Consciousness. Infinite Being Publishing, 2006.

Weaver, Donald A. Survival of Civilization: Problems threatening our existence on Earth. Hamaker-Weaver Publishers, 1982.

Weirauch, Wolfgang. Nature Spirits and What They Say: Interviews with Verena Stael Holstein. Floris Books, 2005.

Wilcock, David. Divine Cosmos - Convergence, Vol. 3. Information on Soul Growth, Ascension, and Consciousness, 2006. Visit www.divinecosmos.com.

Wilson, James L.N.D., D.C., PhD. Adrenal Fatigue: The 21st Century Stress Syndrome. 2001. See also: www.smart-publications.com.

Windrider, Kara. Doorway to Eternity: A Guide to Planetary Ascension. Heaven on Earth Project, 2003.

Winters, Owen. "The Shift": The Revolution in Human Consciousness. Infinite Being Pub. LLC, 2005.

Winters, Randolph. The Pleiadian Mission: A Time of Awareness. Arkansas City, Kansas: Gilliland Printing, 1994.

Za Kai Rans. Ascension Master's Toolkit: Pictures of Ascended Masters. www.zakairan.com.

Zukav, Gary. The Seat of the Soul. New York: Simon and Schuster, 1999.

Young Bernard
354 8786

ECKanKar by Harold Klemp or/and
Paul Twitchell

The SHARIYAT-KI-SUGMAD
(Way of the Eternal by Paul
Twitchell, BOOK I , Banyon
                         Books.
              Book II

by Harold Klemp,
" Autobiography of A Spiritual
Master? , in the library

LaVergne, TN USA
08 February 2011
215739LV00007B/20/P

9 781450 231718